Kent State University European Studies

4

Series Editors

Marcello Fantoni Fabrizio Ricciardelli

Italian Pop Culture

Media, Products, Imageries

edited by Fabio Corsini

viella

Copyright © 2018 Viella s.r.l. - Kent State University
Tutti i diritti riservati
Prima edizione: giugno 2018
ISBN 978-88-6728-939-4

Kent State University European Studies is a peer-reviewed book series.

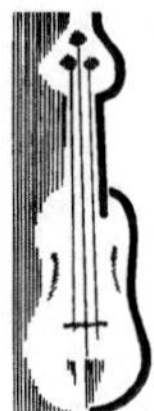

viella
libreria editrice
via delle Alpi, 32
I-00198 ROMA
tel. 06 84 17 758
fax 06 85 35 39 60
www.viella.it

Contents

Fabio Corsini

Introduction: Working Out the Puzzle of Italian Popular Culture

Pop culture is made of many things. Raymond Betts states that "it's almost without definition, so all-embracing are its subjects, so far are its effects".[1] In fact, we can easily observe that it is almost everywhere. It is the cars we drive, the food we eat, the way in which we entertain ourselves and, most obviously, it is about all the media narratives by which we are surrounded. Not only is popular culture in many of our daily activities, but most importantly, it affects and shapes all of them: politics, business, even religion,[2] and more in general our every-day life.[3]

Yet, in spite of its complexity and a related lack of unanimous definition within the academic community, it is possible to identify a few of its characteristics that will allow us to better understand what it is. Betts says that popular culture is "chiefly marked by four characteristics: visualization, commodification, entertainment and technology".[4] The first of these characteristics, visualization, refers to the growing importance of the visual culture "from oil painting to television and the internet"[5] for today's making sense of the world. In fact, "human experience is now more

1. Raymond Betts, *A History of Popular Culture. More of Everything, Faster and Brighter* (New York: Routledge, 2004), p. 1.

2. See for this the *Journal of Religion and Popular Culture*, *Project MUSE*, available at www.muse.jhu.edu.

3. Tim Markham, *Media and Everyday Life* (London: Palgrave, 2017).

4. For a critical review of the concept of popular culture see: Betts, *A History of Popular Culture*, p. 3.

5. *The Visual Culture Reader*, ed. by Nicholas Mirzoeff (New York and London: Routledge, 1998), p. 3. On the importance of visual culture see also Richard Howells, Joaquim Negreiros, *Visual Culture, Second Edition* (Cambridge: Polity Press, 2011), p. 3.

visual and visualized than ever before"[6] within the Western (industrialized) world, and we live under the impression that only what is represented through different media exists. The second aspect highlighted by Betts is commodification: namely the commercialization of culture. In fact, it is true that culture has become a commodity, and the many different cultural products of which it is made are produced and sold within a commercial system or somehow exploited for economic reasons. In other words, commodification is when culture meets the market, and popular culture lives because of this fortunate relationship.

The third characteristic of popular culture mentioned is its entertaining nature. This is related to the fact that those products realized by the cultural industries – quite a revealing expression for understanding the essence of popular culture – are primarily focused at entertaining people. Here the problem is defining what entertainment is all about: in fact, it is not necessarily a "bad" thing. Entertainment is visiting the Uffizi Gallery, but also watching an Italian soap opera: both are entertaining activities, equally worthy of our attention, even if they obviously are very different – and with different meanings. But in both cases, there is no such thing as "just entertainment – meaning that – all stories and images express worldviews, conceptions of humor, beliefs about gender, beauty, success and right and wrong".[7] As a matter of fact, we could ironically state that entertainment is a "damn, serious thing". The last characteristic identified by Betts is technology. The industrial process of mass production is in fact technologically driven: the Gutenberg invention of the printing machine with movable types is technology; radio and television are technologies. Similarly, being able to shoot quality videos, edit and finally post them online with a simple plastic and metal device – a smartphone – is still technology. All of these are different forms of technologies that have significantly shaped popular culture, or, like the last one, that are in the process of shaping it today. Technology is driving and shaping media transformations leading to a new mediascape which is dominated by a process of media convergence which is not only technological but also economic and cultural. An aspect that redesigns and redefines also the very essence of popular culture.

6. *Ibid.*, p. 4.

7. Lee Artz, *Global Entertainment Media: A Critical Introduction* (Oxford: Wiley-Blackwell, 2015), p. 4.

John Storey, in a fundamental work[8] on popular culture, makes a similar attempt at identifying characteristics that help us at better "framing" what pop culture is about. Once again, the idea is that even if it is not possible to agree on a unique definition, it is still possible to outline some of its essential aspects. In a certain way, Storey adds other elements to the ones identified by Betts. First of all, he begins by saying that "any definition of popular culture must include a quantitative dimension".[9] It is not necessarily about the masses and the related mass concept as it was at the time of traditional (mass) media, but is nonetheless a reminder of the fact that many people have to be involved and affected by it. A second, very interesting aspect he identifies is linked to the relationship between high and low culture. In his own words: "A [...] way of defining popular culture is to suggest that it is the culture that is left over after we have decided what is high culture".[10] This juxtaposition between high and low, mass and elite, artistic and consumerist has always been vital for popular culture. But what we need to understand is that definitions are not given once and for all. The way certain cultural artifacts are evaluated by a society change with time and circumstances. For instance, if we think about melodrama and opera music, that is a kind of genre that was born as a popular one but that nowadays is considered high culture: meant for an elite of people and not for the masses. As a matter of fact, what is interesting is this dynamic and conflictual relationship: the *tension* that exists between different juxtapositions such as "highbrow" and "lowbrow", "artistic" and "commercial", "elite" and "mass" etc. It is in those *tensions* that the meaning of popular culture is revealed.

Another characteristic, linked to the previous one, is the idea that pop culture is "mass produced commercial culture, whereas high culture is the result of an individual act of creation".[11] In this case the border between high and low is set on the difference that "should" exist between commerce and art. However, we all know that it is not possible to establish that boundary in an unequivocally definitive way.[12] In fact, even in this case, the idea of

8. John Storey, *Cultural Studies and the Study of Popular Culture*, Sixth Edition (Edinburgh: Edinburgh University Press, 2012).

9. *Ibid.*, p. 5.

10. *Ibid.*

11. *Ibid.*

12. On this see the classic of Walter Benjamin, *The Work of Art in the Age of Mechanical Reproduction* (London: Penguin Books, 2008 [1936]).

authorship is a slippery terrain because while on the one side this category applies always more and more to some of the most traditional examples of popular culture,[13] on the other side a lot of what we consider high culture – paintings and sculptures for instance, have been realized on commission. Finally, a last characteristic "contends that popular culture is the culture that originates from the 'people'".[14] When it is produced by the cultural industries, it is "for the people" to be intended as the target of a commercially driven activity. But there are other cases, thanks to the spaces made available by the new technologies, in which that culture it is also made directly "by the people". In fact, the boundaries between production and consumption are far more porous than we can imagine, and more importantly, these boundaries disappear when instead of the idea of audiences engaged in "consuming" products we think of them as "interpreting" cultural symbols.[15]

After highlighting some of the main characteristics of popular culture, it is now important to insist on the relevance of the media and mediated culture for contemporary societies. In fact, it is undeniable that, with the growing relevance of the media of communication in our everyday lives, pop culture becomes always more central for understanding culture in its broader sense. The complex set of narratives produced by the different media of communication – traditional and new ones – allow us a deeper understanding of the reality in which we live. Media representations produce narratives that result in mediated experiences:[16] a new way to make sense of the contemporary world. Quoting John B. Thompson:

> The growing availability of mediated experiences thus creates new opportunities, new options, new arenas for self experimentation. An individual who reads a novel or watches a soap opera is not simply consuming a fantasy; he or she is exploring possibilities, imagining alternatives, experimenting with the project of the self.[17]

13. We can make reference to the example of "quality television" as a style of TV drama that wants to be distinguished by "all the rest of television programs" because of a set of specific characteristics among which, authorship. On this see Kim Akass, Janet McCabe, *Quality TV. Contemporary American Television and Beyond* (London: I.B. Tauris & Co, 2007).

14. Storey, *Cultural Studies and the Study of Popular Culture*, p. 9.

15. On this see the work of Ien Ang, *Desperately Seeking the Audience* (New York and London: Routledge, 1991).

16. John B. Thompson, *The Media and Modernity. A Social Theory of the Media* (Cambridge: Polity Press, 1995).

17. *Ibid.*, p. 233.

Media content, as any other type of cultural ingredient such as language, religion, norms, and habits, is used as a symbolic material for producing identities: both personal and cultural ones. Even if these ingredients are produced by an industry, namely the cultural industry, for a mass market audience, it doesn't change the fact that these symbols, aesthetics, languages, narrative forms and genres are fundamental elements of our lives and consequently they are worth being investigated.

More importantly, these symbols carry meanings that reveal part of the wider picture of what a culture is all about. It then becomes essential to understand these symbols as well as the ways in which people appropriate them. There is a long tradition of academic research, the Cultural Studies,[18] that has proven the validity of this perspective in relation to the importance of popular culture in contemporary society. This strand of research is about understanding media messages, how these media messages are interpreted by audiences, and how these acts of interpretation finally translate into practices that affect important concepts such as identity, gender, race, class, ethnicity sexuality and so forth.

This book is about mediated popular culture: the one produced and conveyed through the media of communication in Italy. We could say that mediated popular culture looks like a big puzzle made by many different cards: media products, genres, aesthetics, formats, narratives etc. In this volume, all the authors are focusing on one or more than one of these aspects in order to find out more about the Italian popular culture and how that is intertwined with the Italian cultural identity and Italian history. This is not the first time that researchers investigate Italy through the lenses of the media. It is enough here to make reference to the works of authors such as David Forgacs, Stephen Gundle, or Fausto Colombo, to name a few, to understand that this volume is inserted within an already existing tradition.[19]

18. It would be impossible to mention all the authors that contributed to the birth and establishment of the Cultural Studies. See at least: Raymond Williams, *Culture and Society* (Harmondsworth: Penguin, 1963); Richard Hoggart, *The Uses of Literacy* (Harmondsworth: Penguin, 1990); *Cultural Studies*, ed. by Lawrence Grossberg, Cary Nelson and Paula Treicher (New York: Routledge, 1992); Stuart Hall, *Representation. Cultural Representations and Signifying Practices* (London: Sage, 1997); Storey, *Cultural Studies and the Study of Popular Culture*; Simon During, *The Cultural Studies Reader, Third Edition* (New York: Routledge, 2007).

19. On the role of popular culture and the media in Italian culture see at least: David Forgacs, *Italian Culture in the Industrial Era, 1910-80* (Manchester: Manchester University

Yet, this book is also an attempt of critically discuss what popular culture is today in Italy. The complexity of the definition of the concept of which we have talked in the first pages of this introduction, is in itself indicative and it highlights something important. Popular culture is a dynamic field of research that implies multiple aspects of our everyday lives and that requires an interdisciplinary approach: a multiplicity of perspectives from which we can look at cultural phenomena. This volume through the lenses of sociology, political philosophy, literature and media studies, makes an attempt at describing Italian popular culture by also re-defining it. The attempt is one of highlighting the imageries on which Italian identity is anchored, recognizing the native and foreign influences, and identifying those imageries – built on images, sounds, words, schemas, patterns as well as genres – actually recognized as Italian.

Every contribution is connected to one another, and they need to be read and understood as if they were pieces of a bigger puzzle. In this sense, each *card* is an attempt of either framing the wider picture of Italian pop culture or adding an essential detail that characterizes it and makes it recognizable, understandable and finally, meaningful. Since popular culture lives on the cross-references among different media – the narratives and the themes that are adapted according to the time, the medium, or the audience – each *card* we add to the final puzzle is a further step into a less stereotypical and formulaic representation of the Italians. And yet still, every article is also autonomous and can be detached from the puzzle, looked at from a closer perspective and analyzed by itself. In fact, each contribution provides an in-depth investigation of a specific theme, genre and medium by making reference to specific scientific literature and discussing single case studies or wider scenarios.

The articles are listed in alphabetical order, but this is not just the outcome of the lack of imagination on the side of the editor. On the contrary, it is an attempt not to make the same mistakes of the detractors of popular culture. Trying to restitute the complexity of the wider puzzle, it is nonsense to keep producing categories to juxtapose and divide into sections. The reader is invited to work out this puzzle with the only indication that, like in any puzzle, we begin with

Press, 1990); David Forgacs, *Italian Cultural Studies: An Introduction* (New York: Oxford University Press, 1996); Fausto Colombo, *La cultura sottile* (Milan: Bompiani, 1998); David Forgacs, *L'industrializzazione della cultura italiana (1880-2000)* (Bologna: Il Mulino, 2000); Stephen Gundle, *Between Hollywood and Moscow: The Italian Communists and the Challenge of Mass Culture* (Durham: Duke University Press, 2000); David Forgacs, Stephen Gundle, *Cultura di massa e società italiana 1936-1954* (Bologna: Il Mulino, 2007).

the frame, but every piece of the frame is equivalent to the others. And all the articles of this collection have to be considered as equal pieces of an "ideal" frame that allow the readers a deeper unnderstanding of Italian pop culture.

The first contribution, "Understanding Italian Comics Culture: Hugo Pratt, the 9th Art and Politics" by Paolo Biondi, is an investigation of the figure of Hugo Pratt and his role in Italian comics as well as his influence in comic culture in general. More importantly, Biondi highlights the existing relationship between comics and politics in Italy. In bringing together (and bridging) media studies and political philosophy, the author reveals the political dimension of Pratt's comics as well as the importance of redefining the very idea of what is "political".

"*Stil Novo*. The Legendarily Adventurous Route of Italian Music in Search of Pop(ular) Maturity" is the second article by Marco Bracci and Edoardo Tabasso. The two authors analyze the music sector of the Italian cultural industry. Through a detailed sociological analysis rich in data, they describe the making of Italian popular music from a cultural and consumerist perspective. In their contribution, it is discussed the role of pop music in the making of Modern Italy from the Fifties onwards by comparing different genres and different cultural traditions, like the British and American ones, and how Italy was finally able to develop its own style.

Milly Buonanno discusses the role of domestic TV drama for popular culture. "Fallen Heroes and Anti-Heorines: The Mafia Story in Italian TV Drama" provides a detailed description of the Italian television drama's history of the last three decades by focusing on mafia stories. The author, television studies scholar and sociologist, analyzes this case for demonstrating the evolution of a genre that since the time of *La Piovra* has grown in popularity but also in variety. In fact, as Buonanno demonstrates, the narratives produced are more complex, allowing space for a plethora of "good" and "bad" characters as well as a growing presence of strong female leading roles within the genre.

"Italian Webseries: The New (yet Old) Way of Storytelling" by Fabio Corsini takes into consideration webseries as a new storytelling format which is always more important. In his contribution, the author highlights the characteristics of these narratives directly produced by the users of the web in relationship to the idea of popular culture. Corsini then continues investigating the Italian web series scene outlining which are the main domestic imageries they have produced so far, by stressing their direct link to the other Italian traditional media (mostly television) and the Italian cultural identity.

The fifth contribution by Flavia Monceri is about pornography. In "Porn(ography) as a Cultural Product" the author discusses in an original way the importance of considering pornography as a cultural product as a way for "empowering individuals". The political philosopher, beginning with an overview on porn studies in Italy and abroad, suggests avoiding mainstream pornographies and takes into account the specific case of pornography and "disability" for highlighting the political potential of pornography as a tool against the heteronormative able-bodied regime.

Anna Lucia Natale discusses the role of the radio in Italian pop culture by focusing on light entertainment. In her "In the Beginning There Was the Radio… Contexts and Genres of Radio Entertainment" the author reconstructs the role and the "place" of radio in Italian culture from the mid Twenties onwards. With the sensitivity of a media scholar Natale describes the different genres of light entertainment, music, quizzes and prize contests, and finally talks about how the medium reinvented itself after the appearance of television first and the arrival of rock and roll second.

Nicoletta Peluffo is the author of "*The Adventures of Pinocchio*: An Outcome of Popular Culture". In her essay she describes the popular novel by Carlo Collodi as a perfect example of cultural product: originally published in different installments in a magazine, adapted by the same author in a book with a different ending, and finally overcoming geographical and cultural borders becoming a movie, in Italy and abroad. Peluffo describes from a literary perspective Pinocchio as a "universe in constant transformation" which has been widely adapted and re-written.

Still from a literary perspective, Kristin Stasiowski analyzes the case of the *Divine Comedy*. In "A *Divine Comedy* for All Time: Dante's Enduring Relevance for the Contemporary Reader" the author explores the case of Dante's masterpiece by highlighting two main points. The first aspect is the popularity of Dante through the many re-writing and interpretations from the first lectures of Boccaccio to the references made in contemporary pop culture products such as television shows, movies and videogames. But more importantly, Stasiowski wants to assert that Dante's lessons are not only popular but also relevant to the contemporary reader and to the contemporary society.

The last contribution by Bernardo Valli, "Italy and the Search for Modernity: At the Origins of *made in Italy*", fall out of the traditional conception of popular culture and discusses about the origins of *made in Italy* as a "brand". With a detailed historical and sociological reconstruction, the author investigates the foundations of the popularity of *made in Italy* starting with the cases of Olivetti and Fiat until the birth of the Italian Fashion System thanks to the role of Giovanni Battista Giorgini. In his essay, Valli talks about the making of a modern Italy as a country engaged in an on-going dialogue between the Catholic, Communist and American cultures.

***

I would like to conclude this introduction by thanking all the people that made it possible for this book to be published. First of all, many thanks to Paolo Biondi, Marco Bracci, Milly Buonanno, Flavia Monceri, Anna Lucia Natale, Nicoletta Peluffo, Kristin Stasiowski, Edoardo Tabasso and Bernardo Valli, the authors that collaborated to this collective enterprise. The original idea of this book was born out of the many lectures, conferences, reading/viewing/listening suggestions, and friendly conversations that we have shared together along the years. Thank you not only for your scientific rigor but also for your willingness to talk to the non-specialists, and in so doing making this text accessible to the wider audience.

Another essential thank you is for the editors of the Kent State University European Studies book series that host this volume. Fabrizio Ricciardelli, Director of Kent State, Florence Center, and Marcello Fantoni, Associate Provost of Global Education at Kent State University. Thank you both for the opportunity you gave me: for embracing the spirit of dialogue among disciplines and exchange among cultures as this volume is interdisciplinary and it brings together the Italian and the American academic traditions. But mostly thank you for your sensibility on considering media and popular culture narratives an essential aspect of the Italian and European cultures.

Finally, in the spirit of pop culture and cultural studies, aware that the every "text" is the result of the work of the author as well as the work of the readers, I would like to thank all those people that are about to read this volume. My wish, not only for the foreign (non-Italian) readers, is that this book it's only the beginning of a more personal and richer journey into the many narratives that shape the Italian culture. I trust readers and their ability of finding the best itineraries through the different *cards* of the puzzle that we tried to design. Your contribution is essential for making this work meaningful, and for finally working out the puzzle of Italian pop culture.

Paolo Biondi

Understanding Italian Comics Culture: Hugo Pratt, the 9th Art and Politics

Hugo Pratt is considered one of the masters of Italian comics. As Luca Boschi explains, he deserves the title for authoring, in 1967, *Una Ballata del Mare Salato* (*A Ballad of the Salty Sea*, hereafter the *Ballad*), "*un romanzo a fumetti* [a novel in the form of comics] that will be a model also for the English speaking and Northern American authors, followed, in 1978, by Will Eisner's *A Contract with God* and, in 1980, by Art Spiegelman's *Maus*".[1] The *Ballad*, moreover, introduced also the character of Corto Maltese, the pirate-sailor that would have been celebrated "by authoritative readers such as Woody Allen, Frank Miller and Umberto Eco".[2]

By considering Pratt's oeuvre as a case in point, this article wants to suggest that in order to understand Italian comics culture and the importance it acknowledges to its main authors, it could be useful to adopt a "political" perspective, highlighting the relation comics have entertained with politics in the history of Italian pop-culture. This is not to say that Italian comics implicate politics in the sense that they are filled with political ideologies or messages more than those produced elsewhere. Rather, this is to say that the appreciation tributed to Italian comics masters, and to Pratt in particular, can be explained by the readers' attitude to project political meaning onto comics, using them both to express one's own political identity and position, and that of other people. In this sense, Italian culture seems to be marked by a tendency to see comics as a set of objects whose possible *political*

1. Luca Boschi, *Irripetibili. Le grandi stagioni del fumetto italiano* (Rome: Coniglio, 2007), pp. 36ff.; Giovanni Marchese, *Leggere Hugo Pratt. L'autore di Corto Maltese tra fumetto e letteratura* (Latina: Tunué, 2006), p. 4.

2. *Ibid.*, p. 45.

meaning is questioned, due to different and contrasting possibilities to read and interpret them. However, arguing for this approach to the specific relation of the 9th art with politics requires, in the first instance, to stress more than it is currently done the role that variety and diversification have played in the development of comics in Italy. Moreover, it requires a broader conception of "politics" than the one equating it with the actions and behaviors of established political authorities and centers of power.

1. *Variety and diversification as central traits of Italian comics culture*

The word "fumetti" translates into Italian the English "comics". "Fumetti" has nothing to do with the reference to the funny stories evoked by the English term. Rather, the Italian term comes from "fumo", which stands for "smoke". The literal meaning of "fumetti" may be rendered in English as "little smokes", highlighting that, when the word was introduced in 1942,[3] the Italian speakers' attention was caught above all by the text balloons accompanying the images, which looked like little clouds of smoke.[4]

One of the main features of Italian comics culture comes from its delayed development into a mature form of expression aimed also to adults and not only to children. Contemporary discourse about Italian comics seems to converge on the following position:

> Originating in the United States at the end of the nineteenth century, comics first came to Italy in 1908 through a *Corriere della sera* supplement for

3. See Marco Pellitteri, "Cinque parole da tenere a mente sul fumetto italiano d'oggi", in *Scrittori e scritture nella letteratura disegnata italiana*, ed. by Mario Allegri and Claudio Gallo (Milan: Fondazione Arnaldo e Alberto Mondadori), pp. 222-234; Fabio Gadducci, *Notes on the Early Decades of Italian Comic Art* (Pisa: Felici, 2006).

4. The general trend in comics studies and research is to conceive national comics productions as they were different languages or system of signs, overlapping more or less with the communities of speakers of the different national languages. The fact that different national languages use different words to refer to comics (for example, fumetti, manga, etc…) evocking non-coinciding images and meanings seems to support this conception. However, such theoretical trend has been put under question in relation to the long-standing problem of defining "comics". On this see at least: *A Comics Studies Reader*, ed. by Jeet Heer and Kent Worcester (Jackson: University Press of Mississippi, 2009), pp. 101-171; Neil Cohn, "Un-Defining 'Comics': Separating the Cultural from the Structural in 'Comics'", *International Journal of Comic Art*, 7/2 (2005), pp. 236-248; Aaron Meskin, "Defining Comics", *The Journal of Aesthetics and Art Criticism*, 65/4 (2007), pp. 369-379.

> children, *Corriere dei piccoli*. Over time they became a vehicle for expression and diffusion of the collective imagination although, given the relatively poor organization of cultural production in Italy, comics remained in an incubation phase up until the early 1960s.[5]

Such a position stresses two distinct elements. The first: comics occupy an important place in Italian culture. No matter how much the adventures of characters like Tex Willer, Diabolik, Valentina or Dylan Dog are actually read and followed, they are well known to the general public and perceived to be truly Italian. The second: in the evolution of Italian comics culture the Sixties represent a sort of turning point. On the one hand, during the decade comics became a mature form of expression able to speak also to adults rather than merely to children, and, on the other, a generalized appreciation and valorization of comics' authorship took place.

The latter element is particularly relevant here, since it refers to a view of Italian comics history which is correct under many aspects, but at the same time appears to be a little simplistic. It is true that Italian comics history had been marked by a kind of "original sin", consisting in the initial tendency of the cultural elites of the country to intervene politically on comics. But to say that this attitude took comics into an incubation phase up until the Sixties misses to consider how much the same attitude triggered variety and diversification in comics production.

Back in the year 1908, comics made their first appearence in Italy on the pages of the journal *Corriere dei Piccoli*. *Corrierino*, how it was affectionately nicknamed by its readers, imported from the USA some of the early syndicated daily-strips and Sunday pages originally aimed at a mixed young and adult readership – such as *Buster Brown* (renamed *Mimmo Mammolo*), *Happy Hooligan* (renamed *Fortunello*) and the *Katzenjammer Kids* (renamed *Bibì e Bibò*) –, readapting them for the public of the Italian bourgeois families' children. The strips were dismantled and collocated into a rigid graphic scheme, usually presenting eight or twelve square panels per page vertically disposed in four lines of two or four; balloons were regularly deleted and two lines of rhymed captions were added below each image. In short, the final result had nothing to do with the originals, for form as well as for contents. In this sense, in Italy comics not only became products specifically made for children, which was not the case

5. Franco Manai, "Comics", in *Encyclopedia of Contemporary Italian Culture*, ed. by Gino Moliterno (London: Routledge, 2000), pp. 177-179, p. 177.

in the English speaking world – at least in the beginning –,[6] but they were also treated as cheap products with little or no value in their own right, to the extent that every kind of intervention was legitimate, included those distorting and violating their authors' intentions.

Juri Meda notes that it is possible to isolate many possible explanations for the choices of *Corrierino*'s editorial staff.[7] The director Silvio Spaventa Filippi, like many other Italian liberal intellectuals of the time, believed that it was the case to imprint a pedagogical twist to comics. As Meda puts it:

> In their original version, comics were a new way to make social satyre, parodying the American middle-class miserable habits and taunting its poses and contradictions; when passed through the Italian adaptor's table, in contrast, they entirely abdicated that role and became the colored and gaudy background against which new narrative characters were put on scene, targeted at those descendants of the Italian bourgeoisie doomed to see the failure of all their attempts to go off the grid of customary morality and who were forced, finally, to endure a ritual rant.[8]

Here Meda alludes, as many other Italian commentators do,[9] to the fact that, in comparison to the US originals, the Italian versions looked far more saturated with bourgeois moralism and conformism, because of a precise strategy[10] of the cultural elites of the time to use comics to influence society, thus heavily affecting their subsequent development. The elimination of the balloons reveals another relevant feature of this early attitude, that is to say the well-established belief in the superior value of written texts, associated with "highbrow" culture, against that of the visual component of comics, associated with "lowbrow" culture.

To put it briefly, the insertion of *rhymed* captions below each panel betrays the fear that, becoming too familiar with simple colored images instead of written words, the little Italians of the future would distance themselves from the idealized vision depicting them as "Un popolo di

6. See Roger Sabin, *Adult Comics. An Introduction* (London: Routledge, 1993).

7. Juri Meda, *Stelle e strips. La stampa a fumetti italiana tra americanismo e antiamericanismo 1935-1955* (Macerata: Edizioni Università di Macerata, 2007).

8. *Ibid.*, pp. 18-19.

9. For instance see Franco Restaino, *Storia del fumetto da Yellow Kid ai manga*, (Milan: Utet, 2004); Claudio Carabba, *Corrierino, Corrierona. La politica illustrata del 'Corriere della Sera'* (Florence: Guaraldi, 1976).

10. See Fausto Colombo, *La cultura sottile. Media e industria culturale in Italia dall'Ottocento agli anni Novanta* (Milan: Bompiani, 1998).

poeti, di artisti, di eroi, di santi, di pensatori, di scienziati, di navigatori, di trasmigratori" ("A people of *poets*, artists, heroes, saints, thinkers, scientists, sailors, transmigrators", my italics), according to the widespread nationalist rhetoric of the time, later perfected and exploited also by the Fascist Regime. The above quoted motto, indeed, was pronounced in 1935 by Benito Mussolini himself and can still be read on the facade of the Palazzo della Civiltà Italiana in Rome.

A further explanation has been found for the *Corrierino*'s redrawings. The editorial staff of the journal considered the allusive language of the original balloons too hard to understand for the Italian children of the time, because it referred to a highly urbanized socio-cultural context, considerably different from the Italian, still largely rural, one.[11] In this sense, the very commercial success of the journal appeared to be tied to the re-adaption of the originals according to the taste and experience of the Italian public. Given this, it can be said that when one considers Italian comics in an incubation phase up until the Sixties, a combination between the introduction of the logic of serialization into cultural production and the political use of cultural products is evoked to explain the phenomenon. What is implied is that serialization mechanisms were put in the service of a kind of ideological manipulation intended to educate the people, which considerably delayed the emergence of Italian comics as a self-standing form of artistic expression.

What is missed in this view, however, is the variety of solutions that the general tendency to mix the 9th art with politics and ideology was able to originate, and the possibility to consider how this variety may have affected the Italian readership. Indeed, although *Corrierino*'s format remained the dominant one for more or less thirty years, other actors did emerge, proposing slightly different alternative models. Starting from the 1922, various comic journals sponsored by the Fascist movement were published (like *Il Giornale dei Balilla* or *La Piccola Italiana*). In general, those journals substantially replicated *Corrierino*'s scheme, but superimposing to it stories produced in Italy by Italian authors propagandistically introducing graphic realism and promoting themes like religious faith, courage, the sacrality of work, military discipline and heroism.

The diversification of Italian comics landscape was even increased in the Thirties, when more market-oriented publishing houses – such as

11. Meda, *Stelle e strips*, p. 18.

Lotario Vecchi's SAEV or the Florentine Nerbini – started to publish US adventure strips like *Tim Tyler's Luck* (italianized as *Cino e Franco*), *Flash Gordon*, *Phantom*, *Mandrake* with minor interventions, definitely abdicating to the system of the rhymed captions and adopting balloons.[12] Such journals, the most famous of which were *L'Avventuroso* and *Topolino* (publishing Floyd Gottfredson's *Mickey Mouse* and still in press today), were instant successes, thus becoming the model also for *Il Vittorioso*, another highly influential comic journal born in the same years from the initiative of Catholic organizations and distributed also through the omnipresent network of churches and parishes. *Il Vittorioso*, however, published only materials produced in Italy, with the precise intention of contrasting the diffusion of American comics that appeared too much licentious and morally dangerous from a Catholic perspective.[13]

The tendency to diversification that became possible with the appearance of a plurality of centers of comics production and publication was reduced, but not eliminated, by the adoption of economic autocracy by the Fascist Regime at the end of the Thirties with the approaching of World War II. Notoriously, the restrictions to the import of US materials did not touch Disney's comics until 1942,[14] and the pressing imposition of the Fascist rhetoric on all the media was in a way less compelling for Catholic publishers.[15] The availability of different models of comics was still present in the post-war years and continued to be tied to the ideological contrasts emerging from the political landscape. While influent journals like *Corrierino* and *Il Vittorioso* survived the war and comics continued to be largely associated with "lowbrow" culture, the most influent political formations of the time, the Christian Democrats and the Communists, put them at the center of complex internal debates about the influence they might exert on youngsters and society.

Those debates were also fostered by the unofficial diffusion in the country of the comic books "imported" by the US occupation army that triggered an enormous amount of imitations and clones,[16] and whose

12. Fabio Gadducci, Leonardo Gori, Sergio Lama, *Eccetto Topolino. Lo scontro culturale tra fascismo e fumetti* (Eboli: NPE, 2006).

13. Meda, *Stelle e strips*, pp. 48ff.

14. *Ibid.*, p. 74.

15. *Ibid.*, p. 60.

16. See for example *Dick Fulmine. L'avventura e le avventure di un eroe italiano*, ed. by Gianni Bono and Leonardo Gori (Milan: Motta, 1997).

success appeared to be based on the excessive depiction of violence and on the exaggerate sexual allusiveness of their female characters. A similar criticism was directed also to the *albi a striscia*, a new comic book format consisting in very cheap little strip-shaped booklets of two or three black and white panels per page horizontally disposed, invented by the "independent" Bonelli publishing house (named CEPIM at that time) that introduced in 1948 the longest-running Italian character, Tex Willer, as well as an autochthonous standard for the adventure genre still alive today, even if with relevant modifications.

This is not the place for a detailed analysis of the Italian debate on comics in the post-war years, in which various themes were implicitly woven together – such as the distinction between "high" and "low" art, Americanism and anti-Americanism, the hopes triggered by the incipient democratization of the country and the fears of falling back again into totalitarianism or into Bolshevism.[17] Anyway, it seems important to note that the positions toward comics of the Christian Democrats and the Communist Party (involved itself in various attempts to enter the field of comics publication culminating in 1950 with the appearance of the journal *Il Pioniere*) remained largely ambivalent, thus furthering the variety of the Italian comics landscape of the time. On the one side, they continued to criticize comics, especially those similar to Bonelli's ones, but, on the other side, they tried to put them in the service of their respective ideologies. In this sense, it can be said that at the beginning of the Sixties comic art in Italy was seen either as cheap entertainment or as a potential instrument to educate the masses.

This attitude is commonly considered to have changed during that decade, pinpointed by the birth of the magazine *Linus* in 1965 "whose editorial board included authors and intellectuals such as Oreste del Buono and whose first issue hosted a round table on comic strips featuring Umberto Eco and Elio Vittorini".[18] *Linus*, named after one of Charles Schultz's well known characters, was an anthological review juxtaposing Italian and foreign products imported mainly from the USA. What was new about the magazine, however, was that it presented for the first time strips such as

17. On this see at least Leonardo Becciu, *Il fumetto in Italia* (Florence: Sansoni, 1971); Ermanno Detti, *Il fumetto tra cultura e scuola* (Florence: La Nuova Italia, 1984); Meda, *Stelle e strips*.

18. Simone Castaldi, *Drawn and Dangerous. Italian Comics of the 1970s and 1980s* (Jackson: University of Mississippi, 2010), p. 13.

Peanuts, *Lil'Abner*, *Popeye* with philological accuracy, and accompanying them with critical essays assessing their aesthetic and cultural value, thus definitely presenting comics as something worth of attention by the well-educated adults. *Linus*, in other words, is commonly held to introduce the distinction between comics aiming primarily at commercial success and the so called *fumetto d'autore* (literally: *auteur comics*), a category that has become since then fundamental in Italian comics culture.

Fumetto d'autore refers to a way of conceiving the 9th art doomed to gain space also on journals like *Corrierino* and on more Catholic-oriented publications in the following years, finally acknowledging "legitimacy to the [comic-makers'] professional work, [thus welcoming] Italian authors who would not have being given space in large and standardized editorial enterprises".[19] Such Authors – with a capital "A" – included in their ranks Dino Battaglia, Guido Crepax, Guido Buzzelli, Sergio Toppi and, obviously, Hugo Pratt, "the most popular of this group [...] who also had a strong European following, especially in France".[20] On the pages of *Linus*, and of the many magazines that more or less closely adopted a similar approach along the Seventies and the Eighties (like *Sgt. Kirk*, *Corto Maltese*, *Eureka*, *Il Mago*, *Orient Express*, *Frigidaire*, etc...), they found enough space to experiment more freely than before with comic language, in this way definitely affirming its artistic and expressive potential and opening the road for the subsequent generation of Italian great comic artists like Milo Manara and Andrea Pazienza.

However, even if *fumetto d'autore* is the most critically celebrated kind of comics in Italy, it can be hardly said that it was the only one targeted to adults, or the more consumed one, or even the dominant one. Some years before *Linus*, in 1962, another standard-form for adult comics was introduced by Angela and Luciana Giussani's *Diabolik* (still in press today). Published in cheap black and white books considerably smaller than *Linus*' tabloid format, each presenting self-conclusive episodes with darkly colored covers and plots largely inspired by crime novels, *Diabolik* could be immediately identified by the readers as radically different from any other available product, both for form and contents. In a short time, the publication generated an enormous amount of imitations and clones that, in the following decades, ranged from gothic to truculent and morbid

19. Manai, "Comics", p. 179.
20. Castaldi, *Drawn and dangerous*, p. 24.

tones, from poor quality eroticism to explicit pornography, also originating the phenomenon of the so called *fumetti neri* (literally: black comics), whose seminal value for the future development of comics in Italy has been recently reconsidered.[21]

2. *Hugo Pratt's oeuvre and the relation between comics and politics*

Hugo Pratt's *Ballad* was partially serialized in 1967 on the magazine *Sgt. Kirk*, and later fully reprinted by *Linus* in the same way. At that time, Pratt was already a professional comic maker who had worked in Argentina for several years (with Héctor Gérman Oesterheld) and collaborated with *Corrierino*. The *Ballad* has been seen as groundbreaking for its narrative strategies and graphic/visual construction, clearly capable of fascinating adults more than children.[22] Not least, it was conceived as a kind of literary work, a long self-standing story far from the rigid simplicity and linearity imposed by serialization rules largely put in the service of comics' ideological use.

Thanks to the *Ballad*, Pratt is considered the first and most important representative of the above mentioned *fumetto d'autore* genre. But such qualification is usually credited to him on the basis of a view which identifies the peculiar trait of Italian comics culture in its delayed development and which adopts aestethic or stylistic criteria. However, how it will be clarified in the following, in this way Pratt's work risks to appear scarcely innovative, if compared with that of the other great Italian comic artists of the same generation. A better explanation of the reason why Pratt deserves an important place in the history of Italian comic art can be achieved stressing his ability to exploit the political potential comics enjoyed in Italy; a potential resulting from the fact that since their first appearence they had been seen as a field of intervention by a plurality of authorities and centers of power.

Pratt differentiates himself from other authors of the same generation in that his fame and reputation are tied to the character of Corto Maltese more than to his style. In the graphic representation of his many adventures,

21. *Ibid.*

22. See Castaldi, *Drawn and dangerous*, pp. 24-25; Daniele Barbieri, *Breve storia della letteratura a fumetti* (Rome: Carocci, 2014).

however, the fixity exhibited by the sailor puts him close to the prototypical serial hero of commercial comics. Thus, the validity of the opposition between higher quality auteur comics and lower quality market-oriented ones, usually adopted to describe Italian comics history in terms of a more pronounced artistic awareness of the formers, is in a way mined by crediting Pratt as the first and most important representative of the *fumetto d'autore* genre. For instance, the peculiar mix of fake cynicism and romanticism marking Corto Maltese's personality is so unalterable, recognizable, and captivating that even recently it has been possible to think to enlarge the series of his adventures without the contribution of the original creator both in written (see Marco Steiner's series of novels) and graphic form,[23] suggesting that they may indeed go on indefinitely. From the point of view of seriality and serialization, a character like Guido Crepax's Valentina could appear in comparison far more groundbreaking, being subject to radical modifications, like those connected to childbirth, mental disease, and to a complex relationship with her partner, that somehow prevent her graphic adventures to go on forever.

If we move on to consider the formal aspects of Pratt's oeuvre, the issue risks to become even more confused. From a narrative point of view, it presents elements (one for all, its exoticism) that are clearly derived from the XIX century adventure novel and *feuilleton*, that is, from those literary forms that contributed enormously to the adoption of market-oriented serialization strategies into the field of cultural and artistic production. Moreover, from the visual and graphic point of view, Pratt, who was a self-taught artist, proposes a quick and incisive style highly indebted to Milton Caniff, that is similar to the one adopted by commercial comics *á la* Bonelli and that, in his late years, evolved toward a syntheticism similar to Disney's comics. In short, we can say that Pratt's style is far both from the graphic experimentalism typical of other great Italian Authors – again, with a capital "A" – like Crepax or Sergio Toppi, and from the realistic mimeticism characterizing Manara or Tanino Liberatore, all of whom received a traditional education in drawing and constantly confronted themselves with "high" art.

Finally, if we shift to Pratt's professional life, it could be difficult to consider him a representative of the new relevance comics authorship was

23. Jualian Diaz Canales, Rubén Pellejero, *Corto Maltese. Sotto il sole di mezzanotte* (Milan: Rizzoli-Lizard, 2015).

assuming in the Italian context, given that Pratt's fame has been tied to only one of his many characters, and that it is well known that he was constantly struggling to obtain more remunerative hiring conditions.[24] It seems quite hard, therefore, to fully justify the value usually attributed to Pratt's oeuvre using only aesthetic and stylistic criteria. Beyond that, if we try to explain his centrality in Italian comics culture through his well-known love for written culture pressing him to fill his works with "high" literary references in order to make comics worth reading also for the well-educated, we will be at risk of being easily contested. Indeed, he himself highlighted quite polemically that "in speaking about London, Shakespeare, Thomas More, I also give to someone the curiosity of reading them. I had never read Thomas More *Utopia*, neither Corto Maltese did, but, because of me, some readers want to go and see what is in that work".[25] In short, it is unquestionable that Pratt was a great artist and one of the first to fascinate also adults, but the problem is how to justify this statement.

A possible alternative explanation could refer to the political significance that Pratt's oeuvre assumed in the Italian comics landscape. The author himself puts us along this interpretative path, declaring, when asked by a French interviewer to explain why people loved Corto so much, that "Maybe it is because he was born in 1967, before the great juvenile contestation of 1968. At that time, everybody had the urge to undertake the research for liberty, to contest official culture, to have a change. And then, Corto Maltese had in himself something libertarian that made people dream. He was born under a good sign".[26] But in what sense may Pratt's work be considered political? Obviously, it is quite difficult to speak about a direct or explicit political intention, since Pratt's efforts to remain within the boundaries of entertainment comics are evident, if compared, for instance, to those of Guido Buzzelli. Gaetano Strazzulla, one of the founding fathers

24. Oreste del Buono recalls this point in an episode of the famous television program *Fumo d'inchiostro*, available at the following link: https://www.youtube.com/watch?v=PzaZgtMAja4. See also Boschi, *Irripetibili*, p. 45. For a portrait of Pratt from the perspective of his private life see Silvina Pratt, *Con Hugo. Il creatore di Corto Maltese raccontato dalla figlia* (Venice: Marsilio, 2008).

25. Hugo Pratt, Dominique Petitfaux, *De l'autre côté de Corto* (Paris: Casterman, 1996), p. 166.

26. It was not possible to identify the original source of the filmed document, which however, is available at the following link: https://www.youtube.com/watch?v=ePZjYwQPlUM.

of comic criticism in Italy, gives us a useful indication towards a tentative answer, when he writes that "today a huge and heterogeneous public accepts, consciously or unconsciously, the way of thinking, of speaking and of acting suggested by comics".[27]

Writing in 1980, Strazzulla interrogates himself about the possible long-run effects of the global phenomenon of comics diffusion. However, interpreting his words as simply indicating that, for example, an increasing number of people were imitating the behavior of comic characters seems quite superficial. Probably, Strazzulla's words may be better read as the attempt to identify a *sensibility* toward comics, pressing in some ways people to take them "seriously". Following this suggestion, also Italo Calvino's experience with comics[28] may illustrate how and why such sensibility acquired a specific political relevance within the Italian context. In *Six Memos for the Next Millenium*, remembering how he shaped his ability to read comics dealing with the *Corrierino* in the Twenties, he writes:

> The [journal] redrew the American cartoons without balloons, replacing them with two or four rhymed lines under each cartoon. However, being unable to read, I could easily dispense with the words – the pictures were enough. [...] I would spend hours following the cartoons of each series from one issue to another, while in my mind I told myself stories, interpreting the scenes in different ways – I produced variants. [...] When I learned to read, the advantage I gained was minimal. Those simple-minded rhyming couplets provided no illuminating information; often they were stabs in the dark like my own, and it was evident that the rhymester had no idea of what might have been in the balloons of the original, either because he did not understand English or because he was working from cartoons that had already been redrawn and rendered wordless. In any case, I preferred to ignore the written lines and to continue with my favorite occupation of daydreaming *within* the pictures and their sequence.[29]

Calvino highlights the extent to which the peculiar way of presenting comics introduced by the *Corrierino* demanded an imaginative effort by the readers that survived even after the acquisition of reading skills, given, in most cases, the hardly avoidable incongruities between images and rhymed captions. But, in his words, such imaginative effort also colors itself with

27. Gaetano Strazzulla, *I Fumetti. Vol. 1. La storia - gli autori* (Florence: Sansoni, 1980), p. 61.

28. As quoted in Meda, *Stelle e strips*, p. 6.

29. Italo Calvino, *Six Memos for the Next Millennium* (Cambridge: Harvard University Press, 1988), pp. 93-94.

political tones, in that it brings the readers to speculate about the role *other people* may have played in comics production. In other terms, Calvino's words suggest that it was indeed possible for the readers to use comics to position and identify themselves in front and in comparison of those people, speculating about their possible intentions and motivations, and evaluating how and in what sense the possible consequences of their previous actions on comics might be relevant for the readers' own action of reading them. In short, taking together Strazzulla's invitation to focus our attention on the readership sensibility, rather than on the products themselves, and Calvino's contribution, it is possible to open up an alternative "space" to articulate a relation between comics and politics specifically relevant for the Italian case.

Such "space" can be called "political", because the readers' actions, the publishers' actions, the authors' actions, and possibly, also the actions of all those involved in putting comics in the hands of children became in a sense available to reflection, being inextricably intertwined together. It is not a space in which comics-reading qualifies as an emancipating activity in itself. Rather, it is a space in which comics are put at the center of a struggle for appropriation among different possible interpretations (those of the publishers, of the readers, of their authors, etc…) about their meaning and scope, and a space in which comics are carefully scrutinized and examined to identify oneself and the others. Finally, it is not a space emerging from the readership ability to find a sure way to detect, within comics, precise political messages coming from established authorities or centers of power (for example, political parties or organizations). Rather, it is a political space that theoretically precedes the establishment of any given authority or center of power, since it is built on the possibility to attribute motivations, intentions and scopes to other human beings, as well as to use *instrumentally* ideological labels to qualify them, in this case starting from comics. In short, it is a space built on *uncertainty* and on the possibility of multiple interpretations and *misinterpretations* of other people's behavior.

In this sense, the sensibility evoked by Strazzulla's words may well be interpreted as the sensibility to make comics the objects of a political reading, which frequently adopts ideological qualifications and labels. Umberto Eco[30] gives us further exemplification of this peculiar political

30. Umberto Eco, "Fascio e fumetto (Eja, Eja! Gulp!)", in Umberto Eco, *Il costume di casa. Evidenze e misteri dell'ideologia italiana negli anni sessanta* (Milan: Bompiani, 2012), pp. 266-283.

sensibility, and of how much it could be exercised not only towards the other people involved in comics production but also towards other readers. In an article originally appeared on the weekly magazine *Espresso Colore* in 1971, Eco, one of the first intellectuals to introduce the study of the 9th art in universities, confronts himself, moving from a research sponsored in the same years by the University of Parma, with the hypothesis that the *fumetti neri* genre might contain the residual and dangerous presence in the country of a Fascist and totalitarian culture.

It is surely true that *fumetti neri* often exploited Nazi symbolism and were in general poor quality products. However, when re-examined today, Eco's article may be read as an exercise in discriminating safe comics from dangerous ones. For him, the genre displayed an important element differentiating it from the more "intellectual strips diffused by *Linus*".[31]

> [Their heroes] are not good ones fighting against the evil, but bad ones fighting against the good; as such, they are blameworthy in words but fundamentally likeable: they demonstrate day by day that crime pays; often, they assume for themselves vengeful functions and pursue their mission without considering social parameters, being legitimate by the simple act of superior will constituting them as generators of a personal law. With those dark heroes, it is constituted in Italian comics the principle by which the hero, from now on, may have all the characters of the evil one, without being, because of this, less heroic, rather, quite the opposite.[32]

In his opinion, such peculiarity enabled *fumetti neri* to vehicle messages and values clearly in tune with the culture of the Fascist Era, while at the same time making them appear a ridicolous exposition and public condemnation of those same values and messages. Apart from racism and anticommunism, Eco insists in particular on "the cult of violence [...]; the cult of virility (with the annexed contempt of the woman, of sentimentalism, of homosexuality, but of no other possible sexual deviation)",[33] considering such things, which were easy to find in the *fumetti neri*, as characterizing also the prototypical Fascist mentality. Eco did not see the overproduction of *fumetti neri* as the cause of a possible return to fascism, but considered the genre as the ideal kind of entertainment for those culturally deprived "sub-proletarian masses"[34] that could only access popular and mass

31. *Ibid.*, p. 266.
32. *Ibid.*, pp. 276-277.
33. *Ibid.*, p. 270.
34. *Ibid.*, p. 278.

products to elevate themselves, thus indicating how much those masses were at risk of enlarging the ranks of the neo-fascist groups still alive and well in the country.

The point here is not whether Eco, a reader of comics himself, was right or wrong in his evaluations,[35] but that his own act of comics reading produces an identification of "other" readers and of the intentions, motivations and scopes shaping their reading preferences. Eco's article, then, seems to illustrate how the relation between comics and politics in the Italian context has consisted in a specific sensibility by the part of the readers to give a political interpretation to comics often using them to identify other readers, and how much this operation was tied to the possibility of misinterpretation and to the instrumental use of ideological qualifications and labels. Indeed, Eco argument seems instrumental to the defense of his own reading preferences and use of comics, to the extent that it seems hard to conclusively demonstrate that exaggerated virility, machismo, the condemnation of (male) homosexuality and the contempt of women are exclusively traits of a Fascist, or totalitarian, culture or mentality.

Trying to approach the relation between comics and politics starting from the readership sensibility to interpret them politically is something distant from the more usual way to understand this same relation. Federico Vergari, remembering how little the matter has been studied in Italy exemplifies well the mainstream conception. He considers comics as an "alternative way to communicate politics", and consequently the scope of his study is to show how much "comics language can tell about politics".[36] However, in Vergari's perspective comics acquire political value only when they *explicitly thematize* politics, that is, to the extent to which they refer to those "facts and events which regulate the world daily".[37] The point is that in his conception the term "politics" is used in a "strict" sense, thus generating two relevant consequences that contribute enormously to legitimate the exclusion of a large amount of comic products from his analysis, Pratt's ones included.

In the first instance, Vergari perspective seems to imply the idea that an institutional authority or center of power does actually exist, whose

35. The contemporary trend in Italian comics research seems to reverse his judgment. On this see Castaldi, *Drawn and dangerous.*

36. Federico Vergari, *Politicomics: raccontare e fare politica attraverso i fumetti* (Latina: Tunué, 2008), pp. 12-13.

37. *Ibid.*, p. 18.

function is to deal with a finite set of facts and events regulating the world daily and that in this sense would be "political" by nature. In this framework, a political value can be assigned to cultural products such as comics only to the extent to which they explicitly refer to the decisions and behaviors of that authority. By doing so, however, the circumstance is underestimated that a huge amount of the things and actions to which political significance is attributed, are based just on the examination of – and possibly on questioning – the legitimacy of established authorities and political institutions. Among other things, this results in strategies and actions that include, more often than not, acting, speaking and communicating *as if* those authorities did not exist. In other words, Vergari's conception lose sight of the fact that doing politics and acting politically mean to confront oneself with the following constellation of always open questions: *who* decides (or *who* must/should decide) which are those facts and events regulating the world daily? And *whose* world? And in *whose* interest?

In the second instance, Vergari's vision, which can be said to be correct under many aspects, privileges the daily strips of political argument (such as *Doonesbury*). But in this way he seems to overlook that a huge amount of the global comics production – from *Buster Brown*'s tricks to the transformations of teenage losers into superheroes, from the crimes of a punk like Pazienza's *Zanardi* to the adventures of a lone pirate-sailor like Corto Maltese – would result far less interesting if the readers were not able to find in them a contrast with established authorities and institutions that may well be labeled as political, even if only from a personal or subjective point of view. Be it as it may, the relevant point is that if we accept a strict interpretation of "politics", the political dimension begins in the same moment in which a political authority is established and would be meaningless without it. However, there is at least an alternative way to conceive the term "politics" that can be helpful in broadening its meaning. Gilles Deleuze and Felix Guattari implicitly identify the origin of politics with the origin of philosophical thinking itself. They write:

> Philosophy seems to be something Greek and coincides with the contribution of cities: the formation of societies of friends or equals but also the promotion of relationships of rivalry between and within them, the contest between claimants in every sphere, in love, the games, tribunals, the judiciaries, politics, and even in thought, which finds its condition not only in the friend but

in the claimant and the rival [...]. It is the rivalry of free men, a generalized athleticism: the agon.[38]

Deleuze and Guattari suggest that it is not possible to separate philosophy from politics because it is not possible to separate the former from the birth of the Ancient Greeks' city. It was there, within the *polis*, that individual human beings, forced to share a limited portion of space and time, started to reflect on the possibility to see one another not only as friends, but also and at the same time as possible competitors. In this perspective, then, the emergence of the political problem (as Westerners know it) *precedes* the emergence of a given political authority, because authority itself becomes no more than *an attempt* to solve the problems connected to the cohabitation of different individuals. But there is another relevant consequence of Deleuze and Guattari's position. If politics coincides with the very exercise of thinking, then everyone can do politics, as far as it can be said that everybody "thinks". And this is not because a definite set of things or themes exists, endowed with *a priori* political meaning imposing themselves to the human mind, but simply because anyone can think any "other" as a possible rival or allied in the realization of one's own desires and scopes, independently from what the "other" may *actually* do, say or think.

In this "broader" sense, politics does not lie in certain places, themes or issues, but, so to speak, in the eyes of those who observe those places, themes and issues. In other words, everything is political to the extent that it is recognized as such by someone (to use an idea that is possible to trace back at least to Rousseau's maxim: "Tout tient au politique" and quoted by Miguel Abensour).[39] What is worth noting here is the usefulness this vision may have for the study of comics, in that it enables us to say both that all comics may be "political" and that the value of excellent comics makers may depend also on the ways in which their works suggest political readings even if they did not explicitly intend to "be political" or to "make politics".

38. Gilles Deleuze, Félix Guattari, *What is Philosophy?* (New York: Columbia University Press, 1994), p. 4.

39. Miguel Abensour, "Du bon usage de l'hypothése de la servitude volontarie?", *Réfractions*, 17 (2006), pp. 65-84.

3. *Discovering the politics of Corto Maltese*

From the above discussion, it should be clear that adopting a "strict" conception of the term "politics" in examining the relation it entertains with comics loses sight of the fact that in Italy, probably far more than in the English-speaking world, comics were seen as something political since their first appearance and quite independently from the "stories" they presented. Since the rhymed-captions era inaugurated by *Corrierino* in 1908, the 9th art was understood as a pedagogical instrument to intervene on national culture at the aim of making society more similar to what *someone* considered the ideal, more desirable model of society. In this sense, variety and diversification of form and contents can indicate how much the Italian comics landscape came to be characterized by different and even competing forms of intervention by a plurality of centers of powers. The "strict" conception of politics was diffused not only among political parties and organizations, intellectuals and academics, but also among comics professionals and editors. In the year preceding the *Ballad*'s publication, the 2nd Lucca meeting on comics[40] testifies how much important it was, also for them, to clearly define the role of comics in the national cultural policy, to distinguish between "good" and "bad" comics – a qualification which often put on table the question of the "crypto-fascist" nature of these products –, and identify the proper measures to exploit their expressive potential – censorship included – in the most adequate manner.

From this point of view the Sixties, that is to say the beginning of the comics-specialized magazines era, far from being the moment in which Italian comics were supposedly freed from external intrusions, did not modify much the situation. As Simone Castaldi interestingly notes, when *a certain kind* of comics started to be perceived as something to be appreciated also by well-educated adults, it was appropriated mainly by the left-wing culture:

> In this climate, the question of the culturally and politically ambiguous position of adult comics, by now a legitimate periphery of official culture, became extremely problematic. On this subject, the case of *Linus* is certainly paradigmatic. Almost from its inception, its readership was primarily left-wing supporters, either independent or tied to the Communist Party –

40. AA.VV., *I fumetti. Atti del convegno di Lucca. 24 settembre-2 ottobre 1996* (Rome: Istituto di Pedagogia dell'Università di Roma).

comic book aficionados who enjoyed the Italian and American Golden-Age reprints, those mostly interested in progressive American political strips such as *Doonesbury* and Feiffer's one-pagers, and those who enjoyed the new Italian maestros such as Pratt, Crepax, and Battaglia. However, most of them superimposed a strict ideological reading on *Linus*'s offerings (one which the editorial staff encouraged to a certain extent). Walt Kelly's Pogo, for example, was regarded as a strip with strong leftist innuendos, as were, by way of bizarre hermeneutical strategies, Al Capp's *Li'l Abner* and Hart's *B.C.*[41]

Castaldi suggests that the politicization of Italian comics culture was something emanating in a significant part from the readers themselves, probably because they were been educated and encouraged, so to say, to read comics politically by a long history of political interventions on the 9th art. This is also the reason why, in order to evaluate Pratt's oeuvre, it might be very useful to turn to the attitude of the readership and to its interpretative ability. But how can this be done? According to Castaldi,[42] Pratt was able to gain the title of "master" only confining himself into the neutral and sure terrain of adventure comics. However, this view seems to overlook the circumstance that Pratt was able to traverse almost all the development of Italian comics innovating and professionally influencing it. As soon as 1945, he was among the protagonists of an experimental comics-specialized magazine, *L'Asso di Picche*, which transformed for a short time a group of young artists into their own publishers, in a way anticipating the do-it-yourself philosophy. He was able to become famous abroad before than in Italy, forced, as remembered also by del Buono in the already mentioned interview, to emigrate to make a living out of comics. He had the chance to test on himself the effects of *Corrierino*'s pedagogical approach. Moreover, he was probably the only Italian comic-maker to see two high quality magazines entitled to his characters. The first was *Sgt. Kirk*, produced by a simple but wealthy fan named Lorenzo Ivaldi and aimed at the publication of high quality comics.[43] The second was that same *Corto Maltese* on the pages of which his stories were juxtaposed to those realized by authors of international reputation like Frank Miller and Alan Moore. In the course of all those professional peregrinations Pratt never wanted to find a home, so to say, and was able to move freely thanks to the appreciation of his public.

41. Castaldi, *Drawn and dangerous*, p. 31.
42. *Ibid.*, p. 32.
43. Boschi, *Irripetibili*, p. 18.

In sum, many reasons seem to be there to say that Pratt's work might acquire also a political meaning to his readers' eyes. Pratt might appear, in a way similar to Corto himself, making no compromises, be it with *Linus* or anyone else. He might appear, in other words, "a rockstar", to quote the expression that Pazienza used to define himself in one of his stories, and whose evocative power may be understood only considering the fascination exercised by some English words on the Italian speakers. Beyond that, the efforts of the *enfants terrible* of Italian comics like Pazienza, Liberatore, Scòzzari and Tamburini[44] to preserve their own professional freedom could not be fully understood without considering Pratt as their forerunner.

There are also more aesthetic and stylistic reasons able to highlight the ways in which the readers could attribute political significance to his works. As noted before, Pratt's drawings and simple dialogues highly differentiated him from the more experimental style adopted by other contemporary great Italian authors. In this sense, they might illustrate well what Pratt meant claiming for himself the qualification of *fumettaro*, using the pejorative transformation of the word *fumettista* which usually translates in a politically correct way the English "comic-maker".

Reading Pratt's works of the Sixties it is clear that to say something new and revolutionary it was not necessary to break all the rules and schemes, or to resort to frontal contestation and intellectualism, even if these latter solutions probably seemed to be the only viable roads in that moment. But what could we say about the contents and characters of his most popular works? It will suffice here to remember what Corto reveals in the *Ballad*. Discovering, as a child, that he did not have any fortune-line on his hand, he made himself one as long as he wanted, with his father's razor-blade, in this way highlighting that it is possible to build one's own fortune simply refusing to accept as true and objective any ready-made interpretation of reality. It seems, then, that Corto and his author were able to speak about politics, and to do politics, in a broad sense, without explicitly talking about the behaviors and actions of the established political authorities and doing as if they did not exist, so suggesting that it is possible to live an equilibrated life without the recognition of any authority apart from one's own.

It seems difficult to maintain that this political dimension of Pratt's oeuvre was not available to those who appreciated it. On the contrary, it seems that it was also because of the presence of this political vein in his work that

44. On these authors see Castaldi, *Drawn and dangerous.*

Pratt can say: "I have found a huge number of people [...] believing to be Corto Maltese [...], being always convinced to have something in common with the personality of this character, of this individual, of this cartoon [...]. A good mate Corto Maltese, anyway. The mate that many people [...] many would like to have".[45] In this sense, the value of Pratt's oeuvre is that it reveals how much comics in general and his own in particular were at the center of a political struggle for appropriation among different possible interpretations. It will not be so surprising, then, to discover that in 2011 Corto Maltese was the object of a public debate sponsored by Casa Pound, a contemporary radical right-wing organization, and indicatively entitled "Camerata Corto Maltese" (that may be translated as: "Corto Maltese, the Comrade"), juxtaposing to the name of the character one of the most clearly recognizable Fascist epithets and pointing to make the character part of the Italian right-wing culture.

The initiative justly registered the condemnation of Pratt's relatives and friends. But this event, as ridiculous as it may seem, is an important one to remember, since it indicates, from the one side, that on Pratt's oeuvre different and even opposite political readings are projected, contrary to what is usually assumed, while on the other side, it suggests that it deserves a more careful political reading also from the viewpoint of research. It seems today the case to stress that Pratt was a master in playing the role of the "independent" in Italian comics culture, for the way in which his history and his stories remember us that in Italy comics-making, and hence culture-making, is a political matter in and for itself. And, last but not least, for the way in which, in declaring to be a "son of all those who recognize themselves in official culture, but also of those that the same culture does not recognize",[46] Pratt has demonstrated that there is not an absolute necessity to be recognized by an authority which pretends to exist regardless of individuals, and that such an authority could only limit one's own possibility "to sail" freely. A message, this one, that can hardly be ultimately and exclusively appropriated by any possible political ideology.

45. Pratt's word are quoted from an interview originally released for the Italian public television cult show *SuperGulp!*, which was broadcasted from 1977 to 1981. A partial transcription of the interview can be read on-line at this link: http://www.451online.it/radio-3-su-carta-hugo-pratt-e-altre-latitudini/.

46. Pratt's words are reported in Vincenzo Mollica, Mauro Paganelli, *Hugo Pratt* (Montepulciano: Editori del Grifo, 1980), p. 52; these words are also quoted in Marchese, *Leggere Hugo Pratt*, p. 8.

Marco Bracci and Edoardo Tabasso

Stil Novo. The Legendarily Adventurous Route of Italian Music in Search of Pop(ular) Maturity[1]

1. *Once upon a time in Italy*

Until 1945, the record market in Italy was hardly sizable: a million and a half records were sold, and in 1950, the number raised to 3 million. Italian record companies offered a limited amount of international hits, but sales would soon undergo a hike thanks to the production of 45 rpms. Unlike the US radio system, where for decades private and commercial networks had played a significant role in the spreading of pop music, in Italy the state broadcast Rai still had full ownership.

In 1953 RCA, the largest US record company, opened an independent branch in the Italian market, settling in Rome in a building with state-of-the-art equipment. As for the movie industry and the television in Rome, the center of gravity of the Italian discography was shifting, searching allies in movies and radio programs to create ideal synergies to launch the records. The arrival of RCA in Italy marked the end of the pioneering phase of Italian discography, and the opening of new perspectives, where marketing acquired a significance never seen before, and where the American business philosophy paired the value of production.

In 1956 Elvis Presley's single *Heartbreak Hotel* was published; soon to be nicknamed "the Pelvis", Elvis was white but sang like a black, and swung on stage in a way that was then considered obscene and demonic, upturning the quiet American society. Elvis was young and sang for the

1. The planning, contents and entire coordination of this chapter was carried out by the combined work of the two authors. More in detail, the authors developed the paragraphs together.

youth; teenagers revered him like an idol because he sang about love and pain, therefore close to their universe of feelings. Nevertheless, only in 1961 did Elvis reach the third position in the Italian hit parade, but was able to keep it for a very short time; moreover, it was with *It's now or never*, a cover of the very Italian song *'O sole mio* and ranked only seventeen in the yearly classification.

As Gino Castaldo wrote in an article in *La Repubblica* on July 18, 2007: "The rock 'n' roll revolution that had shaken the social order in the US was a lukewarm event in Italy". In 1957, Italy was not ready: true, the Italian audience did not welcome the new music style eagerly, but let's not forget that in those same years, our musicians were dazzled by the new sound and new American rhythm. 1958 was the real divide, the year when RCA distributed the first songs by Elvis Presley in Italy and produced Domenico Modugno, who topped the *Festival di Sanremo* with his *Nel blu, dipinto di blu*, otherwise known as *Volare*; exported in the USA, it sold 22 million copies all over the world; "only" 800,000 copies in Italy, yet an amazing amount for the Italian market.

While all of the USA were listening to *Nel blu, dipinto di blu*, its success spread out in Europe too; in 1958, the single was launched on the British market in nine different versions: the original one, four American versions, and four played and sung by English bands and singers. The following years, over 250 performers, some of which rather questionable, tested themselves with this Italian and international hit, translating it in several languages and arranging it according to various musical tastes and fashions. Even David Bowie and Frank Zappa, to name two of the most significant innovators in the recent history of British and US pop music.[2]

The history, genre, and use of *Nel blu, dipinto di blu* are therefore Italian, but in the course of the years, they have become international; a sort of unceasing hybridity, a mingling of musical traditions and modernity; a bridge across the before and the after; a symbolic representation of the cultural, social and economic shift that Italy was experiencing in the late Fifties and early Sixties. This scenario embraced the new musicians who started looking at the UK and the USA, and the reference points they offered, for the production and the consumption of pop music in Italy.

2. Maria Cristina Zoppa, *Nel blu, dipinto di blu. Modugno, 1958 "Volare" e il sogno possibile* (Rome: Donzelli, 2008).

2. *Launching discography between juke-boxes and summer hits*

In May 1955 the first juke-box made its appearance in Italy from Chicago, about twenty years later compared to its arrival in the USA. Juke-boxes had an alternative role compared to the radio, which did not broadcast songs with lyrics about subject that could have jeopardized the righteousness of a nation that had just started its process of cultural modernization. Juke-boxes were so successful that in 1958, Italy counted 4,000 coin-operated machines, and their number increased considerably in the following years.

To fully grasp the effect of their appearance in our country, we should mention the deep, swift change Italy was experiencing, aided by the social shift featuring a strong urbanization, abandonment of the countryside, and the increasing population density in the cities, which were becoming the cornerstone of working life. The combo of juke-boxes and summer hits was, and still is, an Italian distinctive feature. The summer-holiday 45 rpm in vogue in the early Sixties was invented by the minds behind RCA; those few people had the merit of grasping the change in the Italian society, of spotting the new sound, and letting new artists stand out, thus leading them to success. These record producers had fully understood that the economic boom was also affecting music consumption, as revealed by the fact that people had the possibility to spend more money to listen to music.

The Beatles represented the real cornerstone, marking the net border between the before and the after in the international and Italian musical scenario: the hairy nonconformist "rebels" who mingled rock and pop. Through vinyl records and, for the lucky few, live concerts, Italians learnt all about the four kids from Liverpool (George Harrison, John Lennon, Paul McCartney, and Ringo Starr) who held eight concerts in June 1965. In the meantime, the partnership between music and movies was reinforced by the current of movies put together in the wake of the success of a song, from which they smartly took the title, and the popularity of its performer. Almost all the Italian singers in the limelight in the Sixties participated as stars or co-stars; Celentano, Morandi, Mina, Rita Pavone, Bobby Solo, Caterina Caselli, Little Tony, Al Bano and Romina Power.

These movies were a great help to record companies, as they contributed in strengthening the appeal of renowned artists, or helped those still finding their feet. Thanks to the capillary distribution of the over 20,000 movie theaters spread out all over Italy, those movies brought music and performers also in the areas not reached by the TV signal or where subscribers were still scant.

Movies derogatorily nicknamed "musicarelli", *b-movies*, that is, low-budget movies of an average cost of 20-30 million liras, able to obtain large financial recoups, sometimes around the billion. Shot in the late Fifties, these movies helped turn Italian music into a show and were a formidable advertisement, forerunners of nowadays music videos. For instance, the movie *I ragazzi del juke-box* starring Adriano Celentano, directed by Lucio Fulci, appreciated and quoted by Quentin Tarantino.

As Giandomenico Curi stated, the directors and screenwriters of these *musicarelli* completely put aside the social problems that marked the music of the late Seventies, as well as all the incentives and contaminations that brought forth on the one hand the Italian beat, and on the other the early definition of the singer-songwriters. Curi adds that there was no deep analysis of the new relation with the American sound, nor a realistic awareness that the youth were creating a world apart, marked by the widening gap with the previous generations.[3]

Around the late Fifties, rock 'n' roll had dropped its wild features, now aware that this form of musical communication was something through which the youth were able to express themselves, their aspirations, and their hopes against the social order. The music industry was taking over the distribution process and the rules of production, alongside television and movies. The golden period was coming to an end, but the music arriving from the UK kept the transgressive features: rock 'n' roll was a new musical genre but also a life style. Rebelling against school, social order, family, politics was a new cultural means able to kindle the demons of the youth renewal against the post-war quietude of the adults. The seeming order was being upturned by the youth reacting against the adults converting to the social pacification immediately following the dreadful world war. In the shift from rock 'n' roll to rock, it was thanks to the British music that pop music gained a new status, its own respectability, thus becoming not a mere commercial phenomenon, but obtaining a leading role in separating the youth from the adults. Not yet in the name of a so-called class struggle, as was the case with the European revolts at

3. Giandomenico Curi, *I frenetici: storia del cinema musicale dal rock 'n' roll ai nostri giorni* (Rome: Arcana, 1992).

the end of the decade, but as the uprising and pondering of a culture, or rather, as someone defined it, "subculture".[4]

The British working class youth adopted new musical timbres to be distinguished from their respectable peers; the *teddy boy* style come into being in England before the advent of rock 'n' roll, reinforced and renewed its ties with the American music. It was also thanks to music that girls caused deep changes, influencing also new relations in gender identities. Teenage girls of the post-war period started to create new spaces of freedom outside their homes, for instance in colleges, but also within their homes. The so-called *bedroom culture* of British and American teenage girls started to invade the whole of Europe, and Italy as well. Girls gained a space in their bedrooms that allowed them to express their nature through cultural consumptions: they could hang posters of their *teen idols*, revealing a premarital erotic imagination well before the sexual revolution that would go off in the late Seventies.

The much more different Italian context featured similar dynamics, but the processes of public representation of the youth, the moral revolution that in the other European countries had started to settle and develop in the previous decades, burst out in the second part of the Sixties as a bombshell, favoring the creation of much more structured, proactive, and bubbly youth movements.

3. *The new attention-seeking youth*

In the second part of the Sixties, Italy was going through a period full of contradictions; modernization was taking place while the economic boom of the previous years was giving way to recession. Prices were starting to go up and inflation was already lurking. Many of the social questions that had been left unanswered or had been treated lightly, hoping they would magically solve by themselves, started to surface. As in all the other Western countries, starting from the USA, the protests of 1968 gave the unanswered questions the opportunity to merge.

The Italian protests lasted very long, over 10 years covering two decades, from the second half of the Sixties well into the Seventies. The

4. Dick Hebdige, *Sottocultura. Il fascino di uno stile innaturale* (Genoa: Costa & Nolan, 1983).

youth didn't merely want to claim the change of moral and family habits, or the exhibition of sexual behaviors until then deemed inappropriate. The claims to change of the students and the workers became political prerogatives in the common target of revising the power relations. In Italy, thanks to mass education, the numbers of students in secondary schools and universities increased: in 1968 the students between 15 and 23 years were about 6 million, and in the early Seventies over 600,000 attended university.

In their radical reformism and sometimes irresponsible wishful thinking, the youth protested for better schooling, better work conditions, and fairer salaries. In 1967, the priest of a small village in Mugello, north of Florence, father Lorenzo Milani, edited a book titled *Lettere ad una professoressa* (*Letters to a professor*), written by the students of the school of Barbiana that he managed. A true best-seller, the book was the manifesto of that generation, passionately denouncing the new social distress. We must point out that in Rome, in April 1966, violent clashes between youths of different political factions had taken place; in the same year, several youths showed their need to commit themselves, rushing to Florence after the ghastly flood of the river Arno, to dig the books from the mud and offer help to the deeply wounded city.

The 1968 protests showed its farcical side and the psychodrama of a generation also animated by useless nihilism, weary of its duties and oriented towards the deprecation of values for the sake of change that originated no realistic solution. What music did those youths listen and danced to, while their hair grew and their fathers' suits and ties and their mothers' knee-length skirts stayed in the wardrobe? The same skirts that Mary Quant, in the 1963 *Swinging London* shortened to show the girl's shockingly provocative legs, thus launching a fashion that quickly spread out in the world?

Italy was just starting to experience the teenager takeover, where a new awareness generating omnipotent feelings but also deep angst. The youth easily lost the sense of reality and the limit of their capacity: any kind of wish seemed attainable, but Italy of the post economic-boom did not make wishes come true, therefore, just like their foreign peers, the Italian teenagers and youths found solace in a consolatory self-pity only able to criticize something or someone, and unable to face the hardship.

A survey in the magazine *L'Europeo* in January 1964 taken on a group of youths between 15 and 19, from different social classes, stated that they bought at least a record per week, preferably a 45 rpm. They favored modern songs, their songs. A young worker commented that she liked both the fast pieces and the slow, blue songs. It must be said that the unfavorable economic conjuncture caused by the productive crisis of 1963, did not hinder the upward trend of the Italian record industry, as shown by the 23,000 record stores at the beginning of that decade selling records, and the number of juke-boxes reaching the amount of 20,000 pieces. Sales went up, and at in the late Sixties, 45 rpms reached the amount of 37 million pieces, and 5 million LPs sold. There were, to be honest, a few standstills to mention: for instance, the records of the 1965 *Sanremo* edition, deep in the conjuncture, sold only half than in the previous year, "only" three million.

A survey carried out by the Doxa – the Italian opinion poll company – on behalf of the Italian Union for Chambers of Commerce, stated that in 1965 teenagers were the largest consumers of music: they had purchased 400,000 record-players and had spent five billion lire worth in tokens for the juke-boxes. For their cultural consumptions, they had spent 540 billion per year, a billion and a half per day, and had bought 70% of the 27 million records sold that year. That is when music became progressively portable: magnetic tapes came in several different sizes: RCA produced 8-track tapes, while the smaller music tapes launched by Philips started prevailing, also thanks to the fact that Philips introduced means of reproductions that were much more simplified and cheaper than record players; they offered a mechanical device that allowed as many duplication as you wanted off vinyl records. Small devices you could take with you everywhere, and easier to install in cars. In the USA first, and everywhere else soon after, the spreading out of magnetic tape recording caused car radios to become a standard accessory. And the word "copy" became increasingly popular among the youth who started creating their own personal choices of songs to tape and exchange with friends. Unfortunately, this phenomenon favored music piracy. In Italy, tapes started flanking the record market in 1965, surpassing the number of LPs in the following decade, thus contributing to the gradual decadence of 45 rpms.

But well before all this, the commercial ascent of 45 rmps continued. The market introduced the portable record-player, in Italian, "mangiadischi", literally *record eater*. The plastic device had a slot for 45 rpms, a button to expel them, and a volume control knob. It needed batteries and could be carried around with a shoulder strap. The early models were expensive, but between the late Sixties and early Seventies, some ultrathin and very colored models appeared on the market.

The year 1964 marked the first 45 rpm that was able to go past the threshold of a million copies sold in Italy: *Una lacrima sul viso* sung by Bobby Solo. The song reached the 1,700,000 copies sold, and following the fashion of that time, it inspired a movie with the same title. In that period, Italy came up with the idea of promoting the first personalized covers, replacing the colorless ones with the hole in the middle, thus transforming records in a real item to sell and purchase. These 45 rmp covers became coveted goods among collectors and music enthusiasts. RCA inaugurated a graphic department dedicated to record covers, and Ricordi emulated it for the LP covers that were designed in book shape.[5]

4. *All night long*

The Piper Club was inaugurated on February 17, 1965. In the course of the years, more than a dance hall or simple meeting place, the Piper became the brand of the times, and it still exists in Rome, in via Tagliamento. It was founded by the lawyer Alberto Crocetta, by the entrepreneur Giancarlo Bornigia and their partner Piergaetano Tornielli. Sensing the changes that were occurring in the new musical scenario, on the wake of the British bands, the three partners had grasped the extent to which nightlife was starting to play a significant role in the social life of the youth. They sensed that night fun should not be confined to the dance halls during the summer holidays, but should instead be available all year long in the cities. That this new way of enjoying nightlife was becoming a worldwide phenomenon and the need to escape everyday life was invading New York, London and Rome. With the notable difference that Italy did not have a club comparable to the British or American ones, something more than the average night club.

The number of TVs had gone up from 2 million in 1960 to 6 million in 1965. Therefore, radio and TV were acquiring an increasingly significant role for songs to acquire success. The song festivals, such as *Sanremo* early in the year, *Il Cantagiro*, *Un disco per l'estate*, *Festivalbar* in the summer, and *Canzonissima* in the fall, generated an actual music TV planning. Each season was covered and a cycle of competitions similar to a popular ritual had been planned, to hold the interest of the viewers and create loyal customers.

5. Gianni Borgna, *Storia della canzone italiana* (Milan: Mondadori, 1992).

Within the changes occurring in the cultural environment, compared to TV shows, the radio programs had more freedom to experiment, as they were able to avoid the grip of censorship the Italian music system was slowly trying to escape. Until then, those who wanted to listen to music could do it through juke-boxes, since although transistor radios were slowly appearing in Italy, programs dedicated to the youth and to their music were non-existent.

5. *The sound conspiracy of the Italian beat*

The Seventies were the "miraculous decade of rock", an innovative art form grasping the new life style in the cultures it helped emerge. As the youths that at the end of the decade would be named "flower children" were experimenting with the new borders, the *hippie love generation* was a jumble of claims for freedom affecting both the private and the public scope: breaking the social rules; pacifism; communes as a critical alternative to family; the early forms of feminism and environmentalism; exoticism towards the far east; light drugs. All this was associated with the youths' generational identity, through a process of mobilization and political attention-seeking behavior on a world scale featuring nonconformity, separation from the adult world, refusal of social conventions, need to affirm oneself, all through the denial of the established order.[6]

The United Stated exported the utopic, naive notion that everything had to be changed, starting from sexuality that by listening to music found a new rituality; rock 'n' roll had already started the process, but lacked a true awareness and a political project. This change of route involved billions of youths, forever debating between defiance, the need to change, and the urge to consume.

Bob Dylan gave voice to that music turning it into a "communicative mediation". He may not have influenced rock as a music genre, since he started new from popular music, but he may take credit for giving voice, words, contents, and the opportunity to reflect, to the music that Elvis Presley, Chuck Berry and others had played until then, trying to translate into sound and poetry that generation's dreams of freedom and anger. Dylan committed himself in giving his defining moment to rock 'n' roll and turn

6. See Marcello Flores, Alberto De Bernardi, *Il Sessantotto* (Bologna: Il Mulino,1998).

it into rock, by introducing the electric guitar in his famous performance at the *Newport Folk Festival* in 1965, and with *Blowin' in the wind* (1962) and *The times they are a-changin'* (1964), gave music new rigor.

Eager to break free from family traditions, the youth found their source of inspiration and cultural élan in the beat generation of the Fifties, namely in Allen Ginsberg, Jack Kerouac, William Burroughs, Gregory Corso and Lawrence Ferlinghetti: a literary and artistic movement for which art was a place to experiment, a form of rift and liberation. California became the world's magnet with its own 45 rpm anthem *California Dreamin'* by Mamas & Papas and the LP *San Francisco: Be sure to wear flowers in your hair* that included the song *I left my heart in San Francisco* sung by Scott McKenzie. Both were internationally successful, and in Italy Dik Dik wrote a cover of Mamas & Papas' song, calling it *Sognando California* (*California dreaming*).

The Italian beat represented the passage to the British-American pop rock, from which it took the artistic and commercial dynamics in a period of great social and political turmoil that Italy, like the rest of the world, was going through in the second half of the Sixties. In 1965 the band Nomadi was put to shame for the song *Dio è morto* (*God is dead*) written by Francesco Guccini, whose broadcasting was banned by RAI while Radio Vaticana played it. The lyrics read "God is dead / along the edges of the roads / in the cars paid in installments / in the summer myths". The author unsuccessful tried to explain that the text drew inspiration from the Allen Ginsberg's poem *Howl.*

Inspired beat songs were able to interiorize the little social conscience that, as Edmondo Berselli pointed out, was needed to interpret at its best the generational conflict that several Italian families were experiencing, Bands such as Nomadi and Rokes had spread out a scheme, separating the world and society in two: "us" and "you". The youth, and everybody else, the adults. "A separation fully based the generation gap: the youth against the rest of the world".[7] The Italian movement showed several rhythmic leftovers from the Fifties, but the lyrics made the difference when mixed with the pop rock of the Sixties. Often stolen from British and American songs, the lyrics were rearranged by Giulio Rapetti, aka Mogol. The Italian beat was such that even in its songwriting and pop offshoots, it involved the whole Italian music system.

7. Edmondo Berselli, *Canzoni. Storie dell'Italia leggera* (Bologna: Il Mulino, 2007).

6. *From dusk till dawn*

In 1968, the first concept album by Fabrizio De André, *Tutti morimmo a stento*, was released, thus opening the road to more intellectually exacting and sophisticated work compared to the 45 rpm production. No longer a number of songs, but a connected unit of texts that created an unbroken narration between one song and the other. This LP and *Fabrizio De André Vol. 1* topped the Italian charts in 1968. The magazine *Musica e Dischi* realized that the pulse of the music market was expanding, and LPs were already playing a significant role. Up to then, charts only reported the sale of singles, but when, in 1967, the Beatles' *Sgt. Pepper's Lonely Hearts Club Band* was released, the magazine decided to publish also the LP charts; it was a shift in the trend of the purchases of the listeners and in music production, towards a much more complicated product, able to grasp and assess the value of an artist in the collection of their work, no longer limited to the hurried listening of the 45 rpms.

The astonishing era of singles and pop music had marked its personal evolution. From simple soundtrack of society, like someone had hastily defined it, in its visual setting and sound, it had been able to acquire a new role, a new social and cultural significance, capable of marking the public and private moments of contemporary history. Music was no longer a mere "entertainment planet", but the founding place of the acknowledgement of identity. In 1969, in London, on the rooftop at No. 3, Savile Row, the headquarters of the Apple label, the Beatles played live together for the last time, just before they broke up. In the same year, Brian Jones, guitarist of Rolling Stones, died of an overdose, and in the next two years Jimi Hendrix, Janis Joplin and Jim Morrison followed.

Bands like Jefferson Airplane, Grateful Dead, and several other artists of the West Coast, led the American youth towards a collective experience never experimented before, and indirectly, perhaps also towards the end of a naive, deceptive dream: we are speaking of the 3-day-long Woodstock festival in 1969, the ideal conclusion of an incredible decade, the end of an era. The "long summer" of the Sixties was slowly ending, and with it, the golden age of the history of rock; the Seventies were opening with the mass intervention of the big record industry, destined to make large profits and to manage rock music in an increasingly entrepreneurial and calculated way. The major American record companies realized they could manage an oligopoly in music production, since LP cost productions were too high for independent labels. In this scenario, innovation and music research made way for the excessive power of few artists.

And if between the late Sixties and early Seventies the Italian easy-listening music had triumphed in its target to obtain popularity, the next move was to start managing its creative boost, to conquer new listeners in the cultural and commercial comparison with foreign rock pop music. Covers became relevant in numbers and quality in Italy, a sign of the cultural phenomenon that caused positive developments for our music system which finally started a relation with foreign pop music. By rearranging, or rather, reinventing the songs in Italian, the covers introduced English songs to the language-illiterate Italian public. A form of appropriation and readjustment of styles, sounds, artistic and social contexts that were disciplined and translated expressly for the Italian public, thus creating a process of song localization.

Nevertheless, Italian songs had not succeeded in producing a music synthesis that only the Italian progressive rock would achieve from the Seventies, and the singer-songwriters later, who were experts in merging the best tradition of international pop music with their Italian roots.

7. *Music asynchronies*

In the late Seventies the international situation was once again shattered by civil wars and the nightmare of a nuclear war was ever looming. In Italy, the social stability obtained during the economic boom and the carefree attitude of the Sixties was history of the past. The 1970 5.1% inflation rate reached an incredible 21% ten years later, causing the increase in prices and unemployment that for the first time affected the youths. Yet, consumption increased: in 1977, 97% of Italian families had a TV, 94% a fridge, 79% a washing machine, and 64% a car.

Those were the years of the first bombs on trains, in banks, in public places: the neo-fascist attack in Piazza Fontana in Milan in 1969 was the first in a series in a decade tormented by the politicization and violence of the far-right and far-left terrorism alike. In such a political, social and economic situation, the record market continued its growing trend. A concentration among the few record companies was taking place: RCA, Messaggerie Musicali, Ricordi, EMI and RI-FI, later joined by the US WEA and CBS, and the three British companies Virgin, Island, and Chrysalis.

In 1972 the Italian market of recorded music exceeded the threshold of 40 million records sold, and had almost reached the amount of 67 million by the end of the decade. Despite the fact that 45 rpms still took the lion's share, LPs and tapes were surfacing in the market; so 34 million 45 rpms were sold in 1969, but sales decreased all through the Seventies, with a yearly average of 25 million. The sale of LPs increased in the entire decade: from 4 million sold in 1969 to almost 21 in 1979; the same applied to music tapes, nip and tuck with LPs: the former sold 3,5 million in 1970 and reached almost 18 million in 1979.

The early Seventies marked the slow, inexorable crisis of the *Festival di Sanremo*, which recovered a newly found music identity only the following decade. The other music festivals were not in better shape either: in 1970 *Cantagiro* closed down, followed the next year by *Festival della Canzone Napoletana*, and in 1975 by *Un disco per l'estate*, which started over in 1980, but only until 2003; only *Festivalbar* was able to hold on. Times had changed, and that kind of live shows, based on the competition among singers, couldn't last any longer. At the same time, 45 rpms were losing their consumption value, juke-boxes were paying for it, and music festivals were no longer able to carry out the fundamental role of advertisement vehicle in a record market that was entering a new phase. For this same reason, record companies were not as generous as before in funding the organization of the festivals.

On the wake of what was happening in the other countries, Italy was discovering the new dimension of live music enjoyed together in the squares and in the outdoor meetings. Being together as a political experience, enjoying the new vibrations that offered original ways of feeling part of a group, that went well beyond the anachronistic traditionalism of the now questionable *Sanremo*. Music shows on TV continued to offer successful programs such as *Milleluci* in 1974, hosted by two of the favorite women in the business, Mina and Raffaela Carrà; the program registered an average of over 23 million spectators glued to the TV set on Saturday nights.

Radio programs had a more innovative role compared to TV. For instance, the program *Bandiera Gialla*, run until 1970, contributed in demolishing the dusty formats of the Rai programs of the time. The show was based on a simple but innovative structure for the time: the live public, mostly the youth that animated the night life of places such as the Piper Club, listened to foreign tracks and voted for them. Or *Per voi giovani*, that concentrated on the quality of the music, and introduced new trends and new international artists, especially from the UK and the USA; for instance, rock signature tunes such as *Glad* by Traffic, *Moby Dick* by Led Zeppelin or *Thick as a brick* by Jethro Tull. The program run on weekdays in the early afternoon, and continued until 1976 when its host Renzo Arbore started presenting another show that marked the history of Italian radio programs, *Alto gradimento*. *Per voi giovani* introduced Jim Morrison and his Doors, Jefferson Airplane, Pink Floyd, Genesis, and other artists that were an absolute novelty for the Italian youths. The program showed special consideration for the new Italian singer-songwriters and contributed significantly to their diffusion, offering them a springboard to success. Lastly, the historical program *Hit Parade* on the Second Channel of Rai, that started on January 6, 1967, continued in its original version until the end of 1976, a date marking a watershed for music in Italy, as it was the year when the public monopoly of Rai ended, and private stations improved the radio market.

"I love the radio / because it reached people / it comes in the houses / and speaks to you directly / and if a radio is free / but really free / I like it even better / because it frees your mind". These are Eugenio Finardi's lyrics to his song *La radio*, celebrating in 1976 the appearance of pirate radios in Italy. In the same year, over 200 free radios in small towns and larger cities became legal after the sentence of the Constitutional Court that shattered the Rai monopoly, thus opening the radio-TV market also to private competitors. Often born for political reasons, these early radios were based on self-funding, creative improvisation and amateur organization. They allowed people to listen to Italian and foreign pop music at all times, and not just in the short programs Rai channels dedicated to it, thus creating communities of loyal listeners. Around music, free airwaves became also freedom of expression, communication, discussion: a fundamental identity place for the generation of youth of that decade.

This epochal change in Italy destroyed the stiff music scenario that was no longer able to spread out the sound novelties the record market could offer. Many private radios preferred a more general program, as they were trying to attract various segments of listeners, and were increasingly funded by local and national entrepreneurs. To all intents and purposes, private radios became commercial radios, with increased professionalism, more complex organizational structures, and closer relations with the Italian and international record industry. In other words, real companies working in the media system.

8. *Opportunities and music challenges within and without traditions*

The features that pop music acquired in that historical period – namely, increased professionalism, stately use of new technology and equipment, ambition to show off high artistic abilities by the musicians, search for deep lyrics whose meaning was often hard to catch – matched the choice of LPs as vehicles to offer complex works, full of sense, in other words, concept records.

Rockers and singer-songwriters were starting to feel the need to widen the music format, thus privileging concept as basis for every LP; a choice, or need, that in the early Seventies met the favor of the listeners, now culturally inclined towards that direction. The audience felt like they could participate in the creative act of a record; thus, the imagination of the composers nourished that of the listeners, allowing the latter to enter in a relationship with the contents of the records. In a way, the audience seized the records, the stories told, ideally turning from addressee to music interlocutor. What surfaced in those years was the need to find new paths, to practice music and productive testing so that they would not be an end in itself, but would allow the development of the artists; the latter, in turn, in longer-lasting records, could create art, innovate, and test new waters. All this was possible thanks to LPs and to the spreading of concept albums in the record market.

In that period, the imagination of the artist turned into the imagination of the listeners who could catch the most intimate and personal meanings in what the artist had created and put at the disposal of the audience. But without bonds, imagination risks to become a sterile, fleeting exercise of style, without being able to convey a meaning to what is being said. Therefore, music must have some tools, the most significant of which being the story it is telling, and therefore the narration that may involve the audience, and be so emotionally strong to captivate the listener.

The stories that started being a significant part of rock operas, usually featured well defined themes to convey. From this point of view, the history of progressive rock and of the singer-songwriters are linked to an expression mode that started using LPs to convey a concept. Concept albums tried to adequate themselves to the 33 rpm format, but it aspired to make rock music more noble,[8] by overcoming the notion of the song-form

8. Paolo Prato, *Dizionario di Pop e Rock* (Milan: Garzanti, 1996).

spread out in the pop environment, that was considered simple, to reach some complexity. In the late Sixties Europe witnessed the takeover of the UK, that was better than the USA in nurturing and raising rock music. Since that moment, British rock music officially recovered its creative part, acquiring the role of cultural media able to create a change, to produce something new in the music field but also under the point of view of the production and of the relationship between artists and audience.

9. *A change of air. The rock turnabout in Italian pop music*

Italian progressive rock grew in the wake of the British music inspiration, where the most significant band lived, swiftly spreading out their influence in some European countries such as France, Germany, but most of all Italy. Progressive rock will be recorded as the main character in the rock scene between 1969 and 1976; after its naive childhood in the Fifties and its teenage years in the Seventies, pursuing the struggle and the conflict against the adults, progressive rock became the bridge to rock music in its adult phase Progressive rock featured three main elements: the increasing presence of suites, the long pieces made by connected movements; the massive use of the keyboards; and the use of committed lyrics, suited to accompany complex and articulated music compositions, obviously referring to other genres, jazz, blues and classical music.[9] Sophisticated music for an educated audience that required thoughtful listening to grasp the emotional and imaginative side of the artist.

The most sagacious record majors invented dedicated sub-labels that could manage progressive rock (EMI – Harvest for Pink Floyd); in the UK, independent labels were able to maintain their power to decide.[10] Progressive rock required a band to play it, due to the several instruments used and the technology needed to synthesize natural sounds and classical instruments such as piano, violin, winds and the like. Sequencers were made to fit in electronic keyboards, now more favored than electric guitars, as they allowed the repetition of music phrases; the early electronic tools were invented, the so called "moogs", synthesizers that allowed the reproduction of music covering a wide variety of feelings, freely used by

9. Cesare Rizzi, *Progressive* (Florence: Giunti, 1999).

10. Donato Zoppo, *PROG. Una suite lunga mezzo secolo* (Rome: Arcana Edizioni, 2011), pp. 149-150.

ELP (Emerson, Lake & Palmer), Pink Floyd, and in Italy by Banco del Mutuo Soccorso and PFM (Premiata Forneria Marconi): the *refrain* of the renowned *Impressioni di Settembre* was produced on a *minimoog*.

In Italy, progressive rock had important proselytes, both artists and producers, and between 1971 and 1974 progressive rock even reached the LP sales charts. This music caught on in Italy because the musicians that fell under the category had music competences rooted in the repertoire of classical music, jazz and Italian beat music. The series of concerts that since 1969 brought Jethro Tull, Atomic Rooster, Led Zeppelin, Pink Floyd, Van Der Graaf Generator, and Genesis to Italy was crucial for the beginning of Italian progressive rock, as they contributed to the forming of new Italian bands and the change of the existing ones, as the progressive transmutation of the band Le Orme.

Despite the general lack of interest of the main traditional Italian magazines, the Italian progressive rock was able to spread out quickly, especially thanks to the help of special magazines such as *Ciao 2001* and to the intense season of pop music festivals, such as the *Caracalla* in Roma, the *Palermo Pop*, the *Davoli Pop* in Bologna, the *Festival della Musica d'Avanguardia e delle Nuove Tendenze* in Viareggio, and the first festival organized by the counter-cultural magazine *Re Nudo*. The latter helped the merging of music and politics: all through the Seventies, progressive rock was one of the main contexts of the youth protests and the implementation of the social clash. Therefore, Italian progressive rock bands such as Le Orme, Area, Il Banco del Mutuo Soccorso e in particular PFM, found in live concerts the best way to speak to an audience that would have been hard to reach otherwise.

PFM, a band formed in Milan off the ashes of I Quelli, a beat music band that numbered collaborations with Italian pop music stars such as De André, Celentano, Mina, and Mogol/Battisti, made its debut as progressive rock band in 1971 at the Teatro Lirico in Milano as support band to Yes, obtaining appreciation of both critique and audience. After making a name for itself at the first *Festival di Avanguardia e Nuove Tendenze* in Viareggio in 1971, the band published their first single *Impressioni di Settembre*. In 1973 *Photos of Ghosts*, first LP made for the international market, made it to the American chards on *Billboard*.

Between 1973 and 1976 the band toured Italy and abroad, in particular the UK, the USA and Japan. In 1974 the LP *L'Isola di Niente* was released in the English version *The World Became the World*. The first official live album, *Cook*, was edited in Italy as *Live in Usa*. And in 1975 *Chocolate*

Kings made it to the British Top 20. After the fourth tour in the UK in 1976, PFM ended the progressive rock phase that had brought the band to reach unexpected targets.

Italian pop music had been able to make itself heard abroad, and to be successful with the audience, the reviewers and the market. It may be said that the Italian authors and interpreters of progressive rock, featuring a significant heterogeneity of trends and styles, was able to invent an original Italian way to rock music. All this within a nation that was disadvantaged compared to the mainstream international record production, where Britain and the United States reigned undisputed, as they could count of music they had invented themselves, rock music, that for at least two decades had reached the status of cultural institution, and had survived unharmed creative crisis, and epoch-making music and technological changes.

Italian music, despite the initial gap, and thanks to its personal revision of progressive rock, assimilated both by popular and more sophisticated artists, was able to walk the path of its consolidation. Italian progressive rock was able to develop significant professionalism in music creation and execution, that were not ripe in our music production of the times; not so much because Italian musicians were not talented or were not gifted in terms of inspiration and creativity, but because they could not count on an executive organization of the record industry. With its limited resources, Italian progressive rock made a virtue of necessity and learned from more advanced productive environments what making music meant. The early *made in Italy* rock music put together its artistic abilities to mature experience and produce music where genuineness and authenticity could become common heritage for those who would want to embark the same journey in Italy. At the same time, Italian progressive rock proved its denigrators and the inattentive media that this complex, hybrid music, could be successfully accepted by the national and international public. Moreover, in the following decades, after losing its initial driving force, – we are speaking of 1976 circa – it became a consistent reference point for many rock bands, and thanks for the European and world revival of progressive rock, it has generated an arousal of interest in the younger generations. Lastly, in all its peculiarities, Italian progressive rock can well fit in the channel of the most important European music scenarios of the Seventies, and when it started declining in Italy, it slowly began to spread out abroad, especially in Japan, the United States, Mexico and Latin America.

So far, we've discussed the music dimension; the singing shift instead was led by the singer-songwriters, both the old leaders and the novices, the absolute beginners.

10. *Until the victory. Singer-songwriters between wings and roots*

The singer-songwriters of the Seventies carried out the significant role of giving sense to a social actuality that was becoming increasingly complex and incomprehensible. Their role was to be cultural mediators in their artistic commitment to rebalance the ambitions of the youths, urging them not to fall prey of disenchantment. At the same time, they tried to have them remain practical, telling them that dreams need to stay dreams, because when they come true, they are not what you were expecting. So the lyric of their songs offered imagination recalling the news, roots and history of a nation full of contradictions and unresolved contrasts.

To fully analyze the shift of Italian singer-songwriters in the Seventies we need to go back to 1958, when Nanni Ricordi and Franco Ceprax founded Ricordi, the label that stood out for the role it covered as real makers of the strengthening and renovating process of the Italian song, experimenting new voices and proving to be a true hothouse of talents. Such as, for instance, the new generation of authors who wrote quite eccentric lyrics for the times, but meeting the expectations of an audience incessantly searching for novelties. With connoisseur's nose, the record industry Ricordi decided to have the authors sing their own songs, thus inventing a new figure, the singer-songwriter, the Italian *cantautore*, neologism created by the actress-author Maria Monti and by Ennio Melis and Vincenzo Micozzi in the RCA studios. Thus, some of the most renowned artists of Italian music found their own creative space and a great feedback from the public: Gino Paoli, Luigi Tenco, Fabrizio De André, Bruno Lauzi and Paolo Conte. This new figure of singer and lyricist played an increasingly important role in the Seventies, and helped rethink the notion of LPs.

The best singer-songwriters were constantly on the verge of an existential crisis. Gino Paoli attempted to take his life in 1963, Tenco unfortunately succeeded in his purpose during the 1967 edition of *Sanremo*. These heterogeneous singer-songwriters were serious, but never solemn; deep bur rarely boring; they were "committed", a typical term of the time, in giving value to words more than to the form of their songs. Contents had to prevail over form, and were, and still are, a reference point for those who wanted and still want to make music in Italy today. In the Sixties they wanted to create a style reference point that was not confined to the rhymes of "cuore e amore" (heart and love), but also cultural, and at time, political.

People such as De André, Tenco, and Lauzi molded a new language, always keeping a watchful eye on novelties coming from France and the United States.[11] The artistic encounter between Paoli with Mina in the song *Il cielo in una stanza*, 1960, where she stood out as one of the most significant female singers of all times in Italy; or the encounter with Ornella Vanoni in the song *Senza fine*, 1961 and *Che cosa c'è*, 1963, started a new genre: "The genre of quality songs, that music reviewers are too busy following the conflicts between melodious, screamers, and singer-songwriters to notice".[12] Such as many other songs, *Marinella*, to name one, written by De André, but brought to success also thanks to Mina's interpretation. Or *Sapore di sale*, Gino Paoli's 1963 evergreen, labeled Ricordi; a song that in the first instance could hastily be considered a summer song, but is still today an unrivalled masterpiece of quality songs but at the same time of successful pop song.

11. *The shadow line. Singer-songwriters, the new storytellers*

The shift from youth to adulthood of Italian pop music also featured the singer-songwriters, who in the Seventies succeeded in taking up significant space in the Italian audience's heart, gaining an authority still resisting nowadays. To name a few, Francesco Guccini, Fabrizio De André, Riccardo Cocciante, Ivan Graziani, Rino Gaetano, Lucio Dalla, Francesco De Gregori, Antonello Venditti, and many more. Some artists tried to interpret their time under a more intimate and personal point of view, such as Claudio Baglioni and his late-teenager loves echoing in his *Questo piccolo grande amore* of 1972, the single that gave the title to his concept album. The song gave rise to a scandal and was censored in part, for instance the words "naked" and "prohibited things" were replaced with "alone" and "wet shoes" in the 45 rpm version, and became an evergreen of Italian pop music, sung over and over in the years, to the point that 1985 a survey designated it as the "Italian song of the century".

11. Enzo Gentile, *Legata a un granello di sabbia. Storie e amori, costume e società nelle canzoni italiane dell'estate* (Milan: Melampo Editore, 2005), p. 76.

12. Franco Fabbri, *Around the clock. Una breve storia della popular music* (Turin: UTET, 2008), p. 113.

Next to the romantic genre, other trends such as the one followed by the storyteller Edoardo Bennato in his monographic album where, in a successful mixture of rock and folk music, he reenacted the story of Pinocchio in *Burattino senza fili*, remaining in the charts for several weeks in 1977. Other authors offered their personal interpretation of the generations of the Seventies, such as Antonello Venditti, who started his career at the Folk Studio in Rome with Francesco De Gregori, who in turn reached his ongoing success in 1975 with the song *Lilly*, the story of a drug-addicted girl. All these authors were called singer-songwriters, and although they took part in pop festivals, they stayed artists, musicians and singers; and for this reason they cut records, they had them distributed, and sold them: in other words, they were music professionals, aware that they were part of a market that on the one hand may have restricted their freedom of expression, but on the other, it was a resource to promote their art.

They experimented and found new poetic paths to allow the surfacing of the hidden dimensions in our lives, helping create ideas and reflections through music. At the same time, their seeming pessimism left some space to irony and optimism. Their lyrics lapped against the small daily facts, but also against the unresolved social questions. "The new singer-songwriters interpret the uneasiness of the youth, but not just that; they do not confine themselves to the restlessness and malaise, they go deeper, even trying to solve these problems, and they create more sophisticated and elaborate lyrics".[13] A heterogeneous group, comprising both the more committed and militant artists and the romantic ones, who wanted to sing about love, equally challenging the rules of a record market that also in Italy was going through an industrial phase featuring choking patterns that curbed them in the role of committed singers. Instead, they wanted to overturn the Italian song in its tradition, so that their effort could offer pure musical poetry, able to endure time beyond the flattened-out daily reports served on music that was already looking back nostalgically at the lightheartedness of the previous decade.

They were able to resist, adapting to censorship, like one of the forerunners, Francesco De Gregori. All the Italian singer-songwriters of that time had an exemplary reference in Bob Dylan, but De Gregori is the one who was able to embody the figure of the American folk singer in Italy. He donated the income of his 1976 tour to the political group Lotta Continua, but was strongly attacked by some activists of the extraparliamentary left who stepped on the stage interrupting his concert and staged a real process

13. Borgna, *Storia della canzone italiana*, p. 354.

against De Gregori, accusing him of making money out of his music. The same had happened Guccini, Venditti and Finardi, author of *Musica ribelle* (1975), reference song of those same activists that were accusing him. It was an extremely difficult period for De Gregori, who decided to retire from the stage for two years, to make a comeback with his record *De Gregori*, including the song *Generale*.

The attempt of the youth activist movement to control Italian singer-songwriters and music in general was fell through. One of the signals was Dalla and De Gregori's 1979 tour *Banana Republic*, which obtained an incredible success all over Italy and counted an audience of over 500,000 people.

A new epoch for committed singer-songwriters was about to begin, as stated by De Gregori himself in an interview for the newspaper *La Repubblica*: "The times when music was judged thought the political lens is over, when the author was seen as a life example, as a leader. Now the only difference is between a good song and a bad song; the only commitment I feel towards my audience is to offer something at the best of my possibilities: a good song, with nice, well-played music. The real charlatan is someone who plays Bandiera rossa out of tune".

The so-called eskimo, the casual hooded water-proof zipped-up jacket, strictly green, was adopted by the student movement, becoming one of their standard symbols. And Guccini even dedicated a song to the parka in 1978. For the generation of the Sixties-Seventies, to whom the song was dedicated, it's a song of regrets, memories and the stock on their life. For the poet Eugenio Montale, memories are not a sin as long as they bring back pleasant feelings; so, Guccini's song may be assimilated to Dalla's *L'anno che verrà* (1978), the song that captured the urge of the Italian society to leave behind the still-burning signs of a controversial decade.

The environment had changed and the youths wanted to escape the false political commitment that for way too long had stated that fun and music reflection were incompatible and personal life was not worth of being told or sung. Collectiveness shifted towards singleness, and being in a group toward being in a couple, and therefore towards love again, to sentimental education and new sexual experiments. The new generation favored new life styles, transgression and sexual ambiguity, like in Renato Zero's songs, and his *en travesti* pop music.[14]

14. Gianfranco Baldazzi, *La canzone italiana del Novecento* (Milan: Newton Compton, 1988), p. 120.

Authors lived a real boom, thus becoming research, appraisal and reference points, not only for the audience of the times, but thanks to the firm grounds they had created, for future generations. They offered original options to Italian music that could face, with renovated charm, the challenge with international pop music. A brilliant example was given by Battisti and Mogol, who were able to create Italian songs that would find their way through all the novelties coming from abroad with unassuming, but subtle wit. They were able to use the shift that affected pop music and make it understandable for the Italian tradition, using all the possible ideas to mix and synthetize different styles in a modern, never banal way. They did it with a skilled business nose, to spread out as much as they could the results of their music research. Their study was organized and never self-regarding, so that the later generation could still have a song to sing, that would stick in their memories, attuned to the audience that in Battisti, and through his lyricist Mogol, discovered words in music, echoes of their early loves and more mature ones, their frame of mind, and social feelings that were still dormant, such as individualism and responsibility.

Battisti represented the role of a real popstar able to gather around his music the most diverse listeners, from the more sophisticated ones, to the families seated in front of their TV sets; from the young protesters intoxicated by the social songs, and those who listened to all kinds of music, and why not, also to the catchier tunes, as long as they were good, danceable and sentimental. With Mogol, Battisti was all this: he incarnated pop, rock, and soul music, in his way able to direct the instrumental and singing evolution of music.

12. *In between. Headed towards new adventures*

It was the turning point of the Seventies that marked a deep change and the real consolidation of Italian music, the transition towards a more adult and aware phase.

Italian popular music broke up in a fragmentation of music experiences, among which styles and genres on the wake of the influences of the Anglo-American pop music of the Seventies; the singer-songwriters; progressive rock; the light *Sanremo*-style songs; and the more commercial easy-listening music. The reason for this break up was due to the fact that despite the weakness of its record industry and the market, Italian music became fully aware of itself before its increasingly differentiated audience.

As we have analyzed and argued so far, Italian progressive rock played and worked mostly on music experimentation, while the new generation of committed songs felt they were invested with the mission of creating lyrics that would give sense and meaning to words in music able to capture the public and private moments of the Italian society.

We wish to highlight two artistic experiences of the late Seventies that can be interpreted as symbols of that decade and as watershed between a before and an after. We are referring to the 1979 tour that Fabrizio De André performed with PFM and that resulted in a live album published that same year. Singing-songwriting and progressive rock met and mixed, one stimulating the other, and opening up to offer an original artistic alliance that gained the approval of two different kinds of audiences that were seemingly very distant. The lyrics, the poetry, the narration of the outsiders of the Genoese singer-songwriter mixed with the sounds and music competence of Franz Di Ciccio and Franco Mussida's band, producing a unique example of art, generated by the greatest characters of the Italian pop music of that decade.

The second instance was the concert *Omaggio a Demetrio Stratos*, lead singer of Area, often acknowledged as the music group of the Seventies able to embody the political and cultural flurry of that decade. On June 13, 1979 a large group of Italian musicians from the most different traditions met at the Arena Civica in Milano for a live concert with the purpose of gathering funds to help Demetrio Stratos, hospitalized in New York for a rare illness. His death, occurred a few hours before the beginning of the concert, turned it into a farewell that especially singer-songwriters and progressive rock artists wanted to dedicate to him, a homage that gathered on the same stage Francesco Guccini, Eugenio Finardi, Claudio Rocchi, Angelo Branduardi, Antonello Venditti, Roberto Vecchioni, Banco del Mutuo Soccorso, Area, PFM, and many more characters of the Italian pop music of that decade.

13. *From the turmoil of the Seventies to the music hedonism of the Eighties*

The conclusion of the path created by the Italian music of the Seventies was marked symbolically in 1980 when the artistic relation that had linked Lucio Battisti and Mogol since 1966 ended. Later, Battisti started a collaboration with the poet Pasquale Panella, privileging hermetic texts and choosing electronic music with techno-dance influences; he did not want to repeat himself, and therefore decided to try something new, lest he should sound outdated. A new style for a music acrobat who always strived to give the best of his precious talent until he died in 1998, due to a rare syndrome of the lymphatic system. Punk music did not receive significant feedback in the Italian mainstream; nevertheless, some musical experiences within its boundaries found their inspiration and place in the movement. The new influences from Britain and the United States contributed in creating a series of artists who grasped the so called "new wave": an artistic and cultural container that drew inspiration from the punk experience and matched it with glam rock. Abroad, the new wave environment included bands and singers coming from completely different trends and music styles, but sharing the attempt to interpret and convey the ambience and the changes that the late Seventies and early Eighties had brought: Kraftwerk, U2, REM, Police, Cure, Depeche Mode, Duran Duran, Spandau Ballett, Simple Minds, Talking Heads and many more. The bands of the other side of the channel were the protagonists of the second British invasion, able to go up the ladder of the American charts of the early Eighties, and leaving clear marks of the new pop also in Italy. Compared to the international scenario, in Italy the new wave struggled to become a popular genre, also due to the lack of attention the national media dedicated to the trend.

During the Seventies, the *Festival di Sanremo* had failed in adjusting the spirit of the festival to the changed context and times of a society in great turmoil, thus losing the hallmark as well as the liveliness and support of the national song, that had made it a symbolic event in the life and tradition of Italians. In the late Seventies something was changing, requiring the change to affect also the festival, so that is could evolve to hug its identity of popular show. The Eighties marked the revival of the show, also confirmed by the presence of Sanremo-style songs in the charts. Rai decided to broadcast the entire 1981 festival, and the choice was awarded by the almost 80 million Italians that watched the three nights.

The Eighties were marked by a musical culture that defined itself, and wanted to be defined, by the exaggerate display of an esthetic extravagance. The peculiarities of that decade lie exactly in that need to be unique, to make that art unmistakably Eighties, in adapting and readjusting it to the quickly-changing fads and trends. Sounds and images, also supported by the fast spreading out of the new promotional media, the video clips, created an inspiring alliance. Stars were worshipped all over the world, and the music market expanded accordingly thanks to the sale of records, participation in concerts, new artists and bands. The show business reached intense peaks in the tours of some bands and rock stars.

The attention to aesthetics, the choice of inventive and glittering clothes, the study of the gesture and the use of the body in TV shows and concerts; the explicit references to a supposed sexual ambiguity, were all elements stolen from glam rock and readjusted to be slightly more acceptable to the larger audience: to mention a few, Duran Duran, Spandau Ballet, but also Madonna, Michael Jackson, and many more protagonists of the pop music scene in the Eighties and Nineties.

Towards the late Seventies, traditional music underwent a deep fragmentation, which produced the creation of a series of artistic styles. Rock music had lost part of its uniformity, from then on developing new and increasingly extreme trends, absorbing contaminations within a more popular and richer styles, and generating quite an amount of new music and social phenomena surrounding the more defined music identities.

Music was becoming increasingly individualistic: the youth's cultural universe was evidently becoming more evasive and changed at amazing speed. It was following the strategy typical of any cutting-edge movement, accumulating in a continuous reinvention, and continuously updating itself, coming close to the border of unpredictability. The youths reacted inventing new behaviors to obtain a peculiar identity, to opt out of the social roles accepted; it was this behavior that once again placed them at the center of the attention of the same culture that they were striving to attack, but at the same time wanted to surpass.

From the Eighties, styles started to become more extreme, losing their ability to dialogue among each other, while the youths were seeking refuge in a more private life, and choosing to experiment in new life styles, new clothing trends, new ways to express themselves; in other words, different communicating strategies that could coexist in harmony or in antagonism. The target was the new transnational and global youth culture, and the universe of consumerism. An enormous market, exploded in the second half of the Eighties, that became the main interest of the record industry, but mainly of the global advertisers that looked for new communication means based on increasingly effective advertisement campaigns, and synchronized to be launched everywhere at the same time. In this context, MTV was functional to these new strategies that were both cultural and economic.

14. *Between crisis and recoveries. The dance of the Italian record industry*

After the growth registered in the Seventies, between 1979 and 1989 the Italian record industry underwent a period of downturn in the sale of records. In this environment, video clips acquired a significant role in their ability to give new visibility to the artists on the market. Between 1980 and 1985 the turnover coming from the sale of international music increased to 60 billion lire, thus topping the sale of Italian music: in 1980 Italian pop music registered a turnover of 65 billion lire, the international music behind with only 50 billion. The situation changed in 1985: 107 billion lire against 110 billion, and then again in 1989, when Italian pop music made 166 billion lire against the 120 of the international music, although the latter was able to sell 26,2 billion records while Italian music sold only 21,2 billion.[15]

The Eighties marked also a new technologic evolution, when Philips and Sony introduced CDs on the market, slowly scaling down music production, superseding tapes and traditional records. The increasing importance of CDs marked a new period of prosperity for the record market, also thanks to an unprecedented phenomenon called the "stock effect": people would buy a CD of the record they already had in LP format, thus causing an exponential increase in the sale. The passage from analogic to digital was already posing some problems: it was progressively easier to obtain music, and keeping the same acoustic quality and sound fidelity, CDs offered piracy and home tapers new sources from which they could obtain their tapes; and later, with the spreading out of digital-duplicating devices, the basis of the record industry started to have to face a difficult challenge.

Here are some figures to understand how CDs were changing the Italian scenario at the end of the decade. In 1989 the overall turnover of the Italian record market was 452,7 billion lire compared to the 408 of the previous year, not considering the piracy that counted for another 30%. In 1989 the sale of CDs represented 31,9% of the overall turnover, largely topping the sale of regular records, still at 27,8%; and let's not forget that the price of a CD was higher than an LP or tape. In 1989, 15,6 billion LPs 10,5 billion CDs were sold in Italy, but the following year, the sale of CD

15. Daniele Doglio, Giuseppe Richeri, "L'industria del disco in Italia", in *Rapporto sull'economia della cultura in Italia, 1980-1990*, ed. by Carlo Bodo (Rome: Istituto Poligrafico e Zecca dello Stato, 1994), pp. 673-691, p. 674.

(15,8 billion) topped that LPs (14,6 billion). In 1991 the difference was even higher, with CDs at 20.6 billion, almost three times the figures of LPs, at a mere 8,5 billion. Tapes were instead resisting, with 24,7 billion sold in 1989, 25,7 in 1990, and 24,3 in 1991.

CDs changed radically the dynamics of listening, and the consumption of music: even more than tapes, compact discs are suitable to a personalized use of music, as they allow you to skip from one piece to the other, following your personal choice and not the order imposed by the artist. This aspect is part of the change that was happening in those years, a period that featured a strong individualization process. In the course of time, the production of video clips became, in the Eighties, a necessary practice to present new songs; it gave visibility to the song and, by full right, it was part of the vital process of a song, from production to distribution.

15. *On the fringe of the empire. Italy in the rough turning point of the Nineties*

The branch of MTV dedicated to the Italian market that started broadcasting in September 1997 was at the time the only unencrypted free network. Video clips contributed in renewing the programs in Italian TV; music through images was able to discover new market-oriented spaces, dedicated to teenagers and the youth, and even invented a channel offering "all video music". Nevertheless, the gap between Italy and the English-speaking countries was still wide. The Italian record makers often wrongly urged their artists to emulate the English and American video clips, but they could not count on adequate resources.

In 1984, thirteen years before the creation of MTV Italia, Videomusic started off in Tuscany; conceived and founded by Marialina Marcucci and directed by Pierluigi Stefani, it was the first instance in Europe of a channel completely dedicated to music, addressed to a medium-high audience with highly-cultural expectation. The channel broadcasted video clips, but dealt with music also through interviews, reviews and recording of live concerts. Videomusic allowed the Italian youth to discover international artists, and gave them the chance to widen their choice in music consumption. Unlike the previous programs that had attempted to get in touch with the youth, Videomusic imposed a model of television that included the youth's world, embracing their language codes, timings, fashion and symbols. It contributed in lifting up the sales of Italian artists and groups that, starting from the second half of the Eighties, found renewed success. The choices Videomusic made encouraged other productions of video clips, helping Italy catch up, and the Italian videos grew to the detriment of the British and American one.

Starting from the Eighties, live performances turned from cultural practice to real mass phenomena and media events[16] widening the possibilities to enjoy music. In this perspective, live TV started playing the crucial function of amplifying the artistic value of concerts that, by being shown on TV, became common heritage that could be shared, taped and performed again, and even historical documents. The audience had the chance to watch their favorite artists perform, despite their status of unreachable pop and rock stars.

Although this could apply to other fields in the Italian cultural industry, cinema for instance, the Italian music production was left out of the turbulent environments that had been shaking the world's artistic scenario. Many Italian record makers did not understand that the phenomenon of video clips was destined to last, and simply interpreted it as a deterrent to the consumption of records and not as a promotional means. They showed their lack of far-sightedness and that their vision of the market was short-winded, as marked by their skepticism towards Videomusic.[17] Also, they were not able to create new synergies with the film industry, or the new industry linked to the production of advertisement videos, or develop new promotional ideas with the radio and TV, to help music free itself of the secondary role in the media, only functional to short-lived business targets.

There were a few examples of pre-eminence and novelties, but they were extemporaneous or too isolated; while Italy stalled, the fruitful relations between languages and different social contexts grew and spread out exponentially in the United States and in the United Kingdom. Music models were increasingly associated with the industry of fun and the market of imagination linked to fashion (to name a couple, the commercials of Coca Cola and Pepsi Cola starring Madonna and Michael Jackson).

16. See Daniel Dayan, Elihu Katz, *Media Events. The Live Broadcasting of History* (Cambridge: Harvard University Press, 1992).

17. Felice Pesoli, "Il videoclip italiano", in *Catalogo. Music in Film Fest* (Vicenza: Associazione industriali della provincia di Vicenza, 1996), pp. 175-177.

16. *The challenge of Italian pop music. Sound disruption between the old and the new millennium*

Over the Nineties, alternative aesthetic codes were appearing, spontaneous style identities, underground looks, fashions that originated from metropolitan environments, from the nightlife style used by disco and club-goers. Pop music attempted to keep all this together, in a variety of trends and genres whose traditional precept inherited from rock music mingled and renewed itself in new stylistic elements mixed with cultural expressions coming from the verges of productive processes. It is the instance of hip hop in its 30-year-long lifespan. In Italy, the phenomenon never reached high peaks, but during the Nineties, it was able to emancipate itself and turn from a niche phenomenon into a style much appreciated by the youth, as confirmed by the invasion of graffiti on the walls of Italian cities.

Rap music, and hip hop, the wider and more faceted movement that promoted it, started out as a border practice between white and Afro-American cultures.[18] The new black awareness wished to reestablish some differences, still coding a relational music space. In its continuous evolution, in the dance and techno contaminations, hip hop overcame the American boundaries spreading out in the world, Italy included, thus marking an unfinished chapter in the history of pop music. Over time, rap music was able to reach significant levels of appreciation also in the European environment, despite its distance from the urban ambiance of American cities, until in countries like France and Italy, it underwent a total re-localization: rappers would use local music repertoires with lyrics describing their national problems. Over the Nineties, Italian rap music spread like a bushfire from Turin to Milan, from Venice to Bologna, from Rome to Naples, Salento to Calabria. We are thinking of 99 posse, Assalti Frontali, Sud Sound System, Africa Unite, Frankie HI-NRG, Caparezza and Almanegretta. Like new story-tellers, they would privilege their homeland dialect and would bond their personal culture to the rap musical language, and to a movement, hip hop, that did not have limitations or boundaries.

We must mention someone whose debut in the late Eighties had the credit of introducing rap music and its offshoots to Italians. The eclectic Lorenzo Cherubini, aka Jovanotti, first Italian vee-jay for MTV. In 1989

18. Alessandro Portelli, *La linea del colore. Saggi sulla cultura afroamericana* (Rome: Manifestolibri, 1994).

his albums *Jovanotti for president* (1988) in English, and *La mia moto* (1989) which sold 600,000 copies, had rap songs that soon became very popular, such *Gimme five*, *È qui la festa*, *Vasco*, the latter presented at the 1989 *Festival di Sanremo*. Over the years, Jovanotti changed styles and music trends, but he never truly abandoned his hip hop inclination that through his artistic path found its space in songs such as *Serenata rap* and *Piove* in 1994, *Tanto3* in 2005, *Temporale* in 2009, in his album *Safari*, and in more recent pieces that have discreet references to hip hop, rap, and reggae music, amid the idea of genre contamination according to an ever increasing music research we find in his discography.

17. 'Una vita da mediano'

Una vita da mediano (*Life as a midfielder*) is the title of a 1999 song by Ligabue, hinting at soccer and speaking, as the singer declared, about the "effort of living; life is a pleasure, but also something that you must earn by the sweat of your brow. I was not born wearing the No. 10 t-shirt, I was not Platini. And music, others have No. 9 on their t-shirts, Bob Dylan. This does not mean that midfielders don't have their own value, it's a quality role, you have a lot of responsibility, although you are more in the shade".[19] This metaphor perfectly reassumes and embodies the role that Italian music played from the Nineties on, in its ability to be between the local and the global dimensions.

Italian pop music did not aim at changing the world, it just wanted to tell about it in the personal and collective stories, in the knowledge it had gained in composing, producing and making music. After all the changed happened in those decades, in the Nineties it started finding its own features, in the use of increasingly inspired and involving lyrics, thus reconquering growing segments of audiences, accepting and winning the challenge of the comparison with international music, internalizing the best and most functional creative elements, to reach a recovered pop dimension, in some cases even abroad. Therefore, like the midfielder in soccer needs to be in the middle of the field, offending but mostly defending and hitting hard, the Italian music scenario was able to get up again and compete with the

19. Riccardo Bertoncelli, *Paesaggi immaginari. Trent'anni di rock e oltre* (Florence: Giunti, 1998), p. 172.

international scenario, sometimes even winning the match. This is what happened between the ups and downs in the first decade of the third millennium, when Italian pop music left its place to increasingly original hybridizing. An unescapable change, since in the last 25 years, Italian music has found itself in the midst of a globalization process that involved record labels and their marketing strategies.

As of the Nineties, the live music offered became established, and Italy has been gifted with a long and uninterrupted season of great concerts and music shows as had never been seen before in terms of audience and organizational competence. After the major live concerts of Vasco Rossi and Ligabue, significant instances of the big concerts that as of the Nineties started following one another in Italy, different segments of audiences linked by the need to mirror themselves in the common stories the songs told, and by the opportunity to be at the center of a show based on great music.

Becoming more and more natural for Italians, these concerts were decisive in strengthening the fame of already renowned artists, but also in bringing several up-and-coming stars to the limelight. Speaking of concerts, we wish to recall the charity event *Pavarotti & Friends*, organized in 1992 as per Luciano Pavarotti and his wife Nicoletta Mantovani's wishes, to support philanthropic causes. A series of pop starts attracting enough interest to justify the worldwide broadcast, were invited to duet with Pavarotti for an evening in Modena, hometown of the tenor. The show continued until 2007 when Pavarotti died, and it was organized on an almost yearly basis, counting each time on the participation of renowned guests in the international and Italian music scenario: Sting, Lucio Dalla, Zucchero, Eric Clapton, Elton John and many more.

Lately, the trend of Italian pop music has been to attempt the widest contamination possible, trying to combine the typical melody of traditional Italian songs with other languages and forms of music communication, to meet an increasingly complex and syncretistic audience. Some instances stand out: *Il gobbo di Notre Dame* by Riccardo Cocciante, *Pia* by Gianna Nannini, *Tosca* by Lucio Dalla, *Romeo e Giulietta* produced by David Zard, rock operas whose modernity and tradition offer highly qualified results that once on stage meet the favor of the public. In Italy, supply and demand seemed to meet again like in the Sixties, and this seems to happen due to the awareness of both artists and the Italian music industry on their renovated and less provincial role, but also to the increased expertise of the Italian public, finally able to make stylistic and economic choices, from buying a CD to a ticket to a concert, which in turn favors the growth of the artists themselves. In other words, despite the crisis of the Italian and world music industry, undergoing a significant decrease in the number of music on material media, there is a real process of music integration happening that tends to be increasingly competent. The future of pop music in Italy, in particular Italian music, is in debt with the long process started in the mid-Fifties, and will hopefully feature an amplified dialogue among music producers, distributors, buyers and of course listeners. Excluding even only one of these interlocutors from this communication process would result into taking several steps back and thwarting all the effort of the last fifty years of pop music.

Conclusions: Italian pop music as cultural mine

From the mid-Fifties on, Italian pop music followed a rough path, mingling with foreign styles and trends, and welcoming them. In over 50 years, Italy has changed also through the action of the shift of pop music, which, in its several versions, had entire generations of Italians dance, sing, think, protest, grow up and dream. These fifty years have featured the challenge accepted by the Italian melodic tradition against international pop and rock music, with a hybridizing of genres, culture and youth's fashion that have highlighted how much music is able, and has been able, to mark private and public moments of the Italian society, particularly full of challenges and utopias.[20]

20. For a further analysis of the themes investigated in the chapter, the authors also suggest the following works: Marco Bracci, *The Dark Side of The Moon. Viaggio nell'identità dei Pink Floyd* (Milan: Aereostella, 2013); Marco Santoro, *Effetto Tenco. Genealogia della canzone d'autore* (Bologna: Il Mulino, 2010); Edoardo Tabasso, Marco Bracci, *Da Modugno a X Factor. Musica e società italiana dal dopoguerra a oggi* (Rome: Carocci, 2010).

Milly Buonanno

Fallen Heroes and Anti-Heroines: The Mafia Story in Italian TV Drama

Premise

Italy is world-famous for a number of reasons: fashion and style, good food and wine, Tuscan sun, magnificent landscapes, an enviable historical and artistic patrimony, opera, football teams, Ferrari cars, and so forth; but however much we may extend the list, we will hardly find any mention (for better or for worse) of Italian TV drama. Actually the popularity of homegrown television drama remains confined within national boundaries, in sharp contrast with the world renown enjoyed by Italy in the field of cinema.

The invisibility on the international scene does not alter the fact that domestic TV drama holds high cultural significance and has a wide impact on Italian society, as source of entertainment and education,[1] and as a central story-telling system whose tales fuel and help to shape popular imagination. Television everywhere is largely, although not exclusively, a national medium;[2] TV drama, accordingly, tends to draw on, comment, reconfigure cultural and societal features peculiar to any given territory,

1. It is worth recalling that Italian television (Rai) came into existence in mid-Fifties as a public service broadcasting, thus having education – alongside information and entertainment – within its remit. An evidence of this is the profusion of literary adaptations among television dramas for at least two decades after television inception. On this see: Milly Buonanno, *Italian TV Drama and Beyond. Stories from the Soil, Stories from the Sea* (Bristol and Chicago: Intellect, 2012). Although Rai, which is still today the biggest broadcaster in Italy and the leading producer of TV fiction, is criticised for discarding public service duties, something of an educational intent continues to inform and inspire a fair number of contemporary TV dramas.

2. This is not to deny or understate processes of trans-nationalization and globalization in contemporary world television, though. See Joe Straubhaar, *World Television: From Global to Local* (London: Sage, 2007).

in order to convey a "sense of place" and arouse in viewers the pleasure of recognition, the latter being in turn a condition for popularity. Italian television is by no means an exception. TV drama has developed in close dialogue with the country's history and culture and, to the extent it has endeavoured to narrate and address the nation, it can be mined to provide us with insights into different aspects of Italian society, and into the ways in which they have been narratively re-imagined for public consumption.

The chapter will focus on one of the most popular genres in Italian prime-time drama: the mafia story. This choice is certainly not to concur and indulge in all too common trite stereotypes about Italy as per excellence the country of the mafia, rather to point out how the crime storytelling has been reworked and turned into what is in fact an anti-mafia story at the crossroads of reality and imagination.

1. *Mob stories are always hot*

At the end of November 2007 Italian news media and, even more prominently, the international press and internet sites, announced the arrest of a mafia boss hiding in the Zen district of Palermo. Even though he was regarded as a prominent figure in one of the most powerful Sicilian clans, the man was not of such high caliber as to deserve the attention of the international media. But foreign observers were struck above all, and to some extent amused, by the circumstances of his capture. The wanted person, who was smart enough to have fled just a few weeks before a vast police operation that led to the arrest of the clan boss and his faithful followers, had been surprised in his secret hideaway while watching the final episode of *Il capo dei capi* (*The boss of the bosses*, Canale 5, 2007). This was Canale 5's (the flagship commercial channel) successful and critically acclaimed series, which narrated the bloody ascent in the hierarchy of Sicilian mafia power of the Corleonesi clan under the brutal command of Totò Riina. The final episode, broadcast on 29 November 2007, revolved around the capture of Riina; consequently, an effect of *mise en abyme*[3] was created by the parallel fact taking place in real life. "Real life bursts into mafia TV drama", ran the headlines of number of news stories.

3. This French term refers to the containment of an entity within another identical entity: in this specific instance, the televisual re-enactment of the capture of Totò Riina was contained within the actual event of the arrest of a mobster.

Bizarre though the event appears, it is nevertheless emblematic. Besides reminding us that fact and fiction can meet and mix in unpredictable ways, such event provides telling evidence of the diffuse fascination with mafia stories: they not merely appeal to large Italian audiences but also manage to captivate even the members of organized crime. Portrayals of the criminal underworld in film and television are popular among the mafia members who, as well as taking an interest in the media's image of themselves and their own world, find in these portrayals – more often than is believed – models of behaviour and examples of life-styles to follow. The young bosses of the Neapolitan camorra, as Roberto Saviano[4] in *Gomorra* (2006) confirms, regard the characters in mafia films as authentic role models and imitate their behaviour, styles of dress and even the architecture and furnishings of their homes. Just a few days before the mini-sensation generated by the circumstances of the arrest of the fugitive boss mentioned above, the *International Herald Tribune* of November 19, 2007 had published an article which, in referring to the success of *The boss of the bosses*, did not fail to emphasize that the jailed Totò Riina himself was one of the most assiduous viewers of his televisual biopic.

No further anecdotes are necessary to agree with Christopher Moltisanti's statement in *The Sopranos* (HBO, 1999-2006) that "mob stories are always hot".[5] In the comment just quoted the character was reporting the opinion of his cousin Gregory's girlfriend, an assistant of Quentin Tarantino: thus he referred to the cinema. But in Italy it is rather in television that the mafia story seems to have found fertile ground, a potential for artistic achievement, and the right conditions for favourable reception from viewers and (more rarely) critics.

We know enough to argue that stories about great criminals and great crime exert a powerful and almost universal attraction. The Italian public is certainly not unique in showing a keen appetite for organized crime on the small screen. Yet the Italian case, without being as eccentric or folkloric as it may seem in the eyes of sympathetic but stereotype-bound non-native

4. Roberto Saviano, *Gomorrah. Italy's Other Mafia* (London: MacMillan, 2007). This is a gripping and disquieting non-fiction novel that throws a harsh light on the ramifications of the power system of large-scale crime in Naples. *Gomorrah* became an international best-seller and was listed by the *New York Times* as one of the most important books of 2007. It was the inspiration for a much-awarded cinematic docudrama with the same title, made in 2008 by the director Matteo Garrone, and for the widely sold abroad TV drama *Gomorrah. The series* (Sky, 2014-present).

5. First season, episode 8, "The legend of Tennessee Moltisanti".

observers, is undeniably different with respect to other countries. This difference lies in the unequalled profusion of mafia stories – more than one hundred – offered by Italian television over the last decades, from mid-Eighties onwards.

It would be easy and to a large extent plausible to ascribe this abundance to historical roots, the widespread pervasion in many areas of activity in Italy, the monopoly of violence, the huge scale of illegal trafficking: in short to everything that makes criminal organizations and cultures a dramatic and unresolved problem of Italian society. For better (television drama takes on the task of keeping the issue alive in the horizon of viewers' critical awareness) or worse (television drama stimulates and indulges the "perverse" taste for mafia stories widely diffused in a country with a strong criminal tradition: the mafia country *par excellence*, in the stereotype often taken for granted abroad), this kind of specular and referential explanation renders only part of the truth. It is opportune at this point to recall what Robert Warshow, an insightful critic of popular culture, wrote about the gangster movie in the Forties: "The importance of the gangster film, and the nature and intensity of its emotional and aesthetic impact, cannot be measured in terms of the place of the gangster himself or the importance of the problem of crime in American life".[6]

Truth is that within the range of popular genres the mafia story can be regarded as an unequalled inspirational resource for narratives in which the entire panoply of archetypes, motives and ingredients of popular storytelling based on crime is unfolded: positive and negative heroes, one group armed against others, betrayal and revenge, savagery, blood and tears, blackmail, conspiracies, lust for and conflicts of power, greed for money, corruption, punishment, justice. All this, and more besides, is at the roots of the powerful attraction that crime, especially violent crime, and stories about crime have always exercised on the collective imagination in an inextricable mixture of fascination and repulsion.[7] It is not by chance that crime is the main substance of newspaper reports, as it was in the past for the tales of story-tellers. One could not fully comprehend the popularity of mob drama in Italy without recognising that the mafia, as well as arousing

6. Robert Warshow, *The Immediate Experience* (Cambridge: Harvard University Press, 2002), p. 100.

7. John G. Cawelti, *Adventure, Mystery and Romance* (Chicago: The University of Chicago Press, 1976).

repulsion and moral condemnation, does undeniably emanate a fascination, though a perverse one: the allure of evil.

The article in the *International Herald Tribune* that I quoted earlier found it inexplicable that Italian viewers, normally ready to respond to the appeal of mob stories, should have deserted *The Sopranos*. But it is easily explained. By dispelling many myths about the mafia and in particular by featuring a stressed-out and psychoanalysed protagonist, a husband and father and boss whose authority in both his blood family and his mafia family is continually called into question, the HBO series fundamentally altered the expected experiences of the Italian public: these experiences are constructed on, and in turn are constitutive of, an image of criminal underworld that unceasingly feeds on the ambivalent myth – swinging between moral condemnation and secret admiration – of organized crime.

Equally, an even more important: precisely in order to challenge and contrast such allure, Italian TV drama has built its own distinctive narrative canon on the celebration of anti-crime heroes who are, in actual fact, the true protagonists of the bulk of mafia stories. I will elaborate on this key-point at more length later in the chapter, after retracing the origins of the rise to popularity of mob drama.

2. La Piovra. *A phenomenon of popularity*

Criminality, and even more the culture of the mafia, is a long-established evil of Italian society. Nevertheless both the ability of the traditional *Cosa nostra* leadership to cope with its internal conflicts without attracting too much attention, while at the same time ensuring the immunity of its own members – thanks to its network of alliances with institutions and State officials at local and national level – and the tendency of State authorities, for various reasons, to underestimate the problem, allowed the mafia phenomenon to develop in relative invisibility for many years as far as public awareness and press attention was concerned. The situation changed suddenly and dramatically at the end of the Seventies when the criminal Corleone group, hitherto marginal in the geography of the mafia, began its ascent to power and thus initiated a strategy of out-and-out carnage that left over 1,000 dead among the affiliates in just a few years. For the first time in the history of the mafia, the very institutions of the State came under attack: politicians, magistrates and police officers became the targets of deadly attacks. The mafia thus arose as a socio-political "emergency" that could no longer be underestimated. In the early Eighties the Italian Parliament approved a law against the specific crime of mafia membership, while an anti-crime team consisting of an elite of magistrates and functionaries of the security apparatuses set up wide-ranging investigations in Sicily that were to lead to the charging and trial of over 400 mafiosi. The connections and instances of collusion between the mafia, politics and business emerged (at least in part) from the thick cloud of suspicion that had always surrounded them, and began to assume the clearer contours of provable facts.[8]

Consequently the mafia phenomenon in its multi-dimensional and truly tentacular configuration became a prominent and burning issue in public discourse in the Eighties, raising media attention and collective concern about organised crime to levels never previously reached in Italy. Thus public television was encouraged to venture into the uncharted territory of the mafia story; television viewers on their part were favourably disposed to welcome and follow stories that resonated with the top issue of the time.

Interest in, and demand for, narratives that might display unmistakable marks of Italianness were further aroused by the debate (very heated at that time) about television's system and culture. As is widely known, the Italian television scene experienced a far-reaching and turbulent transformation from the mid-Seventies onwards, when the inception of commercial television – the Berlusconi-owned Fininvest, to be later renamed Mediaset – put an end to the monopoly of public broadcasting and paved the way for the Rai-Mediaset mixed system.[9] The advent of commercial television set in motion large-scale phenomena of Americanization in television drama supply. The new private channels that entered the television arena without their own library or any production experience went ahead with massive imports; at the beginning of the Eighties the Italian television market had the dubious honour of being the biggest European importer of mostly US-originated foreign shows.

The new scenario of the mixed system engendered anxiety: commercial channels were blamed for serving as transmission belts of US cultural colonisation, and the risk was felt that public television, under the pressure of

8. See Pino Arlacchi, *Gli uomini del disonore* (Milan: Il Saggiatore, 2009).

9. On this see *Culture and Conflict in Post-war Italy*, ed. by Zygmunt G. Baransky and Robert Lumley (New York: St. Martin's Press, 1990); and Buonanno, *Italian Tv Drama and Beyond*.

aggressive competition from private networks, might yield to the temptation of fighting them on their own ground and thus renouncing to perform its function as public service and major producer of cultural representations of Italy's social reality. Rai responded to the challenge by creating a mafia story that soon turned into a phenomenon of unheard popularity, destined to remain unequalled even in the future. This was *La piovra* (*The Octopus*: *the power of mafia*, hereafter *La Piovra*; Rai 1, 1984-2001).

The case of *La Piovra* is without doubt the most remarkable in the whole history of Italian television drama, owing to the unprecedented popularity and status as an authentic "media event" gained by this mafia story since its first appearance in 1984, when it was soon acclaimed as the "Italian response to Dallas".[10] The huge success of the programme with both audience and critics prompted Rai to carry on with a narrative that was originally conceived as a single stand-alone miniseries; in fact *La Piovra* became a saga, and unfolded over the years into a sequence of ten miniseries before coming to an end in early 2000.

The amazing and enduring popularity of *La Piovra* must be ascribed first and foremost to its quintessential "Italianness", which made it into a "text of identity" *par excellence* of domestic drama. This prerogative emanated from a set of elements endowed with large resonance, recognizability and credibility in collective Italian culture.

Being a mafia story, *La Piovra* revolved around a dramatic issue deep-rooted as much in social reality as in the Italian imagination. As indicated above, the reality of the early Eighties was a fierce power struggle within the Sicilian mafia: the cause of unequalled carnage which in addition claimed a great many lives among representatives of the State (police officers, magistrates and local politicians). However the definition of mafia story does not adequately capture the narrative's ambitious purpose of unmasking the treacherous relationships between crime and power, in their two-fold embodiment: the deadly power of organized crime, and the criminal connections of political and financial power. Inherent in *La Piovra* was a sort of obsession with conspiracy theories,[11] this being the

10. The success of the American prime-time serials *Dallas* (CBS, 1978-1991, in Italy on Canale 5) was instrumental in helping commercial broadcasting to establish itself in the Italian television scene. *Dallas* was regarded and blamed as the Trojan horse of the American cultural colonization.

11. Richard Sparks, *Television and the Drama of Crime* (Buckingham: Open University Press, 1992), p. 143.

main inspiration for its complex and visionary plots involving collusion between mafia bosses and the powers that be, allies in pursuing their mega-interests. Effectively symbolized by the tentacled metaphor of the octopus, the vision of a world infiltrated by crime right through to its innermost institutional mechanisms strongly resonated with the "culture of suspicion" and mistrust of political power which (for a number of historical reasons) is a permanent feature of the Italian collective mentality.

The protagonist Inspector Cattani, to this day an unforgettable icon of all-time popular hero, was for his part a primary success factor of *La Piovra*. Cattani was a typically Italian character in his captivating mixture of honesty and unscrupulousness, exhilaration and despondency, in his vacillation between a desire for justice and a thirst for vengeance, in a deep anarchism betrayed by his impatience with the restraints of legal formalities. Typically Italian, furthermore, was his tragic figure as hero-martyr doomed to sacrifice his life, fated to succumb in the fierce but unequal struggle against the overwhelming forces of evil. Over 17 millions viewers – an unsurpassed record audience – watched the season finale of *La Piovra 4* (Rai 1, 1989), when Cattani fell in a hail of bullets unleashed by mafia killers.

3. *In the footsteps of* La Piovra

It is imperative to acknowledge the fundamental role of *La Piovra* in launching the mafia story on the small screen, an influential role that is entirely analogous with that played by *The Godfather* (Coppola, 1972, 1974, 1990) in the American cinema. Although the Rai had already begun in the Seventies to produce some historical dramas about organized crime, the huge popularity gained by *La Piovra* was a key factor in creating and maintaining the conditions for the plentiful flourishing of the mafia story in the years to come.

After first discovering and exploring the great potential of this narrative genre, public television raised production and offer of mob drama to levels never attained by the commercial counterpart, although the latter has likewise entered the arena: roughly two-thirds of the post-*Piovra* mob dramas have been produced by the Rai. Most of these are in the prestige format of the mini-series. Often enough, however, topics and issues regarding large-scale crime are incorporated into serialized productions, in particular into police and investigative series, for which these issues provide material either for some anthology plot or, more consistently and continuously, for the running plot. There is no recurring hero figure in Italian police series who can avoid, sooner or later, tackling crimes perpetrated by one of the national or international mafias. Actually the mafia story has turned out to be an important pool for ideas and narrative material for short and long running series and serials.

Production and offer of mob dramas have witnessed intensification from late Nineties onwards. This was no coincidence. These same years underwent accelerating growth in the productive capacity of the Italian television industry; and the privileged evening slots opened up as never before to home-grown television drama. Hence the need to fill the prime-time – where highly rewarding ratings are expected and normally achieved – with a surplus of new stories. In such circumstances broadcasters and producers typically prefer to put more trust in genres that have largely proved their worth and in narrative content that has well-tested appeal and effectiveness. There is no doubt that the mafia story can be so described, with the added value of its strong Italian connotation; this was particularly valued in the climate of pride in national identity surrounding the rebirth of domestic television drama (in embodying the Italian response to *Dallas*, *La Piovra* had pioneered the endorsement of the distinctive and successful Italianness of the mafia story). *La Piovra*, again, has set the standards for a hero-centered narrative.

In the filmic tradition the protagonist of the gangster movie or mafia story is normally the criminal: the individual or the organization. The cinematographic construct of a criminal mythology and a mafia mystique has found an effective instrument and consistent support precisely in the prominence of the negative hero as the protagonist, whether an individual personality or a group. There is no need to postulate a necessary or inevitable coincidence between the leading dramatic role and the dominant narrative perspective; but it is true that the diegetic centrality of the negative hero, which arouses fascination and public controversy in equal measure, in principle offers fertile ground for mythopoetic dynamics. Not by chance, the genre itself in its classic film version has codified from the beginnings, as an antidote or barrier against the mythicization of the gangster figure, a narrative structure in the shape of one ascending and another, equally relevant, falling trajectory as the prelude to the tragic and fatal defeat of the negative hero.

However Italian TV drama, especially in the context of public service television, has resisted the embrace of the cinematographic canons of the gangster movie, thus turning the mafia story into a televisual variant that wants its heroes to come from the world of law and order, or from civil society, rather than the criminal underworld. *La Piovra* has set the standards for this turn. Mob dramas that put crime-fighters positive heroes at centre-stage of the narrative largely exceed those centered on criminal individuals and organizations. Indeed, the diegetic centrality of the negative hero is hardly a recurrent feature of made-for-television mafia stories in Italy (I will say something on more recent shifts later). Likewise, well constructed antagonist figures, complex criminal personalities whose facets go beyond cunning and violence or other limited sets of stereotypical characteristics, are seldom encountered. Whether or not this is by deliberate choice, everything in the Italian mafia story happens – with few exceptions – as if the antagonistic and adversarial nature of organized crime were so self-evident and so completely taken for granted, that it could easily and convincingly be personified in stereotypes, simplified characters and conventional *clichés*. As antagonists, these personify and portray the power and criminal threat after the manner of masks rather than individuals. They are the recurring and recognizable avatars – not in the mystic religious sense of the word, but in its metaphorical meaning of iconic simulation of reality – through which the criminal underworlds reveal (or disguise) themselves in Italian television drama.

It goes without saying that, even if they do not perform protagonist roles, or do not embody complex and nuanced personalities, mafia characters in television drama may well function as effective ingredients of the stories, endowed with a strong and lasting emotional, cognitive, ethical and aesthetic impact. For instance, the basically one-dimensional character of Totò Riina in *The boss of the bosses* does not make the tale of the bloodthirsty ascent of the Corleonesi to the heights of *Cosa nostra* any less captivating; nor does it remove from the protagonist himself that grim fascination which is greatly deplored by the many who fear rightly or wrongly that mafia stories in film or television run the risk of showing the bosses in a favourable light. And more romantic than grim, perhaps, is the charm emanated by the simplistically ambivalent character of Tonio Fortebracci, the villain protagonist – already a mythical figure for the members of the numerous fan clubs that have flourished on the web – of the highly melodramatic mafia story *Honour and respect* (Canale 5, 2006-2017).

Having chosen to assign the protagonist roles to the forces of law and order and the judiciary, or to courageous members of civilian society, the Italian mafia story has become a factory of anti-mafia heroes. Whether the characters in the story are completely imaginary, like Inspector Cattani in *La Piovra*, or based on real people, anti-mafia heroes inspire and inhabit a fair number of Italian mob dramas. Doubtless, most of the mafia stories, and their heroes and villains, are the fruit of imagination: not infrequently a melodramatic imagination, with or without social pretensions, which subordinates the repertoire of conventions and stereotypes of the genre to a dramaturgy of excesses that is all too typical of melodrama. However, from the late Nineties onwards, real-life inspired dramas have somewhat undermined the preeminence of merely fictional tales and characters. Both public and, to a lesser extent, commercial television have explored and exploited the biographical variant of the mafia story to re-enact the lives and deeds of the heroes-martyrs who fell in the fight against macro-criminality (*Brancaccio*,[12] Rai 1, 2001; *Paolo Borsellino*,[13] Canale 5, 2004; *Falcone*,[14] Rai 1, 2006; *Il generale Dalla Chiesa*,[15] Canale 5, 2007; *Borsellino i 57 giorni*, Rai 1, 2012; *Il sindaco pescatore* (*The fisherman mayor*),[16] Rai 1, 2016) and those, be they State servants or common people, who proved capable of standing up against mafia power. Real-life persons and facts have also inspired the already mentioned biopic of the boss Totò Rina, of the captain who achieved to capture him (*Ultimo*,[17] Canale 5, 1988), and

12. The mini-series takes the name of the district of Palermo where the parish priest Don Pino Puglisi was assassinated in September 1993. He was well-known for his dedication to saving marginalized young men living in areas of urban deprivation from being "conscripted" into organized crime.

13. The name of the judge Paolo Borsellino is always associated with that of Giovanni Falcone; the two judges had worked together for a long time and finally shared the same tragic fate. Borsellino, who was fully aware of being a "dead man walking" after the attack on Falcone, was in turn the victim of a mafia killing in July 1992.

14. Judge Giovanni Falcone, who had a deep understanding of the mafia's true nature, was one of the most enlightened and perspicacious investigators and prosecutors of mafia crime. In May 1992 he was the victim of a powerful bomb attack just outside Palermo, ordered by the bloodthirsty Corleone boss Totò Riina. Together with his colleague and friend Paolo Borsellino, who was himself assassinated only three months later, Giovanni Falcone was listed in *Time Europe Magazine* (November 13, 2006) as one of the heroes of our time.

15. General of the Carabinieri Carlo Alberto Dalla Chiesa was primarily responsible for the capture of Red Brigade terrorists in the Seventies. In May1982 he became Prefect of Palermo, where a fierce mafia war was raging; he was assassinated in September of the same year.

16. A former fisherman, Angelo Vassallo served as the mayor of a town in Campania, where the criminal organization known as "camorra" is based. His engagement in fighting crime made him the target of a deadly attack from camorrists.

17. Code name of Carabinieri Captain Sergio De Caprio. He directed the operation to capture the boss Riina, who was arrested in 1993 after over 20 years in hiding.

the tale of the rise and fall of Bernardo Provenzano, the real boss of bosses of the Sicilian mafia until it was arrested and put in jail in 2006 (*L'ultimo dei corleonesi – The last of Corleonesi*, Rai 1, 2007). Such docudramatic[18] turn of the Italian mob drama is certainly not without good reasons; reality is an endless source of characters and events that, in addition to being already familiar to the public (a powerful built-in promotional tool), are surrounded by a captivating aura of truthfulness – regardless of whether the fictional re-enactment of the true story makes room for imagination.

Not by chance, the potential for success of the reality-inspired TV dramas is testified by the wide audiences they reach. With *Ultimo* (*The last*, Canale 5, 1998) and *Paolo Borsellino* (Canale 5, 2004), for example, Mediaset achieved two of the greatest successes in its history, while the biopics *Giovanni Falcone* and *Borsellino i 57 giorni*, both produced by public television, were the most watched programmes of the years 2006 and 2012 respectively.

Tab. 1. Top ten real-life inspired mafia stories

Title	Channel	Year	Audience (in millions)
Paolo Borsellino	Canale 5	2004	10,833
Ultimo	Canale 5	1998	8,930
Borsellino i 57 giorni	Rai 1	2012	8,164
La vita rubata	Rai 1	2008	7,604
Giovanni Falcone	Rai 1	2006	7,597
Il capo dei capi	Canale 5	2007	7,284
Il sindaco pescatore	Rai 1	2016	7,000
Brancaccio	Rai 1	2001	6,935
Generale Dalla Chiesa	Canale 5	2007	6,412
L'ultimo dei corleonesi	Rai 1	2007	6,360

Although the stellar ratings achieved by *La Piovra* in the Eighties and early Nineties remain unequalled, the mafia story's appeal to the Italian audiences persists. At the time of writing this chapter in early 2016 the

18. The word docudrama defines the dramatized re-enactment of real-life event.

biographical docudrama *Il sindaco pescatore* (see footnote 16) reached 27% market share: an achievement quite hard to get now in a television scenario of plentiful channels and entertainment on offer.

As I have already indicated, the powerful mental and emotional grip that the mafia continues to exert on a great many Italians is largely predicated on the intriguing ambivalence between condemnation and revulsion for a socially pernicious and morally despicable criminal organization, and the sinister appeal of a power system that epitomizes a success story, albeit a depraved one, in its capacity to expand, make money and rise to power. The refashioning of so many mob dramas into the biopics of anti-mafia fallen heroes, which is especially true for public television, has endeavoured and greatly helped to establish the narrative and moral barycenter of the mafia story on the "condemnation and revulsion" side of such ambivalence: thus adding a flavour of "civic engagement"[19] to popular storytelling about one of Italy's most dramatic social realities.

Does the repeated insistence on the "dramatic social reality" of criminal organization and culture serve to bolster the mythology of the mafia? Or by contrast, does focusing the narrative standpoint firmly on positive characters help to shatter the attraction of evil, by enhancing and honouring the heroes and heroines, real or imaginary, of the anti-crime fight? This dilemma stirs up public opinion in Italy every time the recurring controversy about the mafia story on television is reignited. As it often happens, we are not facing an irreconcilable alternative, rather a coexistence of opposites that in their own way or in unpredictable combinations – depending on different factors and circumstances – help to keep alive in a large share of Italian viewing public the demand and enjoyment for mafia stories on the small screen.

4. *Female mobsters*

This by necessity synthetic overview of one of the most popular genres of Italian TV drama would however be incomplete without bringing into the picture a recently emerging shift. A quotation from *The Sopranos* lends itself well to introduce the argument.

19. The label "civic engagement" is usually applied to films that are characterized by a dramatic structure, a realistic style and the purpose of conveying social and political criticism of the evils of Italy.

In season two, episode four ("Commendatori", February 2000) of the ground-breaking HBO mob drama, the protagonist Tony Soprano travels to Naples to make a deal with a clan of the camorra, the powerful crime organization that reigns in Campania. Tony's attitude to the trip is informed by his nostalgia-inducing imagination and expectation of a southern Italian world (or underworld) where the patriarchal power structure remains intact. Hence, his disconcerted reaction and sneering remark when he discovers that the camorra boss with whom business must be conducted is a woman, the voluptuous Annalisa Zucca who has replaced her senile father and her husband, jailed for life, as the head of the family. "A fucking woman boss? Never happen in the States. Never".

An inconceivable violation of the gendered hierarchies of mafia power, as perceived by Tony Soprano, the access of women to leadership positions within criminal organizations actually happens in Italy: both in real life[20] and, more recently, in fictional representations of mafia and mafia-like groups in TV drama. Female characters who proudly endeavor the rise to power in the quintessential masculine domain of illegal trafficking and bloodthirsty violence have, in fact, performed protagonist roles within the successful prime-time serial dramas *Squadra antimafia* (*Antimafia squad*, Canale 5, 2009-2016) and *Gomorra. La serie* (*Gomorrah. The series*, Sky Atlantic, 2014-present).[21]

Portrayals of powerful women criminals are totally unprecedented in the whole history of Italian TV drama and, more specifically, in the long tradition of the mafia story that has been a staple of TV drama production and consumption in Italy since the Eighties. This is hardly surprising and transcends the Italian case. Action heroines, armed women and violent and criminal women have emerged in different periods of cinema history, and television drama has recently witnessed a similar trend internationally. Current scholarship[22] has especially focused on police and action dramas, exploring the different ways in which television storytelling has engaged, not without limits and contradictions, in transgressing norms of traditional femininity.

20. See *Women and the Mafia. Female Roles in Organized Crime Structures*, ed. by Giovanni Fiandaca (New York: Springer, 2007).

21. See *Television Antiheroines. Women Behaving Badly in Crime and Prison Drama*, ed. by Milly Buonanno (Bristol and Chicago: Intellect, 2017).

22. See *Action Chicks. New Images of Tough Women in Popular Culture*, ed. by Sherrie A. Innes (New York: Palgrave Macmillan, 2004); Amanda Lotz, *Redesigning Women. Television After the Network Era* (Urbana and Chicago: University of Illinois Press, 2006); and Deborah Jermyn, *Prime Suspects* (London: BFI, 2010).

Yet, in television and cinema alike the genre that has mostly preserved the deep masculine connotations of its diegetic world,[23] thus remaining largely impermeable to the rise of female protagonism, has been precisely the mafia story. The mafia story is by generic conventions "male", by reason not so much of socio-anthropological faithfulness to the macho centrality and culture organized crime syndicate as of the deep symbolic connections between violence, power and money – the dominant themes in the mafia story – and the social construction of maleness. The genre "traditionally foregrounds phallic masculinity"[24] and reduces female representation to the dichotomy of usually powerless or ancillary mothers/wives and mistresses/femmes fatales.

Italian public television has doubtless set the standard for a version of the mafia story centered on (mostly although not exclusively male) positive heroes, but the deep-seated attraction of the Italian public for this genre of drama has prompted free commercial and subscription-based television to make inroads into such a lucrative narrative territory. Crime storytelling has thus witnessed a re-configuration and has been, to a greater or lesser extent, re-imagined according to the "logics of distinction" and identity strategies adopted by the competing players, differently positioned within the television system. Canale 5, the flagship channel of commercial broadcasting, without completely undermining the key role of positive albeit flawed heroes, has nonetheless shifted the narrative barycenter closer to the criminal front (see the biopics of mob bosses and other stories of criminal clans and bad guys). It has also lessened the gender gap, paving the way for representations of women in command of mafia organizations in the long-running serial *Squadra antimafia* (*Antimafia squad*, 2009-2016), a captivating mix of action-crime and melodrama. As for Sky, in its ambitious pursuit of the HBO model, the satellite television that addresses niche audiences has chosen to focus on the dark side of Italian society, since its first move into the field of original production (*Romanzo criminale* [*Crime novel. The series*], 2008-2010), and is committed to narrating, in tones of gritty realism, stories of male and female criminals who inhabit a

23. George S. Larke-Walsh, *Screening the Mafia* (Jefferson and London: McFarland and Co., 2010).

24. Catherine O'Rawe, "Roberta Torre's Angela. The Mafia and the Woman's Film", in *Mafia Movies. A Reader*, ed. by Dana Renga (Toronto: University of Toronto Press, 2011), p. 229.

violent and merciless world without heroes or redemption (see the much acclaimed and widely sold internationally *Gomorrah. The series*, Sky Atlantic, 2014-present).

The increased visibility of female bosses on the national media and judicial scene may well have made an impact on, and provided inspiration for, writers and producers of mob dramas. To this day more an experiment (successful, it must be said) than a trend, the advent of criminal anti-heroines in contemporary TV drama nonetheless testify that the long-held tradition of the mafia story, as one deeply shaped by *La Piovra*, is being challenged by the exploration of new narrative paths, more attuned to different demands and tastes, ethic and aesthetic orientations of specific sections of the viewing public. Next years will possibly see more variety of mob dramas on offer: hardly a signal of crisis, rather of resourcefulness and resilient vitality of the mafia story on the expanding Italian television scene.

Fabio Corsini

Italian Webseries: The New (yet Old) Way of Storytelling

Introduction

It is now well established that the phenomenon of the webseries, namely all those productions of audiovisual content available on the Internet that users place on *video sharing* platforms, has assumed a certain level of maturity and popularity. But how does this kind of production contribute to popular culture? What do they add to or take away from it? And, above all, what are they? In this essay we will try to better understand what is meant by the word webseries, as well as investigating what kind of contribution they provide in terms of the production of media content and to popular culture more generally. The attempt is to analyse how this particular type of product fits within popular culture, and at the same time, to try to describe what imaginaries they create. Naturally, all within the Italian context.

In attempting to establish a definition, we can begin by affirming that webseries is an umbrella term that provides an identity to a decidedly vast and, above all, extremely varied group of audiovisual experiments and, consequently, of experimentation in the field of contemporary storytelling.[1] From the word itself – webseries – it is easy to understand that to keep this differentiated aggregate of products together it is, on the one hand, the reference to seriality, and therefore to the serialisation processes typical of the cultural industry; and on the other hand, the use of the web, understood not only as a simple alternative distribution platform but in all its productive and expressive potential. It is therefore in reference to these two elements

1. Mauro Di Donato, "Webserie e nuovi scenari mediali", *Imago. Studi di Cinema e Media*, 13 (2016), pp. 15-30.

and to the fruitful interconnections that derive from them[2] that the nature of this type of content must be understood. Looking in more detail, as Mirko Lino observes:

> The webseries fuses the immersivity of narrative serialisation typical of the TV series with the participatory interaction between users active in cyberspace and the interaction between man and medial format-content.[3]

This definition helps us to focus on the element of connection with the "web" along with the world of the "series" of which Lino strategically refers to the feature of immersivity. At the same time, however, it also opens up to the idea of new format-content forms of relationship that concern both the production processes and the processes of usage/consumption.

The increase in popularity and importance of the webseries phenomenon is also demonstrated not only by the emergence of scientific literature (magazines, monographs, and various mapping works), but also by the creation of national and international festivals and awards[4] that contribute to the growth of visibility of such productions and at the same time try to give a more coherent and organised structure to a complex and elusive phenomenon. In this regard, in addition to the Italian example of the *Rome Web Fest*, now in its fifth year, it is worth mentioning that of the *International Academy of Web Television Awards* held every year in Los Angeles and the source of inspiration for many of the other festivals. These are two important events that contribute to validate this particular emerging form of popular culture within the traditional media circuit of actors, producers, creators, distributors, etc. Finally, in addition to these two aspects, the interest and attention of brands towards these new products should be mentioned. And it is not just the audiovisual market, but more particularly the brands, which through the new web marketing strategies[5] have paved the way for the creation of branded content webseries.[6]

2. See Chiara Bressa, *Fare webserie. La nuova frontiera del filmare in modo indipendente: teoria e prassi* (Rome: Dino Audino, 2015); Simone Arcagni, *Visioni digitali. Video, web e nuove tecnologie* (Turin: Einaudi, 2016).

3. Mirko Lino, "L'interactive storytelling delle webseries. Un percorso tra i generi", *Mediascape Journal*, 7 (2016), pp. 92-101, p. 93.

4. See Janet De Nardis, "Le webserie e il circuito internazionale dei festival", *Imago. Studi di Cinema e Media*, 2 (2017), pp. 127-138.

5. Paolo Bonsignore, Joseph Sassoon, *Branded Content. La nuova frontiera della comunicazione d'impresa* (Milan: Franco Angeli, 2014).

6. See Romana Andò, Fabio Corsini, "Branded webseries: comunicare i brand tra web e serialità", *Imago. Studi di Cinema e Media*, 13 (2016), pp. 61-83.

Reference has been made to the attention of these three different areas because this is the expression of a process of validation which confers the "status" of cultural products to these new productions and, as a result, are now truly part of popular culture. Furthermore, the case of the webseries is also interesting because it manages to encapsulate within a product a number of trends that have significantly changed the structure of the cultural industries over the last two decades, and the very nature of the media content that shapes and gives substance to popular culture itself. Among the most significant aspects are the phenomenon of remediation[7] and the intensification of the phenomena of media convergence, as well as participatory culture and the connective and collective intelligence outlined by Henry Jenkins[8] more than a decade ago.

Moreover, the webseries are an interesting case study through which to observe the transformations of contemporary mediascapes, mainly in relation to the redefinition of roles, content and ways of using new and traditional media, especially television. At the same time, however, the name itself used to describe these productions highlights the importance of the reference to seriality as a typical feature of cultural industries since the time of *feuilleton* and the serial novel. The latter is a feature which shows us that, contrary to popular belief – namely that the new kills the old – the influences of being bidirectional go in both directions, and media as "technology and cultural form"[9] continue on their journey of transformation and constant adaptation.

From what has been said so far we can draw two interpretations regarding the role of webseries within the broader context of popular culture. The first concerns the ever-present phenomena of serialisation and remediation between old and new media, but also between old and new content; the second is about the once again increasing contamination of commerce and the world of culture. The latter is an aspect that John Thompson defined as the phenomenon of "commodification of symbolic forms" and is based on two important aspects:

7. David J. Bolter, Richard Grusin, *Remediation. Understanding New Media* (Boston: MIT Press, 2000).

8. Henry Jenkins, *Convergence Culture. Where the Old and New Media Collide* (New York: New York University Press, 2006).

9. Raymond Williams, *Television: Technology and Cultural Form* (New York: Harper Collins, 1974).

> Symbolic valorisation [as] the process through which symbolic forms are ascribed 'symbolic value' and economic valorisation that translates the fact that "symbolic forms are constituted as *commodities*: they become objects which can be bought and sold in a market for a price.[10]

And, indeed, webseries have both their symbolic relevance as accepted and appreciated cultural forms, as well as an economic relevance that encourages those who produce or distribute professionally audiovisual content to consider them.

1. *The varied (and vast) world of the webseries*

Given the vastness but, above all, the fluidity of online content and the impossibility of assessing every single webseries, we will consider some of the most significant Italian examples which appeared over the last few years with the aim of looking at the formal characteristics of these productions and, above all, the imaginaries they produce. In this regard, it is opportune to reflect on what is meant by significant and relevant. In fact, it should be noted that within the webseries (but not only in these type of contents) the reference to popular is closely linked to the dimension of popularity, namely that of the celebrity. Taken as granted, here we must underline the existence of a shift from popularity to celebrity and from pop culture to celebrity culture.[11] As a result, the most popular productions have been taken into consideration, in other words those that have achieved greatest audience acclaim. To do this, a number of criteria known as "key performance indicators" have been used to evaluate the performance of blogs and websites: visibility, which is a parameter linked to the number of webseries views, audience engagement that measures the number of comments (or of *likes*) for each episode, as well as the number of subscribers to the Youtube channel or to the Facebook page. In addition, we have tried to take into account

10. John B. Thompson, *Media and Modernity. A Social Theory of the Media* (Stanford: Stanford University Press, 1995), p. 16.

11. On this see at least Graeme Turner, *Understanding Celebrity*, 2nd edition (London: Sage, 2013); Sean Redmond, *Celebrity and the Media* (Basingstoke: Palgrave McMillan, 2014); David Marshall, *Celebrity and Power: Fame in Contemporary Culture* (Minneapolis: University of Minnesota Press, 1997).

notoriety, that is to say the product's ability to get people talking about it in other – old and new – media.

But even in this case, some of the characteristics of the web among which openness, mobility, continuous change, and above all speed, make it almost impossible to quantify the webseries phenomenon. By virtue of this, the method used for the selection, rather than being linked to the rigorousness of a scientific sampling, is that of serendipity typical of the intertextual feature of the web made up of continuous references, and the actual links between different productions. A necessary decision, but also coherent with the online space, which, in reference to the webseries, is crucial both for its production and its usage.

The corpus we have examined has, above all, undergone formal analysis. An accounting operation linked to the number of episodes, average duration (and duration of each episode) and, finally, the number of seasons. From this point of view it could be said that the key word describing these characteristics is variability. A feature attributable to two different reasons. The first, more immediately understandable, is linked to the fact that the less rigid the structure of the show schedule, the fewer conscriptions connected to the writing of webseries products according to the methods and the timings of television.[12] Therefore, a webseries episode is not a fragment or a unit that must be placed within a complex show schedule made up of multiple narrative segments, but simply a pause, a break between a "first" and an "after" that exists within a limitless amount of content. Then there is a second characteristic that can be seen regarding the duration. Barring a few exceptions, the duration of a *webisode*, the name for each episode of a webseries, often varies. A variability that this time depends on the fact that this difference in episode length is based on the different narrative needs that emerge for each single episode.

Moreover, it can also be seen that webseries productions tend to be quite short, and in any case even shorter than short formats in the cultural industry (sitcoms for example and, more generally, interstitial fiction designed as narrative segments that serve to fill a gap between different blocks). Finally, the same can be said for the number of episodes: they range from a minimum of 2 to more than 20, with an average episode length anything between 2 and 22 minutes.

12. Bressa, *Fare webserie.*

Therefore, alongside variety, brevity is the second key word that distinguishes this type of content. The latter is a feature, in part, attributable to production difficulties and, as a result, also to the cost of production (both in financial terms and in terms of time) for those working at an amateur and non-professional level. There is, however, a further reason linked to the need for the brevity of the media formats transmitted on the web that allow episodes to be used as "*libraries* of multimedia content, in other words interactive archives of audiovisual productions that can be clicked on, enjoyed, commented on and shared by users pretty much anywhere and at any time"[13] and through any device. This is also connected to the fact that smartphones are increasingly being used to fill the "gaps" of waiting and moving around that qualify our day to day living. Finally, it can also be added that the brevity is imposed by the aforementioned logic of speed, continuous change and transformation typical of the web itself.

A final observation concerns the reference to the seasons. There are very few webseries, almost without exception, that reach a second season, and almost none get to a third. Nevertheless, almost all the productions examined use the reference to seasonality as if, in fact, this was a distinctive feature of this type of content compared to the huge number of videos that are present online. Something that qualifies, in a positive way, the nature of these productions.

Alongside these characteristics borrowed from television seriality, those of the web must also be mentioned. Among these, first and foremost, is the fact that it is about "user generated content" and therefore productions posted on the web by non-professional users. These are serial narratives and stories that come from the community of web users and, therefore, differ from the television and cultural industry in general. This differentiation is perceived as a point of pride or, any way, as a distinctive feature that makes the webseries stand out from the logic of the cultural industry. This aspect is directly connected to the financing methods. In fact, in most cases we see entirely self-financed products, in other words made using the money from the writers, actors and producers (roles that often blend together); or projects that resort to the practice, typical of the internet, of *crowd funding*.

Another fundamental aspect is that of interactivity. This feature, which appears to resemble another tired and abused gulf between audience

13. Luca Barra, Damiano Garofalo, "Ritorno alla realtà televisiva: influenze e riappropriazioni tra webserie e tv", *Imago. Studi di Cinema e Media*, 13 (2016), pp. 31-47, p. 33.

passivity and activity, is in fact often referred to as a distinctive feature of the webseries. In this regard, it is important to cite the example of *Lost in Google* (2012) where the main characters perform actions based on users' comments on previous episodes. In this sense, users are seen as active as they are capable of constantly changing the fate of the protagonists by simply leaving comments and posts. However *Lost in Google*, unfortunately, represents more a *one-off* rather than a model taken up and imitated by other web serial projects. In fact, in most cases users' comments do not directly become part of the narrative but are taken into account, just like, in a rather immediate and direct way, the traditional television industry takes into account viewers' opinions regarding plots and character popularity. However, it is significant that, as happens with other types of content posted online, the comments left by users for the various episodes of the webseries become a sort of secondary text that, for better or for worse, have the power to make those productions even more popular.

Finally, there is another feature, already mentioned at the beginning, and which typifies the webseries: "remediation". The idea of this feature is to remind of the fact that webseries frequently end up quoting, in a more or less direct way, some television series, mentioning titles, remedying their language and sometimes imitating actual characters. *Gli effetti di Gomorra sulla gente* (*The Effects of Gomorrah on the people*, 2014) is an excellent example of this. Not only is there a reference in the title – and therefore a remediation – to the famous TV drama produced by Sky and already broadcast by several television channels around the world, but the entire series lives on parodies of the characters and scenes of the original show itself. The popularity of the webseries is so great that sometimes we find stars from television series making cameo appearances in webseries, in technical jargon known as a "crossover".

Even from this point of view, however, it is worth digressing slightly to remember that remediation is another hallmark of popular culture in general and not just of the web. The repetition of formats, genres and above all of stories within different media and through different languages is something inherent in the history of cultural industries. In this regard, the reference to the television series fits perfectly. Whether they have a journalistic/narrative origin, the serial novel known as *feuilletton*, or they come from a more literary sphere as in the case of the novels with recurring heros, before reaching television they have had also a significant passage on radio. And this story is even older if we listen to even David

J. Bolter and Richard Grusin. In fact, according to them, "remediation did not begin with the introduction of digital media. We can identify the same process throughout the last several hundred years of Western visual representation",[14] discovering in one of the key principles of new technologies something as old as the birth of visual culture.

In light of all that has been said so far, as a first consideration, it can therefore be argued that the expression webseries can be understood as a sort of brand, or a tag to be associated with content that guarantees the web production a higher chance of success and popularity and greater visibility on the net. And this is also because TV drama and seriality more in general are enjoying a certain level of success not only among the younger generation; they represent some of the most sought after content on the web and increase the chances that content will go viral.

2. *Continuity and change*

It has already been said that webseries are a good example of the reconfiguration of the relationship between new and old media to the extent that:

> What is new about media comes from the particular ways in which older media and the ways in which other media refashion themselves to answer the challenges of new media.[15]

But what is the actual scale of such reconfigurations between television and webseries? It is necessary to understand what their significance is for the world of seriality in general and more particularly for television storytelling by trying to review the correlated elements of continuity and change. As a matter of fact, even though this type of production and with it its peculiar production methods, influence all media, we are interested in looking at webseries in relation to television and more particularly in relation to TV drama.

In the emerging Italian academic debate on webseries,[16] the reference to television is a constant characterised by a marked ambivalence. In fact,

14. Bolter, Grusin, *Remediation. Understanding New Media*, p. 11.

15. *Ibid.*, p. 15.

16. *Imago. Studi di Cinema e Media*, 13 (2016), ed. by Janet De Nardis, Mauro Di Donato and Andrea Minuz; Arcagni, *Visioni digitali*; Mirko Lino, "Le fiction delle webserie.

if on the one hand the "kinship" between television seriality and serial forms of the web is recognised, on the other the reference to television language is thought of as a negative focal point. The classic seriality "forces" and therefore limits the stories into rigid and predictable formulas: the formats, genres, and the schedules connected to them and to the traditional (pre-Netflix) practice of content distribution. A language that, although no longer representative of the complexity of the contemporary serial panorama, acquires its meaning if it refers to the production of Italian fiction, and especially generalist networks such as Rai or Mediaset. In fact, one cannot fail to take into account the stigma that especially young generations attribute to such kind of productions perceived as not very believable, out of touch with them, and seen as using unrealistic language, and of having a rather slow narrative pace. A stigma further strengthened with increasing exposure to foreign fiction, mainly, but not exclusively, American.[17]

Analysing the panorama of the Italian webseries provides an opportunity to better understand the complex and ambivalent relationship between web and seriality. But it also explicits the connections between Italian seriality and international seriality. In fact, already from the titles, most of these web productions refer not so much to Italian TV drama, but rather to contemporary international productions. Or, to those Italian productions, not belonging to generalist networks and that Massimo Scaglioni and Luca Barra have actually called "a whole other fiction" referring to Sky productions such as *Romanzo Criminale. The Series* and *Gomorrah. The series*.[18]

On the other side, there is the web that seems, instead, to be the positive focal point characterised by high levels of freedom and creativity where, by virtue of this, one can take risks through new forms of *storytelling*. And this is no longer just transmedia but above all interactive, more and more linked to the gaming experiences that push viewers, not only to enter into

Un percorso tra i generi", *Emerging Series*, 2, pp. 42-53; *Post-serialità. Per una sociologia delle tv series. Dinamiche di trasformazione della fiction televisiva*, ed. by Sergio Brancato (Naples: Liguori, 2011).

17. On this see Romana Andò, Fabio Corsini, Stefania Pizza, "Watchin Television Today. A Comparative Survey of Italian and American Students' Habits in Front of Television", *Journal of Italian Cinema and Media Studies*, 4/2, pp. 283-306.

18. Massimo Scaglioni, Luca Barra, *Tutta un'altra fiction. La serialità pay in Italia e nel mondo. Il modello Sky* (Rome: Carocci, 2013).

the story, but to participate in the writing process in a genuine act of co-creation.[19]

In actual fact, and this is the line of reasoning we want to carry forward, webseries, rather than being the result of a contradiction between the web and television, are an emblematic product of the connection between the two worlds that too often have been thought of as antipodes, and tell of the transformation of the practices – of production and consumption – in addition to the contemporary mediascape. From the point of view of television as a mass medium, these changes fall within the paradigm that Amanda Lotz defined as "post network era" and that is characterised by "increased fractionalisation of the audience across shows, channels, and distribution devices" and "the exponential expansion in viewers' choice and control".[20] It is the era of "anytime anywhere television" about which several scholars have expressed their thoughts in a fairly concordant manner.[21] This reconfiguration of the scenarios is well represented by the arrival of alternative players in the television industry such as Netflix and Amazon that have gone from mere distribution to content production. They have contributed to the transformation of narrative style and language, and not least have facilitated new modes of alternative use (binge watching) that increasingly free television content from television as a device.

Finally, alongside the reference of television and the language of television seriality, which is without a doubt a fundamental feature of the webseries, we must also remember that these productions are "user generated content", an expression of participatory culture. These productions in fact, contain a strong reference to the "ideology of participatory culture, the valorisation of amateur and community media and hopeful ideas about the

19. On transmedia storytelling see Max Giovagnoli, *Transmedia Storytelling e Comunicazione* (Milan: Apogeo, 2013); on interactive storytelling see Chris Crawford, *Interactive Storytelling* (San Francisco: New Riders, 2013); finally on co-creation see John Banks, Jason Potts, "Co-creating games: A co-evolutionary analysis", *New Media and Society*, 12/2 (2010), pp. 253-270.

20. Amanda Lotz, *The Television Will Be Revolutionized* (New York: New York University Press, 2014), p. 48.

21. Fausto Colombo, *Social TV. Produzione, esperienza e valore nell'era digitale* (Milan: Egea, 2015); *Connecting Television. La televisione al tempo di internet*, ed. by Alberto Marinelli and Giandomenico Celata (Milan: Guerini e Associati, 2012); Massimo Scaglioni, Anna Sfardini, *Multitv. L'esperienza televisiva nell'età della convergenza* (Rome: Carocci, 2008).

democratisation of cultural production".[22] An ideology that gives a strong impetus to popular culture as a movement from the bottom to the top, that surfaces outside of the traditional cultural industry. Beyond the reference to the now old idea of prosumer, i.e. the one who produces and consumes content at the same time, coined by Alvin Toffler back in 1980, what seems most interesting is understanding the relationship – one could say with a game of words remediation of relationships – between the webseries and the traditional cultural industry. In this regard, Barra and Garofalo are able to put the ambivalence of the webseries in their transition from a phase of

> independence from the media system, which is hosted on the internet and in those space experiments languages and distribution models" with another phase in which Italian broadcasters are beginning to "become interested in (and approach) this new content, professionals and production systems, and on the other hand the creative groups developed online are looking for, in a more or less direct way, a 'side' of television both to give greater editorial and economic solidity to their work and to address a wider audience.[23]

It is a process of transformation that concerns both areas, and which actually tells us that there is a new form of production to be taken into consideration in order to understand popular culture today.

3. *A look at the imaginaries and genres*

As a final point in this brief delve into the webseries and their relationship with popular culture, we now move on to say something about their content and, therefore, about the stories they tell and about the imaginaries they create. In this regard, while it is relatively simple to analyse the webseries from a formal point of view, the analysis of the imaginaries requires a more detailed study and for this reason the exploratory survey that has been carried out is only able to provide some general indications. Alongside this difficulty, there is also that of an interpretative nature linked to the issue of media genres. In fact, even by using the traditional genres of cultural industries as a starting point, webseries show us even more effectively the principle of Jacques Derrida in relation to the ability to

22. Jean Burgess, Joshua Green, *Youtube: Online Video and Participatory Culture* (Oxford: Polity Press, 2009), p. 12.

23. Barra, Garofalo, "Ritorno alla realtà televisiva", p. 46.

contain (i.e. to separate and distinguish what the genres have) what he calls precisely the law of genre: "It is precisely a principle of contamination, a law of impurity, a parasitical economy".[24] The web world perfectly exemplifies the ideas of "contamination", "impurity" and "parasitism" of genres that are too limiting concepts, especially within a space seemingly devoid of rules such as the web. A freedom that is amplified in the moment of creativity of the writers and creators of stories who do not need to deal with the rules of the market.

Despite all this, especially if we observe that serial web universe that refers to the "classic" story and that could be called web drama as the closest form of evolution of television storytelling through the web, it is still possible to outline the prevailing content, also because it emerges with a certain evidence of the areas of content on which the webseries are based on and that in an apparently paradoxical way they recover the discourse of genres.

As Simone Arcagni also claims, webseries in fact:

> have re-introduced with force the genres into the Italian media system: a narrative dimension that Italy has often embraced, and with excellent results (think of spaghetti-westerns, horror by Bava and Argento etc.). Then, these genres have almost been ousted from cinema and from television more and more geared towards comedy and crime; the most dynamic and experimental genres such as horror, thriller, apocalyptic and science fiction are now returning to independent web productions (and often ultra-independent) as an important resource, not only to attract the viewing public, but also as a narrative method able to propose different interpretations and reflections.[25]

The reference to genre is therefore fundamental even when one tries to get rid of it or overcome it. It is for this reason that in order to look at the imaginary showcased by the Italian web series one has to start from the genres. Below we will try to describe four areas of content that, in addition to being quantitatively significant as they include the majority of the most important productions, are also useful for understanding at least one of the dimensions in which the relationship between webseries, TV series and popular culture is structured more in general. Precisely that of

24. Jacques Derrida, "The Law of Genre", *Critical Inquiry*, 7/1 (1980), pp. 55-81, p. 65.

25. Simone Arcagni quoted in Lino, "Le fiction delle webserie. Un percorso tra i generi", p. 44.

imaginaries, that is the ability that these new forms of narration have to produce meaningful narratives.

The first such content, perhaps the most obvious, is science fiction, sometimes with significant hints of fantasy. This is the case of the aforementioned example *Lost in Google* (2012), or the less popular but still appreciated *Social Dead* (2013). While the first series centred on a sort of short circuit between the real world and the virtual world after the main character finds himself immersed in the web after having searched the word "Google" on Google, the second refers to new technologies used in everyday life, and how their failure, in particular the shutting down of Facebook, the top and most used social media, might actually cause a real disaster.

Horror is another genre that is enormously successful on the net and has given rise to a wide range of imaginaries thanks to the numerous contaminations with other genres. *Freaks* (2012) is an example of an Italian webseries that tries to work, with moderate success, around this type of imaginary in a rather convincing way mixing together horror, science fiction and superhero stories. This webseries, openly inspired by the British TV series *Misfits* (2009-2013), looks at the lives of five main characters who, after being knocked out together, find themselves with special powers. Furthermore, productions such as *Web Horror Story* (2014), again openly inspired by the American series *American Horror Story* (2011-still in production), which tells the story of a blogger with a keen interest in the paranormal who investigates a supposedly haunted house, as well as the best known *Skypocalipse* (2011), which tells the story of the zombie apocalypse during the days of Skype, contaminating, once again, horror with the world of technology.

Horror and science fiction seem to be two imaginaries – in addition to the genres of traditional cultural industries – in which more work has been done in trying to conjugate and hybridise the technological universe, mainly in the direction of new communication technologies, in a new and convincing way. References to Google, Skype and other social networks are a clear allusion to the area in which these productions have been conceived and are consumed/enjoyed. Furthermore, they are a direct reference to usage practices and lifestyles that are a good representation of the younger generations that are more likely to "populate" the web. A first, trivial consideration can therefore be linked to the fact that the imaginaries created reflect the technological universe from which they emerge. Sometimes, it can be added, this also implies a reflection – that is a lucid and critical consideration – on that same universe and on the impact of technology in relation to us as human beings and our place in society.[26]

We must then refer, as a variant of horror, to zombies and zombie stories, which in recent years, but we could say from George A. Romero onwards, have been enjoying a resounding success on the web. It should also be added that these stories seem to be those that best lend themselves to trans-genre contamination ranging from comedy to noir through classic horror. In this regard, with the Italian scene we can not fail to mention the case of horror comedy *Geekerz* (2013) where the main character, a web journalist and video game reviewer, is responsible for the spread of a virus that turns all his friends and residents of his city into the living dead. Then there is *Di come diventai fantasma e zombie* (*How I became a ghost and a zombie*, 2014) which tells in a funny way the cohabitation and mutual understanding of a ghost and a zombie that are the same person; or *Soma* (2014) defined by its producers as a fanta-thriller with an environmental theme that still draws heavily in the imaginary of the living dead but with inserts typical of the action movie, and of course, with marked ecological undertones. These are examples of productions that have achieved audience success in terms of episode viewing figures, as well as a media popularity seen by the number of internet pages dedicated to reviewing and commenting on webseries. To understand how all this popularity on the web is actually the result of a work of remediation – precisely mutation and change – of productions and imaginaries that come from the cultural industry, one merely has to mention the American series *The Walking Dead* (2010-still in production) which has inspired many Italian and foreign webseries. At the same time, however, these productions are also the expression of a cultural and generational appropriation that transforms these scripts and these imaginaries into something else. A rewriting process that is a typical feature of the webseries and extraordinarily indicative of the relationship with the industry and popular culture.

A third imaginary worthy of note is that of diversity, with particular attention to sexual diversity. The world of webseries (not to mention bloggers and vloggers) is actually populated by a fair number of productions that feature openly homosexual characters. Among the latest examples we

26. On this it is impossible not to mention the case of the Netflix TV series (originally born as a webseries) *Black Mirror* (2011-2017). It is a popular culture product that investigates in critical way the relationship between media and our contemporary society.

can mention the much talked about – on the web – *Coming* (2014) which tells the story of the life of a gigolo at the time of social media such as *Grindr*. Or the webseries with a lesbian theme *LsB* (2013) which tells the stories of a "group of friends of various homosexuality [...] focusing on university, friendship and love" as we can read from the Facebook page, and that very closely resembles *The L World* (2004-2009) but this time set in Rome. It is finally important to make a reference to *G&T* (2013), which tells the story of the love affair of two childhood friends and that over the course of two seasons tackles different problems starting from coming out, up to same sex marriage and the desire to become parent. A little-known webseries that, however, over two seasons, thanks to attendance at various European gay and queer festivals and the presence of subtitles in several languages, has achieved over 80 million views on Youtube. The case of *G&T* in particular goes to show that, beyond the aesthetic quality of the production (in this case rather low), to the extent that we are going to build a shared (or shareable) imaginary for a major slice of the audience, these productions can become successful.

Finally, a last imaginary – although it would be more correct in this regard to speak of genre in the strict sense – is that of comedy and parodies. We can start from the aforementioned case of *Gli effetti di Gomorra sulla gente* (*The effects of Gomorrah on the people*, 2014) which exploits the reputation of the homonym *Gomorrah. The Series* (2014-still in production) but above all it is down to the talent of the group of authors/actors and each episode attracts millions of views. Furthermore, it is the case of *Esami* (*Exams*, 2014), that mocks the world of Italian universities and, on the traditional comedy front, *Kubrick una storia porno* (*Kubrick a porn story*, 2012), which reconstructs the events of a group of directors who fail to succeed professionally and who decide to get into producing pornography. An interesting metaphor also of popular culture that contains both "high" culture and auteur films, represented by the reference to the director Stanley Kubrick, as well as "low" and commercial culture typical of pornographic productions.

It is also worth remembering, still within comedy, a long list of productions including *Occhi al cielo* (*Eyes to the sky*, 2012), a sit-com set inside a vestry; *Preti* (*Priests*, 2013) interesting due to the fact it is an animated series that tackles burning issues in a humorous way; and finally the most recent *Il Camerlengo* (2015) which tells in a desecrating way the misadventures of a camerlengo struggling with the organisation of the 2016 Special Jubilee. These three small examples are interesting because they represent religious imaginary, a vital part of Italian culture, in a comical and often irreverent way. An importance that is also reflected in Italian popular culture if one thinks of the abundance of television series dedicated to priests, popes and saints told from various angles and which reconfirms the idea of "a plural Catholicism", an expression that Milly Buonanno[27] borrows from the sociologist Franco Garelli.

There are many reasons for the popularity of comic imaginary – maybe a *primus inter pares* compared to others. In this regard, we can mention the previously stated brevity of the formats, as well as excellent characterisation and, above all, an impressive talent for writing that is fundamental for creating comedy. More generally, we can also touch on the reference to genre in the strict sense. In fact, comedy not only expresses a lightness and a need for escape, but, even more so, offers itself as a language to deal with "important" issues in a lighter and more comprehensible manner. In this regard, one just needs to refer to the importance of the parody that is central to popular culture as "playful, comic or satirical transformation of a single script".[28] A transformation that does not necessarily go from "high" to "low" and which leads to a form of cultural appropriation.

Now, if you look carefully at these four imaginaries: science fiction, horror, diversity, and finally comedy, it is quite easy to see how there are no equivalents in Italian television narrative productions, at least on mainstream television. For different reasons, the Italian television industry, apart from a number of interesting cinematographic experiences, although sporadic, has never developed a horror or science fiction imaginary. At the same time it has gradually reduced the spaces and the production of interstitial narratives of a mainly comic nature; in the same way it has never produced series entirely dedicated to LGBTQ issues and rarely have there been main characters characterised in a credible and convincing way in terms of their sexual diversity. From this point of view one might be led to think that webseries are compensatory narratives that occupy the gaps left by traditional TV narratives, at least by Italian ones. However, all you have to do is take into consideration the world of international television production to see how this is not true and how these four imaginaries exist

27. Milly Buonanno, *Italian TV Drama and Beyond. Stories from the Soil, Stories from the Sea* (Bristol and Chicago: Intellect Books, 2012).

28. Daniel Sangsue, *La parodie* (Paris: Hachette, 1994), p. 90.

and are well-nurtured and, above all, widely enjoyed and shared by viewers on the web. It can be inferred that the web is not only a clearing house where to look for what is not found in traditional television storytelling, but a place of experimentation of languages and genres where, in a more or less expert, professional and competent manner, some users (and user groups) challenge themselves. Even more interesting is observing that through the web certain imaginaries are re-mediated and placed within national contexts where, both for reasons of television audience and for reasons of traditions and production practices, they are not yet well developed. And once again, in this operation of adaptation, borrowing from different countries, contexts, media, and audiences, we end up reiterating the centrality and strength, but also the need for storytelling and stories.

We have relied on these productions in particular, and on the different imaginaries they have built, not to relegate webseries to a second-class product that bridges the gaps of popular national culture. On the contrary. Web series – and with them, once again the narrative need that they express together with the participatory instance of making their voices heard and of making their own talent and potential to tell a story come to light – are to be understood as elements that connect different media and different cultural industries. They are connectors of audiences, languages, mediascapes and different genres. They appear on the web, but often they are conceived outside of it, and on the web they do not die but go on to populate other spaces, and to create new connections. Those who produce webseries today have studied serial language, both that of comics and anime, and, above all, that of national and international television seriality. These productions do not always express a full awareness of these cultural references, but in any case demonstrate the vitality of a language that tries to actively and participatively build, by opposition and by simulation, imaginaries that are able to give meaning to the dimension of everyday life.

Flavia Monceri

Porn(ography) as a Cultural Product

Introduction: Setting the context

As Feona Attwood and Clarissa Smith[1] highlight, it is at least from the second edition of Linda Williams' seminal work *Hard Core: Power, Pleasure, and the 'Frenzy of the Visible'*[2] (originally published in 1989) that we can speak about a dedicated field of studies, pornography studies or "porn studies".[3] This emerging discipline marks the beginning of "critical academic discussion about pornography, moving away from a 'porn debate' centred on disagreement about pornography's harmfulness" as well as of "the gradual development of research focused on the history of pornography, the analysis of its production and consumption, its aesthetics, its significance for particular audiences, and its place in contemporary culture".[4] Indeed, that such development is actually taking place seems to be proved also by the fact that the quoted passage comes from the introductory opening of the first academic journal dedicated to the various dimensions of "pornography" – *Porn Studies* – whose first issue has been published in 2014.

However, this does not mean that pornography has been accepted, let alone "normalized", as a cultural product like any other, and it still holds

1. Feona Attwood, Clarissa Smith, "Porn Studies: An introduction", *Porn Studies*, 1/1-2 (2014), pp. 1-6.

2. Linda Williams, *Hard Core: Power, Pleasure and the "Frenzy of the Visible"*, Expanded Paperback Edition (Berkeley and Los Angeles: University of California Press, 1999).

3. See for instance: *Porn Studies*, ed. by Linda Williams (Durham and London: Duke University Press, 2004).

4. Attwood, Smith, "Porn Studies", p. 1.

true that "researching pornography can be particularly complicated and challenging"[5] not least because of that "resurgence of antiporn feminism" to which Smith and Attwood[6] had previously drawn attention, so confirming that it is still very difficult, both in the academia and in the wider public debate, to speak about pornography without taking a preliminary moral stance. Of course, as also the authors underline, "it would be disingenuous to claim that antiporn activism gets a wider hearing than any other approach – there *are* media spaces for plural and divergent opinions on pornography",[7] although I would be careful as to extent to which this statement may apply for instance to the Italian context. At any rate, it is true that "in the porn studies that have been developed by other feminist academics, by gay male scholars, by researchers with an interest in new media and technology, and by sex-positive, sex-radical, and sex workers activists, there are the beginnings of accounts of the history, production, distribution, consumption, and significance of diverse pornographies"[8] as just the possibility to launch an academic journal dedicated to Porn Studies gives evidence to.

At the same time, however, it should be stressed that "antiporn feminism has proved incredibly resistant to the academic practices of theory and evidence, preferring to counter opposition with appeals to emotional truths".[9] The "new wave" of antiporn feminism deploys even more than before the old tools, especially relying "on 'testimony', though whose testimony counts is still a problem – those who testify to porn's pleasures or sense of liberation don't count in the same way as those who present themselves as addicts, victims, or rescuers".[10] A particular *political* consequence of this position on which I would like to draw attention, if briefly, is that such accounts for which "rethorics rather than reason is the preferred mode of debate"[11] argue not simply for more censorship, but for "providing people with a counter-ideology that both reveals the fabricated

5. *Ibid.*, p. 2.

6. Clarissa Smith, Feona Attwood, "Emotional Truths and Thrilling Slide Shows: The Resurgence of Antiporn Feminism", in *The Feminist Porn Book: The Politics of Producing Pleasure*, ed. by Tristan Taormino *et al.* (New York: The Feminist Press Cuny, 2013), pp. 41-58.

7. *Ibid.*, p. 47.

8. *Ibid.*

9. *Ibid.*, p. 54.

10. *Ibid.*

11. *Ibid.*, pp. 54-55.

nature of consumer ideology and offers an alternative vision of the world",[12] as Gail Dines puts it in her influential *Pornland*.

As harmless and sharable as it may seem, this position explicitly points to the need to *educate* human beings – especially *men* – to a different worldview from which pornography would be totally erased and replaced with "a different vision of heterosexual sex, one built on gender equality and justice".[13] But as it is clear for instance in the positions expressed by Dines, this requires an exercise of power on those same human beings, including the dissenting ones, at the aim to impose on them a particular version of a "feminist ideology", which is to be considered as true and good *for all of us*. This is a necessary move because "a sexuality based on equality ultimately requires a society that is based on equality",[14] especially understood as equality between women and men, by the way excluding the very possibility that human beings might exist who cannot, or refuse to, be identified in either category (i.e. "the rest of us", in Bornstein's formulation).[15] Porn cannot be part of this world of the future, because it is embedded in the current structures of inequality primarily affecting women, given that "nowhere is the practice of inequality so starkly obvious", and that "in porn we are one-dimensional objects who want nothing more than porn sex".[16]

Consequently, if women do want to be equal they must get rid of pornography and claim that also men – well, the entire society – do the same, since "as long as we have porn, we will never be seen as full human beings deserving of all the rights that men have": in short, "in a just society, there is no room for porn".[17] Of course, this would be an ideal situation not only for women, but also for men, because they also strive, as human beings, for values such as equality, dignity and the like. Therefore, they also must and can be increasingly gained to the just cause of antiporn, since "what resistance to porn offers men is a sexuality that celebrates connectedness, intimacy, and empathy – a sexuality bathed in equality rather than subordination".[18] This

12. Gail Dines, *Pornland: How Porn Has Hijacked Our Sexuality* (Boston: Beacon Press, 2010), p. 98.

13. *Ibid*., p. 98.

14. *Ibid*., p. 165.

15. Kate Bornstein, *Gender Outlaw: On Man, Women, and the Rest of Us* (New York: Vintage Books, 1995).

16. Dines, *Pornland*, p. 165.

17. *Ibid*.

18. *Ibid*.

will be surely possible because, as Dines tries to show in her book, men are growingly asking to "be rescued" from pornography, to which they realized to be addicted to in order to be compliant with the requests of contemporary market-oriented society and its "consumer ideology", and not because they really have a need for porn or like it.

Now, in my opinion, for all the merits and attempts by the part of porn studies up until now, the discourse about pornography – including the academic one – seems to be still characterized by the predominance of approaches to pornography as a one-of-a-kind cultural product, which in order to be explained and understood must be first of all *morally evaluated*, no matter if positively or negatively. This gives birth to a debate between pro- and anti-porn scholars and activists who are more similar to each other than they would like to be, particularly in that they do not *interrogate* porn listening to what it has to say, but try to *confirm* the evaluation judgment on which their research is based. As far as I can see, this normative approach is widely and strongly diffused especially in cultural contexts like the Italian one, in which there is not yet a public and academic discourse about pornography worthy of the name. This is of course not to say that there are no scholars in Italy researching pornography from different disciplines and approaches,[19] but simply that their voices are more difficult to hear because of the predominance of positions according to which porn should not be considered as a cultural product like any other because it has to do with "a thing" which is different from all other "things" – that is to say sexuality.

In other terms, the normative approach to pornography and the pornographic products, which seems to me to be diffused especially among philosophers, be they anti- or pro-porn, is closely linked to the still well-alive normative approach to issues relating to sex, gender and sexuality, at least (but not only) in Italy. It originates from the circumstance that when researchers choose pornography as a subject of inquiry they "do it normally – and normatively – with moral and/or juridical concerns: the purpose is to define it in an unequivocal way, in order to sanction what is pornographic and what is not, to identify its more or less collateral effects, and to contribute to keep

19. See for instance Pietro Adamo, *Il porno di massa. Percorsi nell'hard contemporaneo* (Milan: Raffaello Cortina, 2004); *Il porno espanso. Dal cinema ai nuovi media*, ed. by Enrico Biasin, Giovanna Maina and Federico Zecca with an afterword by Peter Lehman (Milan-Udine: Mimesis, 2011); *Porn after Porn: Contemporary Alternative Pornographies*, ed. by Enrico Biasin, Giovanna Maina and Federico Zecca (Mimesis International, 2014).

under control, as far as possible, those ones which seems most detrimental".[20] This is surely the case with those who, like Michela Marzano, take a clear anti-porn stance by explicitly stating that pornography "consists in staging the economic attitude to possess goods and barter them, the exchange that run counter to the irreversibility of the caresses and kisses characterizing human sexuality".[21] However, the same seems to go also for those who, like Simone Regazzoni[22] take the opposite pro-porn stance, because even "an apology of pornography would develop still and again at the same normative level, simply from an opposite perspective".[23] On the contrary, in this article, as a preliminary step toward further and deeper research, I will try to show that pornography is a cultural product like any other having something relevant to say about the heteronormative regime to which sexes, genders and sexualities are still submitted. Moreover, as a political philosopher who does not share the above-mentioned usual attitude, I will also try to briefly highlight the political potential of pornographic products towards empowering non-normative bodies and sexualities.

1. *Making space for pornography as a cultural product*

To consider pornography as a cultural product like any other implies an overcoming of the "repetitive and simplistic discussions about whether pornography should be viewed as either a positive or a negative phenomenon in terms of its cultural influence – discussions that are widely understood to be the legacy of the partisan feminist politics of the Seventies and 1980s".[24] Anyway, this should not lead, as Helen Hester adds, to "the redemptive, or at least overtly celebratory, tone evident within much of Porn Studies", with the result to deny that "not all pornographic material

20. Stefano Bancalari, *Fenomenologia e Pornografia* (Pisa: Edizioni ETS, 2015), p. 8. All translations from Italian quoted works are mine.

21. Michela Marzano, *La fine del desiderio. Riflessioni sulla pornografia* (Milan: Mondadori, 2012), p. 23.

22. See Simone Regazzoni, *Pornosofia. Filosofia dèl pop porno* (Milan: Ponte alle Grazie, 2010).

23. Bancalari, *Fenomenologia e Pornografia*, p. 12. Bancalari refers in the footnote just to Regazzoni's book.

24. Helen Hester, *Beyond Explicit: Pornography and the Displacement of Sex* (New York: State University of New York Press, 2014), p. 2.

is radical, disruptive, progressive, or likely to have a positive effect on sexual minorities".[25] Indeed, if Porn Studies wants to legitimate itself as a scholarly discipline not least by "attaining a properly scholarly standard of critical rigor", to this aim "an appropriately interrogative attitude to pornography" is necessary, which might be put "at risk of being quashed within the largely celebratory intellectual climate in operation within Porn Studies".[26] I agree with this precautionary warning just because, as Hester herself hints to, the relevance of Porn Studies consists in making it possible that "porn is no longer discussed as if it is a single thing to be either condemned or defended, but is instead viewed as being as mutable and multifaceted as any other regime of representation".[27]

Actually, it would be more correct to speak about pornographies in the plural, once you have acknowledged that the range of possibilities covered by pornographic products cannot be reduced to a singular label. In any case, there is surely one characteristic feature of all pornographic products, consisting in their being finalized to a particular kind of "adult entertainment", that is to say sexual arousing and possibly sexual pleasure *through masturbation*. Of course, this is valid in the most basic case in which the pornographic product is consumed by a single individual for their personal pleasure, and not for instance in the case that the same product plays the role of a "sexual tool", so to speak, to accompany the performance of a sexual act between a number of persons (not limited to the so-called "couple"). Although I would be very interested in going more deeply into this second case, I will limit myself to considering the first one, because I find that the fundamental problem with pornography has to do with a still very widespread banning and silencing attitude towards a specific sexual act – i.e. masturbation.

The fact that pornography has to do primarily with masturbation implies that it cannot stick to patterns of political correctness, as moralists of all sorts would have it, because as Barbara DeGenevieve rightly stresses "it is about being aroused in an uncontrollable way and feeling something in your body", "it is about what we fetishize, what we need to get off", and "about fantasy, not reality".[28] In short, the characteristic feature of

25. *Ibid.*, p. 5.

26. *Ibid.*, p. 8.

27. *Ibid.*, p. 2.

28. Barbara DeGenevieve, "The emergence of non standard bodies and sexualities", *Porn Studies*, 1/1-2 (2014), pp. 193-196, p. 194.

porn as a cultural product is that it "is made to get people off", and "in order to do this, bodies must not only be highly sexualized, but objectified, fetishized, exotified and made to accomodate very particular kinks".[29] If this is true, then pornography has immediately to do with masturbation, in that it allows the spectator to be aroused by the "scenes" they are watching because they are able to fit their personal sexual fantasies, to which of course the individual reinterpretations add, to the point that people "get off" through masturbating in the way they prefer.

By the way, this is also the reason why I agree with Barbara DeGenevieve when she refuses the very term "feminist porn", which has gained growing attention,[30] because it is "so heavily front-loaded with rules of political correctness and so inscribed with feminist politics of the 1980s and 1990s that the category itself becomes a turn-off".[31] I also agree with DeGenevieve in "making a distinction here between a feminist pornography that developed in the 1980s and 1990s as a reaction to anti-porn protests and the writings of Andrea Dworkin and Catherine McKinnon, and the more recent third-wave feminism of the twenty-first century" that has given birth to a "more contemporary genre of porn (still categorized as feminist even by the women who make it)", but that "is informed much more by queer theory and queer identity than it is by conventional feminism".[32] And I must add that I find the adherence to the label "feminism" a little bit strange by the part of those who otherwise attack the very existence of clear-cut feminine and masculine identities, to the extent that their persisting self-identification as "feminists" sounds to me somewhat inconsistent.

Coming back to masturbation, I agree with those who underline not only that "porn is *for* masturbation", in the sense that causing or favoring an act of masturbation is the ultimate goal of the pornographic product, but also that "contemporary pornography is, in a significant sense, *about* masturbation" because "the act of masturbation is vital to the stories that the majority of pornographic texts tell us", although this refers especially to *male* masturbation, becoming a central aspect as "to the way in which

29. *Ibid.*, p. 196.

30. See Anne G. Sabo, *After Pornified: How Women Are Transforming Pornography & Why It Really Matters* (Winchester and Washington: Zero Books, 2012); *The Feminist Porn Book*; Rich Moreland, *Pornography Feminism: As Powerful as She Wants to Be* (Winchester and Washington: Zero Books, 2014).

31. DeGenevieve, "The emergence of non standard bodies and sexualities", p. 193.

32. *Ibid.*

masculinity is produced via pornography"[33] in many contemporary societies. However, despite the obvious centrality of masturbation and autoerotic pleasure for pornography, and despite the fact that "masturbation is the most common and generally the first *type* of sexual activity that we experience", the "amount of scholarly attention paid to masturbation compared to other aspects of our sexual lives is extremely limited".[34]

At first sight, the marginality of masturbation within sexuality studies in general, and porn studies in particular, may seem strange, but things change if we consider that such marginality may have to do with the *political potential* of this particular sexual act. As a matter of fact, masturbatory practices, with their stress on fantasy and complete disregard of the rules governing sexuality as a social institution, have shown an ability to put the heteronormative regime in question since its very inception in the history of Western Europe, and have been therefore the target of a repressive sexual politics by the part of various "institutions" (the Church, the state, "science", and so on) that have continuously tried to exercise their power to police the (deviant) masturbating body.[35] Of course, this is so first of all because masturbation shifts the goal of the sexual act from reproduction to (individual) sexual pleasure. However, the most frightening threat posed by masturbation practices to the heteronormative (but also homonormative) regime consists in their assuring a transgressive political use of one own's sexual body through being aroused by sexual fantasies that may go beyond all prevailing categories governing "normal" and "normative" sexuality.

It is in fact undeniable that "masturbation is not limited to any particular type of body by age or gender, and while linked to the sexual imagery, it is not limited to any one sexual orientation", as it is undeniable that "almost every "body" masturbates".[36] Therefore, a deeper consideration of masturbation could surely offer "a way of understanding our sexuality outside of the usual binaries of biology (male and female),

33. Steve Garlick, "Masculinity, Pornography, and the History of Masturbation", *Sexuality & Culture*, 16 (2011), pp. 306-320, p. 307.

34. Greg Tuck, "The Mainstreaming of Masturbation: Autoeroticism and Consumer Capitalism", in *Mainstreaming Sex: The Sexualization of Western Culture*, ed. by Feona Attwood (London-New York: IB Tauris, 2009), pp. 77-92, p. 78.

35. See notably Thomas Laqueur, *Solitary Sex: A Cultural History of Masturbation* (New York: Zone Books, 2003); Garlick, "Masculinity, Pornography, and the History of Masturbation".

36. Tuck, "The Mainstreaming of Masturbation", p. 80.

culture (masculine and feminine) and sexual orientation (heterosexual and homosexual), but one that is still firmly grounded in the visceral realities of our actual sex lives".[37] From a more political viewpoint, this implies that "the masturbatory consequences of pornography are profoundly leveling", and although it could "be argued that this reveals our mutual alienation as much as our liberation, [...] either way it seems an articulation of sexuality that is particularly contemporary, a potential democratization of pleasure".[38] I would only add that masturbation should be rather understood as showing an anarchic, rather than democratic, potential because – as far as I am concerned – the idea of a democratization of pleasure would still run the risk to be submitted to some rules securing equality, respect and so on, that is to say to fall again into the traps of "regulating" sexual pleasure by imposing a version of political correctness on individual sexual fantasies.

Of course, as also Greg Tuck underlines, "no form of sexual practice is in itself revolutionary, exploitative, enriching or degrading", and yet "it seems remarkable that the potential for masturbation to offer and reveal our shared capacity for simple embodied pleasure is still so difficult to contemplate for a society which is supposedly based on the pleasure of the individual".[39] But this could be rooted in the still widespread association between masturbation and the performance of sexuality in a egocentric, selfish, individualized, in short *not sociable* or *asocial* way, so denying the very character of sexuality as a social institution built on whatever notion of *relationship* between human beings. This idea applies especially to the masturbating *male* body, while a few theories, "particularly feminism, have championed masturbation's role in granting sexual satisfaction and autonomy" to women, giving birth to a situation in which "contemporary attitudes are asymmetrical in relation to their concerns over 'wasteful' male masturbation compared with 'empowering' female masturbation".[40] This double standard in evaluating the potential of masturbation for a positive and progressive sexual politics gives nonetheless evidence enough to state that such a potential *might be* more widely recognized. But this would require a definitive acknowledgement, especially by the part of some strands of feminism thinking, that "if we are really to encourage or demand

37. *Ibid.*
38. *Ibid.*, p. 82.
39. *Ibid.*, p. 92.
40. *Ibid.*, p. 84.

a revolution in sexual politics for both genders and all sexualities, men who identify themselves as heterosexual are in as much need for liberation from sexual stereotyping and patriarchal functionalism as everyone else".[41] This could also happen through acknowledging masturbation as an original sexual practice typical of all sexes, genders and sexualities.

Coming back to the main point, the general problem with recognizing pornography as a cultural product just like any other can be individuated in the fact that this would minimize, if not erase, the possibility to construct self-referential, let alone normative, theories of sexuality and the sexual body (both in the singular) that could make an appeal to a consistent identity theory ready to be used for political purposes. Moreover, this would also make much more difficult to speak about the (negative or positive) "effects" of pornography on the "consumers" of this allegedly very flourishing market[42] and hence to argue for normative interventions – be they rules, laws, psychological or educational programs – to "govern" pornography directing it in the desired way. The point is that, just like pornography, even its individual consumers are very often pictured as an homogeneous entity – as a particular unitary "sexual subject" –, totally forgetting that "audiences may engage with porn in a range of complex, nuanced, critical – and yes, contradictory – ways that far exceed a simplistically described cause-and-effects framework",[43] a circumstance that also a serious confrontation with masturbatory practices might help to highlight.

2. *The political potential of porn*

As it should be clear by now, pornography has surely to do with the individual, concrete, sexual bodies of those who "consume" it in order to be sexually aroused and to eventually "get off". Each of them – well, each of us – can do this in their own ways being driven by an infinite number of (individual) motivations and fantasies that are impossible to

41. *Ibid.*, p. 92.

42. For the lack of economic research see Fabio D'Orlando, "The Demand for Pornography", *Journal of Happiness Studies* 12/1 (2011), pp. 275-303; Georgina Voss, "Treating it as a 'normal business': Researching the pornography industry", *Sexualities*, 15/3-4 (2012), pp. 391-410.

43. Sharif Miwlabocus, Rachel Wood, "Introduction: Audiences and consumers of porn", *Porn Studies*, 2/2-3 (2015), pp. 118-122, p. 119.

reconstruct in clear-cut patterns, let alone in an homogeneous picture. If this is true, pornography shows itself as a powerful political tool at the individual level, because watching pornography and being aroused by it and the fantasies it lets emerge at least *might* lead to subvert all norms and conventional rules defining the borders of sex, gender and sexuality within a given context. And this is possible both for people who usually follow the tenets of heteronormative (and homonormative) regime, and for people who are to be considered as deviant according to those same rules and would not easily find acceptance if they were to publicly express and try to act out their non-normative, deviant, abnormal, sexualities.

To be sure, the objection could be legitimately raised to such a position that mainstream pornography is based upon still very widespread stereotypes and prejudices about sexuality fitting the dominant heteronormative (and homonormative) regime. It would be therefore difficult, so the objection could go on, to think about an empowering role of pornography and the pornographic products because they merely reproduce the cultural, social, and political, status quo. Anyway, this objection would acknowledge no role to the power of fantasy in reshaping the usual images of sexuality in the service of one own's pleasure, what is in and of itself a political act of self-affirmation through subversive sexuality. On the other hand, moving such an objection is possible only if we totally discard, or refuse any relevance to, the fact that non-mainstream, alternative products do exist though they are a minority in numerical terms. Such non-mainstream porn has not only to do with "non-normative practices" (such as BDSM, to name only one), but also with "non-normative bodies" that *become visible* through pornography in the most frightening way for the heteronormative regime, because they show themselves capable to be a "turn-on" not only for other non-normative bodies, but also for the normative sexual bodies that are the target of mainstream pornography.

To argue for this particular kind of political potential towards empowering individual sexual bodies by dismantling the claim to normalcy of the heteronormative regime, I would like to conclude by addressing the still thorny case of pornography and "disability". A careful consideration of this case, as well as of a number of other cases,[44] is very promising to deconstruct the idea that pornography can only be discarded or celebrated, instead of taken seriously as a means to put under question well established

44. See for all *The Feminist Porn Book.*

and acritically accepted assumptions about human sexuality. After all, as Tim Dean rightly points out, one relevant feature of contemporary pornography is that "it so notably preoccupies itself with anatomies that can be presented as freakish, whether by emphasizing larger-than-average genitals, breasts, and 'booties'; by highlighting unusual body modifications; or by contrasting normative embodiment with corporeal excess, as in fat porn, midget porn, tranny porn ('chicks with dicks'), and amputee porn".[45] If we abstain from a preliminary moral evaluation of such relevant feature, which would imply answering the discomforting political question about *who* is legitimated to evaluate it and *for whom* – we might conclude with Dean that "more explicitly than freak shows, however, porn eroticizes the non-normative body and its capacities", revealing "how bodily anomaly – indeed, non-normativity in its many guises – can be erotically attractive".[46]

This is so already for mainstream pornography, which aims more often than not to represent the perfect sexual act between/among perfect sexual bodies,[47] what by the way means representing the *fantasy* and not the *reality* of the sexual act, as some authors claim. To give only one example, Regazzoni states that "pop porno is the visual *real-fiction* of the sexual intercourse or the sexual acts, that is to say: a visual *fiction* in which the actors *pretend to do what they are actually doing* – they pretend to carry out the sexual acts that they are carrying out in the reality. Hence, pop porno is a *fiction* (the only form of *fiction*) incorporating, by showing it in detail, the real of the sexual act".[48] However, behind those statements, if inadvertently, there might still conceal a very heteronormative and mainstream idea equating the "reality" of sex with penetrative sex and the male orgasm, which would give evidence to the "reality" of the represented sexual act.[49] Beyond that, if we try to prove that pornographic products give a representation, or better a *presentation*, of the reality of sex by referring to *gonzo* or amateur pornographies, we must acknowledge that even in such cases "it is important to remember that the amateur performance of sex is still *performance*: people do not really

45. Tim Dean, "Stumped: The Pornography of Disability", in *Il porno espanso*, pp. 275-303, p. 277.

46. *Ibid.*, p. 278.

47. See Giovanna Maina, "Piaceri identitari e (porno)subculture", in *Il porno espanso*, pp. 197-227, p. 210.

48. Regazzoni, *Pornosofia*, p. 101.

49. On this see also Peter Lehman, "Postfazione: Come simulare una carezza? Perché è importante la differenza tra hardcore e softcore", in *Il porno espanso*, pp. 461-474.

act as they do when having sex in private".[50] In short, even if pornographic products would like to show the "truth" of sex, their empowering potential lies rather in the fact that they are unable to do so, just because they are cultural products like any other – that is to say *re-interpretations* of "the real" and not "the real in and for itself".

As it is obvious, this is much more clearer in the case of non-mainstream pornographies, especially when they offer the representation of non-normative bodies as *sexual* bodies capable of generating sexual arousing as well as of their non-normative sexual practices as something that is at everybody's disposal for their own sexual desire and pleasure. The point is that according to the heteronormative regime of normalcy non-normative bodies should not be a turn-on for other (especially normative) bodies and at the end of the day should not even be entitled to act out their sexuality in order to avoid that the rules governing sexuality be put in question. This holds true for all non-normative bodies, but becomes especially visible in the case of the so-called "disabled people", for whom "*any* manifestation of erotic desire is regarded as excessive – as if the disabled, in their dependence on able-bodied good will, should behave like children whose imperative is to safeguard our fantasy of their sexual innocence", whereas "to discover that disabled folks are more interested in getting laid than in being pitied can seem like an affront to established notions of victimhood and able-bodied privilege".[51]

Now, it can be surely stated that "pornography's focus on extraordinary anatomies lends itself to the all-too-familiar disciplinary project of regulating bodies by stabilizing their identities, thus rendering them more susceptible to classification and control".[52] On the other hand, however, it can be also stated that "porn's emphasis on action – its relentless displays of what different bodies are capable of doing – works against this normalizing effect by downplaying the significance of identity" and that "insofar as it privileges acts over identities, pornography disperses rather than consolidates normalizing power".[53] As a matter of fact, the political potential of pornographic products, both mainstream and non-mainstream,

50. Simon Hardy, "The New Pornographies: Representation or Reality?", in *Mainstreaming Sex: The Sexuaization of Western Culture*, ed. by Feona Attwood (London-New York: Ib Tauris, 2009), pp. 3-18, p. 9.

51. Dean, "Stumped: The Pornography of Disability", p. 281.

52. *Ibid.*, p. 296.

53. *Ibid.*, p. 297.

lies in the possibility for their consumers to become aware of the infinite possibilities to *perform*, to *act out*, sexuality through sexual practices exceeding by far those considered as normal or even possible under the heteronormative regime to which all of us are still being socialized. In this sense, it is surely correct to assign to pornography a "pedagogical function", especially "when it comes to non-normative sex", at least to the extent to which it "shows how to elicit pleasure from regions of the body that one might have been unaware could yeld pleasure; it demonstrates practices that one may not have previously imagined; it suggests how to cultivate non-genital parts of the body (the hand, the sphincter, the stump) for sexual encounters; and it reveals a greater range of anatomies that may be considered desirable".[54]

However, beyond such pedagogical function, also a political one can be acknowledged to pornography, especially if we take under consideration "disability pornography". In fact, in the very moment in which "disability porn publicizes disabled bodies exercising their sexual agency, it also shows how ability and disability are inextricably intertwined rather than opposed".[55] In other terms, disability porn shows that contrary to what we are used to thinking disabled bodies are actually not only sexual bodies, but even bodies absolutely *able* to sexually desire other bodies and to engage in a variety of sexual practices for the sake of their own sexual pleasure. Hence, being exposed to this kind of pornography can not only have an empowering effect on "disabled consumers", giving them more confidence in the fact that their sexual desires and needs are perfectly "normal", but also and especially a subversive double-effect on "non-disabled consumers".

On the one hand, namely, "non-disabled consumers" are urged to acknowledge that the distinction between able-bodied and non-able-bodied human beings, fabricated through the exclusion of the *ability* to perform sexuality, is but a cultural construct and not something rooted in "nature". This can have the side-effect to put under question the very notion of "disability", by questioning the artificiality of the dichotomy able/disabled and especially by understanding that there is not such thing as "disability", but only a process through which some specific non-normative bodies have undergone a cultural process of being disabled that might be nullified. On the other hand, those same consumers are exposed, and be it unwittingly,

54. *Ibid.*, p. 295.
55. *Ibid.*, p. 301.

to the possibility to find themselves attracted by "disabled" bodies, to find them sexually arousing, to think of them as possible partners for their own sexual performances, so resisting *through their bodily reactions* the very distinction between legitimate ("normal") and not-legitimated ("abnormal") sexual partners. It goes without saying that all of this surely represents a serious danger for the firmness of the conventional presuppositions on which the heteronormative regime of sexuality is still based.

Of course, I am very well aware that disability porn, like other non-normative pornographies, can also be used as simply another tool to exploit non-normative bodies by reducing them to a mere "object" in the service of one own's pleasure and nothing more. But I would fiercely stand any attempt to censor, ban, or negatively evaluate such products because I find that their very existence and accessibility opens the possibility up for an empowering individual politics to be acted out by the concrete sexual bodies. As a matter of fact, pornography, just like any other cultural product, cannot be judged as good or bad in itself but only in relationship to those particular individuals who interact with it, assigning it a *meaning* for their life within a particular spatial and temporal context. Put differently, and to conclude, the positive or negative value of porn(ography), as well as the possibility to actualize its political potential, is not something inherent, but rather something emerging from the interaction between this particular cultural product in all of its concrete manifestations and its consumer's gaze.

Anna Lucia Natale

In the Beginning There Was the Radio… Contexts and Genres of Radio Entertainment

1. *The origins of home entertainment. The pleasure of music*

> No history of entertainment can be written today without considering the explosive effect the introduction of the radio in the homes of Italians had, both in material terms, and in questions of taste and fashion.[1]

Here, Gianni Isola is expressly referring to the central role played by the radio in the development of popular culture in Italy. The radio led to a hugely varied repertoire of entertainment being introduced into the homes of the Italians, ranging from brand new forms of entertainment to adaptations of existing or contemporary art forms, from theatre to novels, from cinema to comics.[2] This repertoire of ideas and creations of the imagination, virtually available to all, within the home's four walls, would be later drawn upon by television productions. So it was that from the Twenties to the Fifties, the radio became the main source of home entertainment, resulting in significant changes in the tastes, fashions, and daily habits of its public, first in the elite and middle classes immediately after its debut, gradually extending to the rest of the population.

The radio was not actually the first medium of home entertainment. It redefined and completed what other media had introduced earlier, in terms of transforming people's free time. The origins of this goes back to the second half of the 1800s, when the separation of social life between

1. Gianni Isola, *L'immagine del suono. I primi vent'anni della radio italiana* (Florence: Le Lettere, 1991), pp. 131-132.

2. Peppino Ortoleva, "Generi", in *Enciclopedia della radio*, ed. by Peppino Ortoleva and Barbara Scaramucci (Milan: Garzanti, 2003), pp. 343-347.

the public sphere (productivity) and the private sphere (family life) combined to give much greater value to domestic life, a trend started by the American and English middle-classes.[3] With free time from work becoming available, the home became the place where family relations, friends and acquaintances could be cultivated, through cultural activities, such as the listening to music.

Live music was first made available in homes through the distribution of the pianoforte, and then registered music, through phonograms and gramophones. Next was the turn of the so-called "circular telephone". Indeed, to use Balbi's suggestive definition,[4] it was "the radio before the radio" to bring news, music and theatrical shows into private homes, through media such as the *Thèatrophone* (1881) in Paris, the *Telefon Hirmondò* (1893) in Budapest, the *Electrophone* (1895) in London, and the *Araldo Telefonico* (1910) in Rome, which inaugurated an experimental service of the circular telephone in Italy, as well.[5]

The telephone then returned to its original use as a one-to-one form of communication with the introduction of the radio, which was wireless and more efficient in connecting, in real time, different parts of the world to one another. The medium contributed in profoundly redefining the relations between public and private spheres, with information, previously accessible to only a restricted public, becoming available to everyone. Activities, such as listening to opera, symphony concerts, and dance music, which had only been possible outside the home, were now taking place in the domestic realm. To use a common metaphor of the time, the radio "brought the world into the home".

The radio became so popular mainly due to the novelty of the technology it involved, whereby airwaves were able to simultaneously carry events from one place to another, differently distributed in space. On this point, Joshua Meyrowitz talked of the weakening of the link between

3. Patrice Flichy, *Une histoire de la communication moderne. Espace public et vie privée* (Paris: La Découverte, 1991).

4. Gabriele Balbi, *La radio prima della radio. L'Araldo telefonico e l'invenzione del broadcasting in Italia* (Rome: Bulzoni, 2010).

5. See on this Balbi, *La radio prima della radio*; Franco Monteleone, "Il momento, magico e irripetibile, della funzione svolta dalla radio italiana nell'ascolto musicale", in *La musica alla radio 1924-1954. Storia, effetti, contesti in prospettiva europea*, ed. by Angela I. De Benedictis in collaboration with Franco Monteleone (Rome: Bulzoni, 2015), pp. 29-55; Giorgio Simonelli, *Cari amici vicini e lontani. L'avventurosa storia della radio* (Milan: Mondadori, 2012).

"physical place" and "social place"[6] (there is no longer the need to be on the spot to experience an event), and John B. Thompson of "despatialized simultaneity"[7] (the same time no longer requires the same place). Whatever the case, the traditional time-space barriers had been broken, with the radio being principally responsible, even before the introduction of television.

Besides being able to "conquer time and space", the radio managed to enter the domestic walls thanks to how it "synchronized" with the new social setup which was being formed, following the adoption of a standard system of time measurement in a number of countries.[8] Right from the beginning, the European State radio was structured around the concept of time, with its transmissions of culture, information and shows going hand in hand with the rhythms of everyday life, and so defining how and where it was used by its increasingly differentiated audience. Due to the peculiarity of the medium, both sonorous and simultaneous, the radio adapted to the time of its listeners, while in the same way listeners were influenced by the time or times of the radio,[9] so creating a model of regulation of everyday life:

> It had become a new social clock which struck the time at varied intervals [...] with heterogeneous forms of entertainment, conversation, information; it was a show made up of time [...], which allowed the individual to freely synchronize their activity with that of an entire nation.[10]

Not only did the radio reorganize time, then, in terms of public spaces, it also began to organize private spaces, occupying typical family settings: the social and cultural gatherings of high society, the kitchen of the most modest homes, seats next to the fireplaces of farmworker's homes.[11] In this way, the radio contributed in reconfiguring the concept of time and space as it was actually conceived in these domestic settings, transforming the home into a choice place for the spreading of products of the cultural industry. This process began to take shape with the Italian radio from

6. Joshua Meyrowitz, *No Sense of Place. The Impact of Electronic Media on Social Behavior* (New York: Oxford University Press, 1985).

7. John B. Thompson, *The Media and Modernity. A Social Theory of the Media* (Cambridge: Polity Press, 1995).

8. Peppino Ortoleva, "Orologio dell'aria, spettacolo elettrico", in *Cento anni di radio. Da Marconi al futuro delle telecomunicazioni*, ed. by Maria Grazia Janniello, Franco Monteleone and Giovanni Paoloni (Venice: Marsilio, 1995), pp. 43-47.

9. David Hendy, *Radio in the Global Age* (Cambridge: Polity Press, 2000).

10. Ortoleva, "Orologio dell'aria, spettacolo elettrico", p. 46.

11. Isola, *L'immagine del suono.*

1928 onwards, with the Unione Radiofonica Italiana (Uri) becoming Ente Italiano Audizioni Radiofoniche (Eiar), when a precise policy concerning the radio's social diffusion was adopted, to help transform it from a status symbol of the elite into a means of popular entertainment.

Radio transmission officially began on October 6th 1924. In the first few years, the radio was purely a homely expression of elitism and escapism, as the costs of radio receivers only made it available to the higher and middle-classes. As such, the programmes transmitted were mainly musical (opera music, symphony concerts, chamber music, dance music). The fascist regime, whose rise virtually coincided with the birth of the radio in Italy, was not yet totally aware of the propaganda potential of the new medium, and the only obligation it imposed on the State radio was the promotion of national artistic-cultural heritage, which was particular rich in music.

At this time, the radio served to spread the "magic of sound" of an opera or a music concert (the most popular programmes of the time), into the homes of the elite, for their family gatherings and social events. Indeed, with the diffusion of receivers with loudspeakers, listeners were no longer obliged to use headphones, so creating new social opportunities, also encouraged by house owners wishing to show off their receiver and offer their guests "the real impression of being actual spectators of an opera", as affirmed by a radio listener.[12] Hence, it was a form of "cultural entertainment",[13] this type of domestic entertainment having already been introduced by the piano, the phonograph and the circular telephone. Through the radio, however, new forms of expression were to be found, not only within the domestic walls, but, with time, beyond them, as well.

2. *Light entertainment. From dance music to radio variety shows*

In Eiar's 1931 annual report, the radio is seen as

> A great public service […] which will give the new market tendencies to a businessman, a highbrow concert (a symphony concert, chamber music) or lighter music (musical shows, dance music, operettas) to a family gathered together for pleasure, the "Cantuccio dei bambini" to the children, the

12. "Posta dei Lettori", *Radiorario*, 46 (1926), p. 7.

13. Anna Lucia Natale, "Sulle onde sonore. Strategie e usi sociali della musica alla radio (1924-1940)", in *La musica alla radio*, pp. 57-79.

"Rubrica delle signore" to the lady of the household, and news, information, points of reference to everyone, which nobody today could do without, not even those in the most isolated places, now in contact with the most advanced civilized living thanks to the radio.[14]

At this point, a concrete scheduling of programmes truly begins, aimed at providing the listener with different forms of information, culture and shows, and satisfying, during the course of a day, the needs of individual members of a family unit. The main priority was to increase the diffusion of the medium where the public was most accessible – in the home and in the family – and through a typology of programmes, to create a daily routine with radio appointments, some aimed at individual listening (businessmen, ladies, children), some aimed at the family nucleus, and some at a wider social setting, such as the evening shows.

What also clearly emerges from the declaration of Eiar is the intention to use the radio as a means to culturally unify a nation, to promote its diffusion in the most disadvantaged sections of society, and in the "most isolated places". There was a clear strategy to "popolarize" the radio, and during the Thirties this strategy began to be interlaced with that followed by the acting political powers to "build a fascist society". The radio became the main medium used by the regime to organize consensus. When the home proved insufficient, gatherings were called to fill the *piazzas*, to assist ceremonies held by the regime to be transmitted on the radio; more over, schools and State community centres were equipped with the radio, and public houses were given incentives to acquire a radio receiver and special license rates.

With the radio being promoted on various levels and the variety of programmes giving ample room for light entertainment, there was in a slow but steady increase in its audiences, with the number of subscribers exceeding a million by the end of 1939. Compared to other countries, the number was relatively small, with 9 million subscribers in Great Britain and 13 million in Germany,[15] and the huge American audience, which sat around the fireplace to listen to President Roosevelt's famous "fireside chats".[16] However, as learnt from a Referendum held for the radio audience

14. Eiar, *Annuario 1931* (Turin: Eiar, 1932), pp. 123-124.

15. Franco Monteleone, *Storia della radio e della televisione. Un secolo di costume, società e politica*, 3rd ed. (Venice: Marsilio, 2003).

16. Erik Barnouw, *The Golden Web. A History of Broadcasting in the United States 1933-1953*, vol. 2 (New York: Oxford University Press, 1968).

in 1939,[17] the number of listeners was particularly increasing among the middle and lower-middle classes, the self-employed, office workers, shopkeepers, specialized manual workers, artisans, pensioners, and students. The radio had also begun to enter the lives of shop floor workers and farm workers. Apart from the news and cultural programmes embued with political propaganda, the programming also included new forms of music, comedy and variety shows, dramas, and sports programmes (football, cycling, and car racing, etc.). This was part of a deliberate policy on the part of Eiar to increase the popularity of the radio.

Music had a particular important place, not only the already popular opera and classical music, but also *ligh*t and/or *dance music*. This kind of music included songs and dance music played by Eiar's own light orchestras (active since the time of Uri), or transmitted live from the dance halls, or, following agreements with the discography companies, reproduced from the playing of records. The radio's contact with the record companies led to recruitment of "radio singers" to be accompanied by Eiar's orchestras, which helped launch some of the most famous singers of the time (Carlo Buti, Alberto Rabagliati, and Trio Lescano), and create a first expression of idol worship.

The work of the radio orchestras also helped the Italians, already keen music lovers, to develop a passion for the new genres of music, such as jazz and its offshoots, which had been introduced from abroad. Jazz music had first been received tepidly by the Italian public, and heavily criticized by staunch defenders of Italian music. In Italy, however, a new more danceable, rhythmic form began to evolve, which became very popular with audiences, particular following the arrival of the American swing in the second half of the Thirties. The success of rhythmic music in combination with a growing interest in dance (already present in the Twenties, among the middle classes and urban shop floor workers, as well) meant that further home entertainment was organized around the radio. Dancing in the home, accompanied by a new enthusiasm for star singers, was to explode into a true phenomenon after the war,[18] but its origins are to be found in the period of growth in the home use of the radio.

17. On the Referendum see: Eiar, *Referendum Eiar 1940-XVIII. Organizzazione e risultati statistici* (Turin: Eiar, 1940); Anna Lucia Natale, *Gli anni della radio (1924-1954). Contributo ad una storia sociale dei media in Italia* (Naples: Liguori, 1990); Antonio Papa, *Storia politica della radio in Italia. Dalla guerra d'Etiopia al crollo del fascismo 1935-1943*, vol. 2 (Naples: Guida, 1978).

18. David Forgacs, Stephen Gundle, *Cultura di massa e società italiana 1936-1954* (Bologna: Il Mulino, 2007).

The genre of programme, however, which really represented that period was a new form of light entertainment, a mix of music and speech: the *radio revue*. This was an adaptation of the theatre revue, which mixed a number of prose, comic sketches, and music, all held together by a storyline and regular characters. This formula of the genre became the first great success in terms of mass radio audience in Italy. Later on, it would develop into the *variety show*, with a show conductor.[19]

The creators behind radio revues were Angelo Nizza and Riccardo Morbelli, whose popularity peaked with *I quattro moschettieri* (*The four musketeers*, 1934-1935). The programme was a remake, or parody, of the famous story by Alexandre Dumas, where elements from the classic literature, theatre, cinema, song lyrics and opera music were mingled with lively dialogues, jokes, and popular music, to create a sparkling mixed genre. Its success led to further editions of the programme, from 1936 to 1938. Apart from the originality of its format, the popularity of the programme was also due to its pairing with a competition with prizes sponsored by the food companies Buitoni and Perugina, which involved the collecting of figurines of the various characters. When the top prize became a Fiat 500 *Topolino* (launched in 1936), a mad rush on mass levels followed in a bid to find the most elusive figurines, resulting in the first phenomenon of integrated communication in Italy, with the production of records, books, and various films, all related to the series and its characters.

Other forms of the radio magazine would follow, but *I quattro moschettieri* remains one of a kind. For the very first time, the radio had managed to create something which was able to reach all stratus of society, irrespective of social class, individual tastes, and ownership of a receiver, as evident through the multimedia quality of the event and the multitude of different forms and copies the programme led to the birth of. It was genuinely "popular", in that it was in "complete harmony with its audiences".[20]

In the late Thirties, the radio was a popular medium, profoundly tied to the domestic environment. The radio was a popular medium not so much for its diffusion among different social groups and classes (while it could no longer be considered a phenomenon of the elite, the number of subscribers

19. Nicoletta Verna, "Rivista e varietà", in *Enciclopedia della radio*, pp. 743-747.

20. Paola Valentini, *La scena rubata. Il cinema italiano e lo spettacolo popolare (1924-1954)* (Milan: Vita e Pensiero, 2002), p. 13.

indicate it was far from being widespread on a mass level), but popular in the profound way it managed to be part of the lives of the public. The very essence of the "popular radio" resided in the spontaneity of private and family listening: it resided in the regular listening to the news (*Giornale Radio*), the pleasure of listening to songs or following a football match, sharing listenings of operas or dancing in the home, and joining in the rush to search out the figurines of *I quattro moschettieri…*

As the home use of the radio grew in popularity, radio audiences tended to outgrow the previous unifying models of cultural entertainment or family get-togethers, and began to be recognizable in social and generational grouping. Apart from the news and light entertainment, every social group (according to the data already cited by the 1939 Referendum) appears to have identified favourite genres of programmes and particular ways (and/or times) of listening. The higher-middle classes and the housewives preferred opera music, while the more working classes opted for radio revues and musical comedies. Women tended to use the radio to keep them company during the day when they were alone, while men liked the news and the Sunday sport. Then, for the first time, among the subscribers were young people: they were lovers of jazz music, songs, dance music, with the radio used to hold improvised home parties, extending the passion for dancing in homes. These young people were also the first ones to use the rudimentary "suitcase" radios (already widespread in other countries), and took them to accompany them in their free time, for instance, on the beaches and in the countryside.

Nonetheless, considerable time would pass before the radio freed itself from domestic ritual. In the meantime, the outbreak of the Second World War and the subsequent fall of the fascist regime led to a change in the use of the radio, compared to the previous twenty years. That said, its social role and the special relationship between the radio and its audiences through programmes of light entertainment would remain, partly due to people's need to "escape" from the hardship of war. This prepared the way for other, diverse "radio pleasures".

3. *The desire for rebirth. Amid songs, quizzes and prize contests*

With the leaving of war, the radio needed to be "reinvented", in line with the principles of the new democratic society. The main objective of Rai-Radio Audizioni Italia (the new name of the company from 1944 onwards) was to provide "a radio for everyone", to quote the promotional slogan used at the time. It encapsulates the idea of a radio open to differences in opinion, encouraging the participation of citizens to public life, capable of reaching all sections of society and all parts of the country. In short, it was a radio set on recuperating its authentic role as a public service.

After the initial phase linked to the reconstruction of the country and the establishing of the political setup (the 1948 political elections resulted in the Christian Democrats, a Catholic inspired party, leading a series of governments), the new face of the radio began to really take shape during the Fifties with the broadcasting reform of 1951, whereby the main functions of the State radio were divided into three different channels: information and news on the National Channel (which replaced the Rete Rossa), entertainment on the Second Channel (previously Rete Azzurra), and culture and education on the Third Channel (in existence since 1950 and modeled on the example of the British BBC).

This division aimed at resolving the persistent problem of maintaining the "responsibilities" the radio had, while at the same time meeting the "tastes" of a public or their need for escapism.[21] This dualism in nature, however, continued to characterize the radio a long time after the end of the war. On the one hand, the radio was meant to "raise" the population, both culturally and morally, such a view being influenced by the teachings of the Catholic Church and the Italian artistic-cultural tradition, while on the other, it needed to meet the demands of a society which was culturally becoming influenced by mass consumption, which had begun with the arrival of the American liberators during the war.[22] Indeed, it is here "that the first warning signs appear of that modernization in the areas of tastes and mass consumption, that revolution in costumes which has dominated society for the last fifty years".[23]

The project of the people's civic and cultural education was to be at its best in the use of the radio to promote the consciousness raising of the Country (thanks to excellent journalism in the production of documentaries), and its presence in initiatives of social solidarity (such as assistance to

21. S. Tatti, "I gusti degli ascoltatori e i doveri della radio italiana", *Radiocorriere*, 29 (1946, Ed. Cento Meridionale), p. 2

22. Monteleone, *Storia della radio e della televisione.*

23. Gianni Isola, *Cari amici vicini e lontani. Storia dell'ascolto radiofonico nel primo decennio repubblicano* (Scandicci: La Nuova Italia, 1995), p. 32.

the population in times of natural calamity), which all helped to build a sense of belonging and identification with the infant democratic society. However, the real "bond" between the radio and its audiences proved to be, yet again, that "healthy, delightful recreation"[24] which the 1951 Reform had assigned to the Second Channel.

The Rai began to promote light entertainment in the late Forties, reintroducing the running of public competitions to find new radio performers, and re-launching the most popular past genres, such as the revue and song. The Thirties radio revue slowly transformed into *variety*, which gave rise to numerous forms, such as the quiz show, amateur, talent contests, and so on. These programmes became the training ground for directors, actors, and showmen: some were destined to become famous, such as Federico Fellini, Alberto Sordi, Mike Bongiorno, and Claudio Villa. There was a productive synergy between radio and other forms of entertainment, from the theatre to cinema, and television.[25] Overall, the broadcasting of these different forms of radio entertainment contributed to giving hope, to the Italians in the period of reconstruction, that "dreams could come true".

From *Il bilione* (1947-1948) to *Rosso e nero* (1951-1957), from *Botta e risposta* (1944-1956) to *Il motivo in maschera* (1954-1956), from *Il microfono è vostro* (1950-1952) to *Il campanile d'oro* (1954-1955): the variety shows showered prizes, great and small, in the form of money, or electrical home appliances, on both participants and the voting audience. Prizes were also used to attract subscribers, where programmes such as *Radiofortuna* (since 1948) gave out top prizes which constituted real objects of desire for the times, such as scooters (Vespa, Lambretta) and cars (Fiat 500).

Programmes for amateur performers also gave hope to younger members of the audience in their pursuit of a successful career in the world of entertainment. They looked up to the cinema stars, but also to the radio stars, who had been a source of comfort and inspiration during the war through *Il Canzoniere della radio* (*The radio song review*). This magazine published the lyrics of the most famous songs and recounted the lives of the stars, celebrating how, despite their modest origins, they had achieved

24. Salvino Sernesi, "Presupposti e problemi sulla soglia del secondo venticinquennio", *Radiocorriere*, 40 (1949), pp. 7, 9, in particular p. 9.

25. Isola, *Cari amici vicini e lontani*.

success, and how stars were often "discovered" just by a stroke of luck. In an Italy which was still poor, agricultural, Catholic and patriarchal, but which aspired to rise up from the ashes of the war, the radio instilled a belief in the future, which promised to be filled with money, material goods and new job opportunities. So why not try your luck?

Aspiring stars, people dissatisfied with their work, or simply those who wished for a moment of glory, all flocked to take part in *Il microfono è vostro*, whereby the best local performances in theatres around Italy were transmitted over the radio. In an article in *Radiocorriere* (the official review of the radio company from 1930 onwards), hundreds of people are mentioned – students, office workers, typists, artisans and factory workers, sixteen-year-old singers, amateur dads and four-year-old little girls, aspiring singers and mature troubadour, lads in military service, hopeful State employees and smiling young ladies… –, all of whom "await backstage for their turn, for 'Il microfono è vostro' to open the gates to sweet success for them, and only them".[26] The programme triggered an interest and participation in the general public comparable to that sparked by *I quattro moschettieri*. Il *microfono è vostro* started up in 1950, with a second edition in 1952, and special versions for the young men in military service. It also inspired a film under the same title as the transmission. The programmes's success was greatly helped by its itinerant formula, the fame of its presenter (Nunzio Filogamo, the unforgettable interpreter of the Musketeer Aramis), and the music of Cinico Angelini (the famous light orchestra conductor from the time of Eiar).

With the variety shows, but not only, light music was continuing to be a roaring success, particular song music. The foundations for its success laid during the fascist regime, continued during the war, and culminated in the *Sanremo Festival*. Not without, however, stirring up old polemics. In the postwar years, the so-called "Italian song" brought pleasure, as did imported music, such as the American boogie-woogie, the French song, and new South American rhythms.[27] In fact, at the beginning of the Fifties, Italian radio went back to broadcasting dance music, in programmes such as *Ballate con noi* (which, in an afternoon slot, transmitted musical pieces

26. Gianni Giannantonio, "In fila per uno davanti al 'Microfono di tutti'", *Radiocorriere*, 44 (1950), p. 32.

27. Irene Piazzoni, *La musica leggera in Italia. Dal dopoguerra agli anni del "boom"* (Milan: L'Ornitorinco, 2011).

from the best orchestras around the world), or transmitting live music played in dance halls. Supporters of the more traditional radio heavily criticized this new music, in particular jazz music and the South American music most in fashion (rumba, mambo, samba), heavy criticism having already been made of jazz music during the fascist period, denigrated as "negroid" music, accompanied by complaints of an "indigestion" of light music transmitted to the detriment of classical and opera music.[28] Now, critics of the new musical sounds contested above all what they saw as audacious elements in some songs, and worked to safeguard more traditional Italian music from the influence of foreign imports.

It was in this climate that the Rai, in agreement with music publishers, founded *The Sanremo Italian Song Festival*. The declared aim was to promote Italian melodies, "those which came from Neapolitan songs and from romances in the line of a notable lyric tradition",[29] and to "promote quality Italian light music, compatible with what proved 'popular' with this kind of music".[30]

In 1951, the Festival rather went unnoticed, but by the third edition in 1953, the Festival had attracted the interest of both the press and the record companies, by introducing a song contest formula which was altered and adjusted over the next few years: the double performance of the songs, accompanied each time by two different orchestras; the audience as jury, chosen by lot from the public in the auditorium and the subscribers; and broadcasting the Festival from Thursday to Saturday evening. If the press and the record companies took their time in gaining interest in the Festival, this was not the case with the general public, who immediately appreciated the novelty of a contest between singers, the discussion of suspected inevitable riggings, and the familiar Nunzio Filogamo, the conductor of the four editions broadcasted on the radio. Winning songs such as *Grazie dei fior*, *Vola Colomba*, *Viale d'autunno*, *Tutte le mamme*, illustrate the predominance of slow and melancholic rhythms and melodies, accompanying sentimental or nostalgic lyrics, inspired by the Italian song. This carried on, with some exceptions, until the whirlwind arrival of Domenico Modugno.

28. See on this Gianni Isola, *Abbassa la tua radio, per favore... Storia dell'ascolto radiofonico nell'Italia fascista* (Scandicci: La Nuova Italia, 1990); Isola, *Cari amici vicini e lontani*.

29. "Il festival della Canzone Italiana", *Radiocorriere*, 5 (1951), pp. 16-17, in particular p. 17.

30. *Ibid*., p. 16.

The Festival was first broadcasted on television in 1955, and marked a turning point in the growth of the mass cultural industry in Italy, with the definitive exit of light music from its homespun collocation.[31] Through the Festival, well-known and new singers (from Alberto Rabagliati to Nilla Pizzi, Claudio Villa, Gino Latilla, and many others) extended their careers; the record and radio industry expanded, as did the gossip magazines on singers; offshoot events took off on the radio, such as the *Festival della canzone napoletana* in 1952. Furthermore, the Festival contributed in depicting an image of Italian society – reconstructed by several historians partly through the lyrics of songs of Sanremo –[32] and successfully exported the Italian Song to the rest of the world. The most effective example is *Nel blu, dipinto di blu*, the winner of the 1958 contest held on television. The image of Domenico Modugno, his arms open wide to the sky, eyes closed, singing the ritornello – "Volare oh, oh! Cantare oh, oh, oh, oh! Nel blu dipinto di blu, felice di stare lassù" – became famous in America, as well. The song's explosion of joy was in net contrast with the slow rhythms and composure of the Sanremo interpretations. It also represented a metaphor of Italy at that time, finally leaving postwar uncertainty behind and embracing the sunny future of the "economic miracle".

Meanwhile, what was perhaps the golden age of the radio was coming to a close. From the Forties to the Fifties, it had managed to both accommodate and stimulate some of the most widespread trends in postwar society, from a desire to escape to the dream of a better future. It had been a springboard for cultural industry, discovered and launched new talents, and had handed out prizes and jobs. It had finally become a medium "of the people", no longer only in terms of its ability to express a common feeling, but also through the number of its subscribers: though the near 5 million (the number significant in itself) subscribers in 1953 were prevalently among the higher-middle classes residing in the North, the number of the middle and lower class subscribers particularly was on the rise.[33] It was

31. Piazzoni, *La musica leggera in Italia*.

32. On this see Gianni Borgna, *La grande evasione. Storia del Festival di Sanremo: 30 anni di costume italiano* (Rome: Savelli, 1980); Gianni Borgna, *Storia della canzone italiana* (Bari: Laterza, 1985); Felice Liperi, *Storia della canzone italiana* (Rome: Rai-Eri, 1999); Leonardo Campus, *Non solo canzonette. L'Italia della Ricostruzione e del Miracolo attraverso il Festival di Sanremo* (Florence: Le Monnier, 2015).

33. Rai, "Sessant'anni di radio. Cronistoria dalle origini 1924-1984", in *Speciale Radio TV*, vol. 2 (Rome: Rai, 1984).

with this radio that the collective image of "Mamma Rai" was born. The arrival of television changed everything.

4. *The turn of television... and rock and roll!*

Television came into existence on 3 January 1954 and became widespread at a speed radio had never known. Within ten years, it established its hegemony over the other means of communication, becoming "the new family fireplace".[34] The growth in popularity of television – from 88,000 subscribers in 1954 to 5 million in 1964 –[35] went hand in hand with the economic boom, which from the late Fifties to the mid Sixties transformed Italy from an essentially agricultural nation to a modern industrial society. The transformation was profound, and in some respects, quite traumatic, engulfing "ways of production and consumption, of thinking and dreaming, how to live in the present and how to plan the future".[36] It permeated both the reality of the Country, as well as its collective imagination.

Television was, in various ways, both the expression and the motor of this transformation: it contributed to the cultural growth through educational programmes (*Telescuola*, 1958-1966; *Non è mai troppo tardi*, 1960-1968) and television adaptations of literary works; it fed the consumer market through commercial advertising, though limited in quantity and even ennobled through the artistic renderings of *Carosello* (1957-1977); above all, it literally portrayed, spread and multiplied images of a rich society, carefree, orientated towards individual well-being, and represented the promise of a better life for all. This image of the society transpires, for example, through the great variety shows of Saturday evening, the highpoint of television entertainment. Starting with *Canzonissima*, a song contest coupled with the State lottery, evening entertainment would be characterized by opulence, from the studios to the scenography, from the dance corps to the costumes. First aired in 1958, *Canzonissima* would go

34. Radius Emilio, "Il piccolo schermo della tv, focolare d'oggi", *Radiocorriere*, 52 (1962), pp. 14-15, in particular p. 14.

35. Monteleone, *Storia della radio e della televisione*.

36. Guido Crainz, *Storia del miracolo italiano. Culture identità, trasformazioni tra anni cinquanta e sessanta* (Rome: Donzelli, 2005), p. VII.

on to be re-proposed for another eighteen editions (continuing then in other formulas, from *Gran Premio* to *Fantastico*).

Hence, the bond between television and the economic boom is inseparable. The main point of reference, in the type of show and collective imagination, is clearly the American cultural model, though adapted to Italian cultural awareness and attenuated by the continuing influence of the Catholic culture.[37] This is evident in the attempts to combine education with consumerism, in the moral checks on the programmes (from *Carosello* to the variety shows) and in the way certain American programmes are adapted for Italian audiences. An example can be found in *Lascia o raddoppia?* (1955-1959), "the most famous quiz show in Italian television history, the basis for all successive quiz shows",[38] which built a show around the exhibitionist inclinations of the Italians, and their desire for success.

The groundwork for these kinds of programmes, based on overseas cultural models and direct public participation, had already been laid with postwar radio broadcasting. Television took this further, creating much of its initial success by drawing on the radio in terms of genres, programmes, and characters. For instance, *Campanile sera* (1959-1962), a group contest, was based on the radio programmes *Il campanile d'oro* and *Il Gonfalone* (1958-1959), and *Il motivo in maschera* which was drawn from radio show *Il musichiere* (1957-1960), idealized around musical riddles. Even the origins of *Canzonissima* can be found in the radio broadcast *La canzoni della fortuna* (1956-1957), which combined the two great passions of postwar Italians, songs and contests.

However, it is the television which really depicts Italy in the years of economic boom, while the radio took a backseat in terms of the interest of the broadcasting company and politics, audiences, and the press. As the radio's role as a public service was downsized, no longer representing the main channel for broadcasting products of the cultural industry, the medium was forced to redefine its *raison d'etre*. At first, it tried to cultivate the most faithful part of its audience by transmitting programmes which had always been successful, such as dramas, opera music, radiodramas. Then, it tried to carve itself out a role as an alternative to television: by valorizing morning and early afternoon slots; broadcasting programmes

37. See Monteleone, *Storia della radio e della televisione*; Crainz, *Storia del miracolo italiano*.

38. Rai Teche: http://www.teche.rai.it/2015/11/ lascia-o-raddoppia-con-danny-kaye.

of light entertainment, made up of news, songs, music and other rubrics; beginning its transformation into an instrument to keep people company, as "background sounds" to other activities.

Not until the late Sixties did the radio have its "second youth".[39] The process of socio-cultural modernization triggered by the economic boom contributed to the rise of the "youth culture", present in Italy as well. This culture consisted of a lifestyle, a particular consumer system with differences in tastes, which distinguished the younger generations from others, with young people most identifying with rock music.[40] Rock music exploded in the USA in the Fifties and reached Europe thanks to the powerful transmitter of Radio Luxembourg, the most American inspired European transmitter, and "pirate" radios, Radio Caroline in particular, which, from 1964 onwards, broadcasted from the international waters off the coast of England.[41] It constituted a new, transgressive form of "making radio" – plenty of music, the figure of the disc-jockey, a mix of music and word – which explicitly contraposed the rigid models of the State European radios. Compared to the transgressive, hard rock of the original American rock and roll, the kind of rock which the European youth went for, was the softer version of the English "beat" groups of the early Sixties, such as the Beatles and the Rolling Stones.[42]

The radio was the medium most responsible for spreading "this music bringing young people together and sometimes making them freer, happier, and more open", as put by an Italian beat singer.[43] With the invention of the transistor (in 1948), the medium became pocket-sized, mobile, and relatively cheap. As television took up place in the more typical social areas of the household, the radio moved into the home's more intimate places (the bedroom, bathroom, kitchen), and finally, outdoors, accompanying the

39. Bruno Barbicinti, "Incomincia per la radio la seconda giovinezza", *Radiocorriere*, 51 (1966), pp. 17-18, in particular p. 17.

40. See Carl Belz, *Storia del rock. Uno studio completo e appassionante della musica rock dal 1950 a oggi* (Milan: Mondadori, 1975); Marc Fisher, *Something in the Air. Radio, Rock, and the Revolution that Shaped a Generation* (New York: Random House, 2007).

41. Enrico Menduni, *La radio nell'era della TV. Fine di un complesso di inferiorità* (Bologna: Il Mulino, 2012); Asa Briggs, *The History of Broadcasting in the United Kingdom, Vol. 5: Competition* (Oxford: Oxford University Press, 1995).

42. Robert Chapman, *Selling the Sixties. The Pirates of the Pop Music Radio* (London: Routledge, 1992).

43. Piero Novelli, "Fischietta Scarlatti il Bob Dylan italiano", *Radiocorriere*, 43 (1966), p. 34.

listener to their place of work, and places of free time. No longer tied to home listening, the medium became ever more individual and personal.

Within this context, Italian radio built itself an identity, adapting content, communication styles and ways of use most "in tune" with the changes in society. The turning point came in 1966 with the programming reform of Leone Piccioni, aimed at the experimentation of new expressive languages and a differentiation of programmes according to social groups (adult males, women, young people). For the adults, the choice remained somewhat in a rut, recalling those consolidated in the Fifties based on a set system of tastes: sport for men, from radio commentary on football and cycling to the new Sunday slot of *Tutto il calcio minuto per minuto* (from 1960 onwards); serial fiction for women continued to be proposed, from *Una commedia in trenta minuti* (1969-1977) to the morning dramas, comprising soap operas, and radio adaptations of classic literature, and original dramas for radio, and would remain a fixed slot right up to the beginning of the new millennium.[44]

Two important new programmes of the period were *Gran Varietà* (1966-1979) and *Chiamate Roma 3131* (1969-1995). While in format the first was a traditional family variety show, its transmission in the morning was a novelty, offsetting competition from television, and offering an accompaniment for the family on their day-off or on excursions. Animators of the programme were the most well known artists from the world of show, who acted as the show's presenters and guests. *Gran Varietà* proving to be "the most successful Italian radio show of all time".[45] With the call-in transmission *Chiamate Roma 3131*, the telephone became the cornerstone of a radio broadcast for the very first time.[46] During a long daily transmission, listeners (mainly housewives and the elderly) discussed their problems and asked advice, with the conductors intervening and experts in the studio giving their opinions. Through this direct involvement with the public, the transmission being built around its participation, the programme *3131* represented the beginning of real revolution in the public radio service.

44. Anna Lucia Natale, *Reinventare la tradizione. Novità e ripetizione nella fiction Tv in Italia* (Rome: Mediascape, 2004).

45. Nicoletta Verna, "Gran Varietà", in *Enciclopedia della Radio*, pp. 373-374, in particular p. 374.

46. Raffaele Vincenti, *La prima volta del telefono. La storia del 3131 dal 1969 al 1995* (Rome: Rai-Eri, 2009).

However, the radio of the Sixties and Seventies was above all the main interpreter of the tastes, needs and tendencies of the new generations. While in Great Britain, pirate radios forced the State radio to introduce a channel mainly dedicated to rock music,[47] in Italy there was a more gradual introduction of rubrics and musical programmes for young people. The effect, however, were no less explosive in the long run. An indication became a few months before the 1966 reform with the programme *Bandiera gialla* (1965-1970), a transmission dedicated to international musical novelties, and reserved "rigorously for the very young", as announced by the opening theme. Created and conducted by Gianni Boncompagni and Renzo Arbore, the programme involved a group of young people being present in the studio, who would be asked to vote "the best song" from the twelve songs proposed in each programme. Amidst applauding fans, the vote consisted in raising a yellow flag.[48]

Apart from the informal language and the involvement of the public in studio, the great success of the transmission was due to the ability of the radio to capture the "spirit of the moment". The year 1965 also marked the first Italian concert of the Beatles, the first edition of the musical magazine *Big*, and the inauguration of the Piper Club in Rome, the first public space created for the shared use of music for the young. Some years before rock music had begun to innovate the Italian music scene, from the first international events (*The Festival of Rock and Roll* in 1957 and 1961) to the phenomenon of Adriano Celentano (exploded in 1959 with *Il mio bacio è come un rock*), to the beat groups of the Sixties (Equipe 84, Dick Dick, Ribelli).[49] The radio has the merit of being the first to provide a mouthpiece for this new reality.

The programme *Per voi giovani* (1966-1976) went even further. The dual purpose of the programme was incorporated into the opening theme, whereby the interest in music was also accompanied by a confrontation between young people: "For you young people, your records, your problems, your topics". In a first phase, conducted by its creator, Renzo Arbore, there

47. See on this Daniele Doglio, Giuseppe Richeri, *La radio. Origini, storia, modelli* (Milan: Mondadori, 1980); Briggs, *The History of Broadcasting in the United Kingdom.*

48. Tiziano Tarli, *Beat italiano. Dai capelloni a Bandiera Gialla* (Rome: Castelvecchi, 2005).

49. See on this Umberto Bultrighini, Claudio Scarpa, Gene Guglielmi, *Al di qua, al di là del beat. Radici e dinamiche del beat italiano: le voci di tre testimoni* (Lanciano: Carabba, 2011); Piazzoni, *La musica leggera in Italia*; Tarli, *Beat italiano.*

was a mix of music, customs and current affairs, with the voice of young people being aired through interventions with the microphone, letters and interviews. From 1971 onwards, Paolo Giaccio and Mario Luzzatto Fegiz reorganized the programme into a series of rubrics (dedicated to different types of music, both Italian and foreign, to mail sent in by members of the public, and to "spoken services"), and dedicated more time to discussion. From school to work, from politics to questions of the heart, to freedom, the programme progressively extended its attention to themes and problems concerning the youth protests, noting moods, political inclinations, musical tastes – by then increasingly differentiated – of the young people of the Seventies.

Last of all, a variety was created which young people liked, as well, that is to say *Alto gradimento* (1970-1976). The duo Arbore-Boncompagni teamed up again to produce a kind of collective enjoyment, made up of music, jokes, eccentric characters, and grammatically incorrect catchphrases, which soon become part of the everyday lingo of the time: the Accountant Affastellati ("Perché non sei venutta? Ping!"), the former fascist Catenacci ("Quando c'era lui, caro lei!"), the Professor Aristogitone ("Quarand'anni di insegnamento…"), and many more. Some scholars have seen there a double link with the Neapolitan "macchietta", or theatre caricatures, and the slap-stick humour which was developing in the American counterculture at the time.[50] Whatever the case, *Alto gradimento* introduced an innovative language, which was fruit of improvisation, slick timing, and the shaking up of established radio rules. It would go on to be "the model of nearly all the independent radio stations in the decade".[51]

The so-called "independent" radio stations first appeared in the late Seventies, but their origins can be found in the general social crisis triggered by the economic boom, when, starting with the youth sector, there were appeals for greater participation in public life, freer speech, and greater access to the media. To a certain extent, the public radio answered these appeals, anticipating – with *Alto gradimento*, and *Chiamate Roma 3131*, and the musical programmes for young people, as well – the main future characteristics of the private radio: music which young people liked, audiences which were participant and centre stage, a new form of entertainment based on improvisation and alternation between music and

50. Peppino Ortoleva, "Alto Gradimento", in *Enciclopedia della radio*, pp. 20-21.
51. Monteleone, *Storia della radio e della televisione*, p. 393.

the spoken word, and the general idea that it was a radio "made by the listeners, for the listeners".

The public radio of that time, then, laid the foundations for the revolution in the Italian communication scenario, which began with a spontaneous proliferation of thousands of private broadcasters (radio and television), gradually evolving into different types number of associations, and leading, in a few years, to the end of public broadcasting monopoly. Whereas public and private television fully established its identity as the medium of home entertainment, the radio became both an "alternative", countering the cultural models of the old radio and television,[52] and "plural", due to the wealth and variety of its new language forms and formats (musicals, chat shows, music and news, all news, and so on).[53]

As the radio gradually captured the interests and cultural activities of young people, it finally reached its goal as a "medium of the people", and regained its central role in cultural industry. In the course of its journey, from time to time, it had changed its forms and entertainment places, according to the growth and differentiation of its public: it had been the reason behind bourgeois family get-togethers in the drawing room of homes; a discreet companion, adaptable to the different types of public, within and outside the domestic walls; the instrument of expression of youth subjectivity, to use and/or perform in the same place of production.

What about the radio of today? It is a continuous entertainment, a bright mix of words, music and information, accessible in every place and in every moment, through the multiple devices which technology has provided (traditional or digital appliances, car radios, computer, smartphone, i-pod, etc.) The integration into the digital world has further extended the expressive possibilities and social use of the medium, giving the radio its umpteenth second childhood.

52. Simonelli, *Cari amici vicini e lontani.*

53. See Giovanni Cordoni, Peppino Ortoleva, Nicoletta Verna, *Le onde del futuro. Presenze e tendenze della radio in Italia* (Milan: Costa & Nolan, 2006); Barbara Fenati, Alessandra Scaglioni, *La radio. Modelli, ascolto, programmazione* (Rome: Carocci, 2002); Enrico Menduni, *Il mondo della radio. Dal transistor ai social network* (Bologna: Il Mulino, 2012).

Nicoletta Peluffo

The Adventures of Pinocchio: An Outcome of Popular Culture

One of the most world-famous Italian stories is Carlo Collodi's *The Adventures of Pinocchio*, a typical outcome of Italian popular culture that, from its appearance, has travelled outside the borders of Italy thus becoming a universal symbol. With *Pinocchio*, Collodi, pseudonym of Carlo Lorenzini, meets the requirements of the rising Italian cultural industry of the late 19th century and its transition from the serialised form into a different medium, the book, represents the first of the many adaptations, abridgements, reductions, translations and re-writings that the story undergoes from its publication. Its imagery is strongly reconfigured after the appearance of Disney version in 1940, when the puppet becomes part of the American cultural industry, too. The aim of this essay is to trace an evolution of the story of *Pinocchio* inside the cultural industry from its early appearance through some re-writings until Disney adaptation for the cinematic version. Carved in a specific period of Italian history, Pinocchio has become a multifaceted icon of adaptation and transmediality.

1. *Carlo Collodi, a journalist and a novelist*

After his studies in seminary, Carlo Collodi works in the Libreria Piatti, a popular Florentine bookshop where he partakes in a rapidly changing cultural and political environment. In fact, Piatti is the place where the offer of editors and writers converges with the public requests and Collodi can detect the two poles of the rising cultural industry of the mid-19th century and convey their respective needs in his production. Furthermore, in the bookshop he is exposed to the works coming from abroad, where, especially in France and England, publishers and writers increasingly focus on a growing middle-class public. In his early works, he writes about his personal interests, namely theatre and music, two popular genres that engaged many writers and critics. Collodi also participates in the social and political life of his time. He lives and writes in a complex period of Italian history witnessing the transitional process of the country that leads to its unification, a change that he actively supports as a journalist and as a citizen. In 1848, immediately after his beginnings as a writer, he engages in the first war of Italian Independence together with his brother Paolo, and in 1859 he volunteers in the Savoy army supporting the unification of Italy during the second war of Independence. In 1864, following the September Convention, the capital of Italy is transferred to Florence until 1871, giving the city an unprecedented political and cultural expansion that Collodi dislikes for its hypocrisy, social disorder and corruption. But the evolution of Italian political scene puts him at the centre of a cultural debate on another matter related to unification: the language. Collodi's works display a middle standard Italian that he has refined through his journalistic writings. His use of satire and irony in a direct, sharp style alternates high and low registers thus reaching all the levels of readers. In 1875 the editors Paggi ask him to translate into Italian the French *Contes* by Charles Perrault, M.me d'Aulnoy and M.me Leprince de Beaumont: since then, Collodi's cooperation with Paggi becomes very intense and it follows the principle of educating the young middle-class Italians in the Risorgimental ideal in compliance with the political and social unification of the country and of the language. Following this purpose in 1877 he portrays a character, *Giannettino*, a young boy protagonist of a school book series used to teach Italian, mathematics and geography. *Giannettino* is soon followed by *Minuzzolo* (1878), a reading book for school kids based on the adventures of another young boy. While his production as a journalist is full of pessimistic sarcasm and disenchanted irony, the effort he puts in the school publications is enthusiastic and optimistic. He follows the educational process of the rising 19th century reading public, an elite which pursues the ideals of literacy and culture, thus encouraging publishers investments in the pedagogic sector. This approach is of the utmost importance in the early development of the Italian cultural industry, which seems subordinate to the pedagogic strategy.[1]

1. Fausto Colombo, *La cultura sottile: media e industria culturale in Italia dall'Ottocento agli anni Novanta* (Milan: Bompiani, 1998).

In 1881, when Collodi publishes the first story of Pinocchio, he can transfer all his journalistic expertise, his ability in depicting characters and portrayals in the new story. Besides this, his knowledge of the readers' requests and of the editors' needs converges in the creation of his new character, who will in short become an unequalled product of Italian popular culture.

2. *The traveling character: From seriality to the novel*

Pinocchio the puppet first appears on July 7, 1881, in the *Giornale per i Bambini*, a new-born publication directed by Collodi's friend, Ferdinando Martini. Through the request of writing a story for a new periodical aiming at educating children, he is in reality invited to take part in a new cultural operation. The *Giornale* addresses to kids aging from 6 to 12 years old. Its price, 25 cents per issue, is not affordable for everyone, probably just middle-class and bourgeois families can buy it. It is sponsored by the entrepreneur Guglielmo Emanuele Oblieght who understands the potential of the late nineteenth century middle-class young public, and for this reason he accepts to subsidise the involvement of important writers such as Collodi. Besides the pedagogical purpose of the publication, Martini aims at introducing a new *genre* that had flourished abroad, particularly in the United States, in England and in France. The editor of the magazine, Guido Biagi (who is totally and genuinely committed to the project), enthusiastically announces the first issue as a pleasant and educating reading, so successful that even the best and illustrious writers would engage in this new adventure. For Collodi, who will be the director of the *Giornale* between April 1882, and December, 1885, it is not difficult to accept this challenge: he has been a journalist for all his life and the developing cultural market is not new to him. Furthermore, he is probably aware of the success of the *roman feuilleton* genre in France, where Eugène Sue's *Les Mystères de Paris* (1842-43) doubled the circulation of the *Journal des débats*.

Pinocchio appears as the protagonist of *The Story of a Puppet* in the first issue of the magazine, on page five. The story is published following the issues of the *Giornale* and it ends after some instalments with the death of the marionette. Pinocchio, carved by the carpenter Geppetto after many rocambolesque adventures ends his journey hung from the branch of an oak tree by the Murderers (Cat and Fox) while they try to steal his gold coins received from the owner of the Puppet Theatre, Fire-Eater. The first, original story has not a positive, open, happy ending. But the readers feel empathic with the puppet and they express their curiosity and disappointment to the editor, who asks Collodi to add other adventures: Pinocchio must come to life again. In 1883, the story appears under the form of a book with a new title, *The Adventures of Pinocchio*, by the editor Paggi. The transformation of the story from a serial format into a novel requires some stylistic and structural interventions from the author, but the language, the narrative, and the style fits the purposes of divulgation: it is fresh, approachable and affordable. The operation conducted by Collodi and required for a commercial purpose represents the first of the many future re-writings of the story. The eminent scholar Emilio Garroni, in his essay *Pinocchio uno e bino* proposes the theory of two *Pinocchio: Pinocchio I*, a story that develops in a fast and synthetic way towards a catastrophic ending and *Pinocchio II*, which starts from chapter XV and incorporates the original story expanding in longer and slower chapters towards the open finale.[2] Asides from the critical appraisals that the re-writing of the story has always generated among critics and scholars, it appears incontrovertible that the particular evolution of its format, from *feuilleton* to the book, is one of the reasons of its success: the public has already met Pinocchio and it is now eager to know more about him and his adventures.

Additionally, the title change from "story" into "adventures" opens the storyboard to new, unexpected narrative lines. After being saved by the blue-haired Fairy Queen, Pinocchio runs across a number of situations and metamorphoses until the final transformation into a boy of flesh and blood. Through this controversial ending Collodi probably aims at reconciling the insubordinate character of Pinocchio to the current morale. In fact, while the characters of Collodi's school books bent towards the idea of family, rigid work and observance of rules, Pinocchio is quite the opposite: he does not accept the adults advices, he loves his father but he cannot help acting as a brat, he does not recognize the power and its rules until the last chapters. At the end of the story Pinocchio shows he has learned a lesson. To do so, he has to make a double epic movement to remove the negative aspects of his personality thus becoming heroic: first he watches behind himself and understands his mistakes, then he looks at his new future with hope. In that, the final chapter portrays a sort of twist of the former anti-hero who acts

2. Emilio Garroni, *Pinocchio uno e bino* (Bari: Laterza, 1975), p. 51.

as a brat to reset the heroic positivity of the character: he becomes a real boy. The constant narrative tension towards change that accompanies the work falls in the very final lines. Looking at the wooden puppet leaning on a chair (his previous identity has not completely disappeared!) Pinocchio says to himself with the greatest satisfaction: "How funny I was when I was a puppet! And how happy I am now to have become a proper boy!".[3] Many critics see in the last words pronounced by the boy a sort of sad farewell to childhood to enter the world of adulthood, full of responsibilities and rules to be followed. Others consider it a suicidal transformation: Pinocchio kills his *alter ego* and renounces to the freedom that he experiences throughout the most part of his life when he was a puppet and a scamp.

As many scholars argue, one of the main features of this character is his extreme flexibility, which makes him suitable to changes in his nature (Pinocchio is subject of many transformations during his journey) but also in his transmigration outside his story.

3. *Pinocchio, a flexible universe in constant transformation*

Flexibility is one of the main features of the character of Pinocchio. Given his wooden nature, Pinocchio appears to be very rigid in his mechanical body, yet, his narrative *status* and his metamorphic essence put the character at the centre of many adaptations.

The puppet can be fixed and repaired in some small parts, like his feet, but he rarely breaks: he rather transforms into something different in a constant movement that leads him towards the end of the story. In fact, Pinocchio constantly runs towards his unknown future pursuing freedom and happiness, and his run is accompanied by many transformations that change his body or the way he is perceived by others, namely adults. The only place where he is recognized as a real marionette is inside the Theatre of Stromboli. This acknowledgement happens in chapter X when, after selling his alphabet book for four pences, Pinocchio can buy the ticket for the Grand Puppet Theatre where all the marionettes on stage recognize him as one of their group:

3. Carlo Collodi, *The Adventures of Pinocchio*, ed. by Ann Lawson Lucas (Oxford: Oxford University Press, 2009), p. 170.

> "It's Pinocchio! It's Pinocchio!" shouted all the puppets in chorus, leaping out from the wings. "It's Pinocchio! It's our brother Pinocchio! Long live Pinocchio!". "Pinocchio, come up here with me!" called Harlequin, "come and embrace your wooden brothers and sisters!".[4]

This short episode stands as a special phase of his evolution, included in the story but at the same time independent and concluded: here his real essence and the reasons of his birth are fully recognized by his wooden brothers. Moments later the owner of the theatre, Fire-Eater, interrupts this suspended atmosphere. As a result, he asks him about his Mama and Papa thus restoring Pinocchio's identity and revitalizing his narrative position inside the plot. In this way, Pinocchio can continue his journey and his search, and during his wandering he is caught by a peasant (the puppet is stealing his grapes) who makes him take the place of the watch-dog. This is not a real transformation, rather an adaptation to a role that the puppet performs until he is freed. In another situation, Pinocchio is mistaken for a fish and he runs the risk of being fried in a pan by the green fisherman. But a real transformation, foreshadowing the final one, occurs in the Land of Toys. Pinocchio follows his new friend Candle-Wick to a place where everything is fun and, above all, there is no school. After five months, the first physical transformation takes place showing his ears and a donkey tail growing. This transformation represents an intermediate step between the wooden puppet and the human being, as if the author prepares the reader to accept the idea that Pinocchio becomes a real boy in his final, permanent metamorphosis. In fact, before the final chapter, no transformation in Pinocchio is permanent, there is a constant evolution and involution. The complete and conclusive transformation happens at the end of a dream, as if the character would need a dreamlike preparation to anticipate his real transformation:

> At this point the dream ended and Pinocchio opened his eyes and was wide awake.
> Now you must imagine for yourselves how amazed he was when, on waking, he realized that he was no longer a wooden puppet, but that instead he had become a boy like the others. He glanced about him and instead of the old straw walls of the hut, he saw a lovely bedroom furnished and decorated with an elegant simplicity. Jumping out of his bed, he found laid out ready a fine

4. *Ibid.*, p. 27.

> set of new clothes, a new cap and a pair of leather boots, which all looked splendid on him.[5]

The real boy is ready now to adapt to a new situation, but the change does not just affect his personality and his body. It sounds like a sudden, probably expected, reformation of a social condition. This new condition impacts on the scenario and on Geppetto himself. If at the beginning of the story the house of Geppetto is very poor, dark and cold, the furniture is an awkward chair, an uncomfortable bed and a broken table, at the end of the story the house is described as a place refined with "elegant simplicity" thus corroborating the passage from poverty to middle-class. Geppetto himself is depicted as a poor carpenter at the beginning of the story, while at the end he is described as a wood engraver. According to Angela Jeannet

> what has emerged, in this century of readings, is the ambiguity of the text, rooted in a complex tradition, and also its oneiric quality, its ability to suggest new readings and to reawaken elusive fantasies. The record of diverse readings is at the same time a documentation of the extraordinary changeability of the readers, of their concerns and biases, of their experiences and desires. A fluid panorama then takes shape, centering on the presence of a powerful name: Pinocchio.[6]

Yet, the "fluid panorama" is seldom outlined in a precise and definite way. The characters interact in a setting where they travel through the countryside and the seaside, there is the school and the house of Geppetto. Besides the many historical and biographical references, the story crosses times and cultures in a vivid and adaptable way. As Umberto Eco states, "It must be said that, though written in the nineteenth century, the original children's novel, 'Pinocchio', remains as readable as if it had been written in our century, so limpid and simple in its prose, and so musical in its simplicity".[7] It is probably this fluidity in the text and the metamorphic power of the character that continuously suggests new readings and new adaptations.

5. *Ibid.*, p. 168.

6. Angela M. Jeannet, "Centenary of a Character: Pinocchio", *Italica* 59, 3 (1982), p. 185.

7. Umberto Eco in Carlo Collodi, *Pinocchio*, ed. by Geoffrey Brock, "Introduction" (New York: New York Review Books, 2009), p. X.

4. *Adaptations: The Disney change*

From its publication in the book format in 1883, the novel has become the subject of translations, reductions, abridgments and adaptations to different cultures and media. As Nicolas J. Perella writes, "no other work of Italian literature can be said to approach the popularity *Pinocchio* enjoys beyond Italy's linguistic frontiers where its only rivals – but only among cultivated readers and scholars – are the *Divine Comedy* and *The Prince*".[8] In 1981 the Italian writer Italo Calvino, in an article on the newspaper *La Repubblica*, focuses on the "genetic power" of Pinocchio, whose strength is to create a perpetual cooperation with the reader thus offering the possibility of being analysed, disassembled and reassembled.[9] Rebecca West highlights the characteristic of the puppet of falling and reinventing himself every time, thus giving the idea of a perpetual rebirth.[10]

Besides the elements of high and low culture combined in the story, one of the reasons of the success of Pinocchio is represented by the illustrations that accompany the story form its first issues in the book format that will be an invariable, distinguishing feature of its dissemination in different media. As Nicola De Berti writes, "Pinocchio presents an extreme case of intermediality insofar as Collodi's book itself, due to its multiple illustrated editions, appears from the beginning as a 'multimediatic' text in which word and image are strictly intervowen".[11] One of the first images of the character is drawn by Enrico Mazzanti, whose illustrations emphasize the carnivalesque, gothic aspect of the novel. The second illustrator for the 1901 edition of Pinocchio is Carlo Chiostri, whose images are more elegant and sophisticated than Mazzanti's. Chiostri tries to depict the dreamlike, fantastic ambiance of the story. In 1911 Attilio Mussino renews the collodian iconography stressing the burlesque, joyful side of the puppet and the other characters. He does not try, as Mazzanti and Chiostri, to translate Collodi's

8. Carlo Collodi, *Le Avventure di Pinocchio. The Complete Text in a Bilingual Edition with the Original Illustrations*, ed. by Nicholas J. Perella (Berkeley and Los Angeles: University of California Press, 1986), p. 2.

9. Italo Calvino, "Ma Collodi non esiste", *La Repubblica*, April 19-20, 1981.

10. Rebecca West, "The Persistent Puppet: Pinocchio's Heirs in Contemporary Fiction and Film", *Forum Italicum*, 4 (2006), pp. 103-117.

11. Raffaele De Berti, "Italy and America: Pinocchio's First Cinematic Trip", in *A Companion to Literature and Film*, ed. by Robert Stam and Alessandra Raengo (Malden: Blackwall, 2006), p. 114.

poetry in his drawings, his purpose being that of translating the readers' imagery in his tables.

A general impression about the many representations of the puppet and of the main characters of the story is that, regardless of the copious illustrations that appeared from the end of the 1890s, the imagery of Pinocchio has been strongly reconfigured after the appearance of Disney's version in 1940.[12] Disney is probably inspired by Yasha Frank's version, created for the Federal Theatre Project in 1937 and by the first translations of the book. Frank's character is sweet and naïve, he is accompanied by helpers, like Geppetto and the Fairy Queen, and by opponents, like Fox and Cat. The first translation of the story arrives in the United States in 1892 rendered by Mary Alice Murray and then, six years later, it appears in Boston under the title *Pinocchio's Adventures in Wonderland* taking advantage of the popularity of *Alice's Adventures in Wonderland.* Between 1898 and 1913, many editions of the story are released, with different titles and different sets of illustrations. When Disney meets Pinocchio, a revision of the entire story and of its protagonist has already been conducted by the first American publishers. Even though Disney knows the original story, the representation of its original values, wit and social enquiry needs to be revisited, not to mention the fact that by the time Disney works at his version the story and the character of Pinocchio is deemed available for change. Again, the cultural industry of the Forties and Fifties is partially responsible of this transformation. The American children's market is flourishing after the Second World War and Collodi's novel offers an array of images that can be isolated and adapted to new cultural identities. Various versions of *Pinocchio* appear in those days, issued with rudimental animations and illustrated by pictures, many in the read and colour version. On the one hand, Disney's adaptations are generally inspired by popular books, in particular tales and fairy tales, on the other hand his cinematic versions has an impact on children readings. In fact, many of the books he adapts become in turn the most read books after the conversions. After identifying the source material, Disney changes and redesigns it: Collodi's novel thus becomes a simulacrum filled with new values and ideals. The movie *Saving Mr. Banks* (2013) displays this Disneyan attitude to adaptation and some infidelities to the source text. In that case, an unsatisfied Pamela Lyndon

12. Richard Wunderlicht, Thomas. J. Morissey, *Pinocchio Goes Postmodern: Perils of a Puppet in the United States* (New York and London: Routledge, 2002).

Travers, author of *Mary Poppins*, openly disagrees with the introduction of animated sequences in the movie. However, at the same time, it is the character of the nanny to be modified: though maintaining her zeal, she is depicted like a sort of fairy queen able to interact with animated animals. The same happens to Pinocchio: he is put at the centre of a new world and culture preserving few of the original values.

5. *Disney's imagery*

The Walt Disney rewriting of Pinocchio differs from the source novel in many aspects. He is probably aware that the wooden puppet described by Collodi is not attractive enough to be the protagonist of a children movie: too skinny, mechanical and scary. Also, his mischievious behaviour would not be suitable for Disney's main purpose: to entertain young public. The length and the strength of the Collodian narrative is another problem: Pinocchio runs and jumps from one character to another, and in his constant movement crosses places and times and every chapter ends with a cliff-hanger. The movie sequences are longer and slower, with less characters and some new entries like the cat Figaro and the fish Cleo. The beginning of the movie shows a storybook titled *Pinocchio* among many other objects on Geppetto's desk centred in the frame. The presence of the book suggests the inspirational source of the novel. Pinocchio has a childlike, fully carved aspect: he wears a shirt, a vest, a big bow-tie and a hat with a feather. His aspect is neither scaring nor mechanical, but in the first scene, when he is not animated yet, he has strings connected to a control bar to reinforce the idea that he is a puppet. He is one of the many dolls in Geppetto's house, a hot and bright place full of wall clocks and a myriad of objects. The village is sort of magic, there are not elements revealing an Italian setting. Geppetto is a carpenter, and the blue-haired fairy queen is a tiny blond woman, a mixture of Tinkerbell and Cinderella. She appears the night after the creation of Pinocchio and she transforms him into an animated doll. The dreamlike appearance of the fairy queen connects the story with the end of the original novel: there, in Pinocchio's dream, the character of the fairy queen leaves the story after transforming him into a child. When Pinocchio wakes up he is a boy and the dream is a narrative passageway that allows Collodi to perform the transformation.

In the opening scene, above the book Jiminy Cricket sings *When You Wish Upon a Star* thus introducing another important element of the film: music. The song is awarded an Oscar for best original song the same year and it is after used to introduce the Walt Disney TV show and later to accompany the logos of Walt Disney Pictures and, as John Wills maintains, it "served as a Disneyfied American anthem".[13] Its lyrics stress the importance of hope and positivity in the pursuit of happiness and self-sufficiency, which is the core of the American dream that Walt Disney fully embodies. Born in a poor family, son of a carpenter, he becomes rich and famous through his hard work and then supports his parents. In this family configuration, Disney reads *Pinocchio* and it is fascinated by this story, where he can find some analogies with his own life.

The musical element of Pinocchio is embedded in the story. *When You Wish Upon a Star* plays often in the background and it becomes Jiminy Cricket *leitmotif* while other characters are accompanied by a different theme: Figaro and Cleo are associated to the *Kitten Theme*, while the song that probably best fits Pinocchio's adventure is *I've Got No Strings*, performed in the Stromboli's theatre. The song follows the puppet awareness of being freed from strings, thus becoming autonomous and able to take decisions without the help of adults. After *Snow White* and *Pinocchio*, music and action are the two elements strongly synchronized in Disney's productions. Since then, music becomes an entertaining and identifying element melding popular and classical forms that goes beyond the movies it accompanies, becoming a Disney trade mark on its own.

One of the biggest transformations is represented by Jiminy Cricket. In Collodi the "talking cricket" is not identified with a name, he appears at the beginning of the story and in some other situations as a voice reminding Pinocchio what are the consequences of an insane behaviour: he is killed by the puppet with a mullet at the beginning of the story. Disney humanizes the cricket: he wears a tuxedo jacket, he carries an umbrella and he functions as a storyteller throughout the movie.

Besides Pinocchio, many characters depicted in the book (Geppetto, Cat and Fox, the Cricket, the Fairy Queen, Mangiafuoco-Stromboli) some settings (Geppetto's house, the sea, the house of the Fairy Queen, the Miracle Field, Paese dei Balocchi - Land of Toys) have developed independently through different delivery channels: comics, books, cartoons, movies, TV

13. Jon Willis, *Disney Culture* (Rutgers: Rutgers University Press, 2017), p. 71.

series, video games, music, and a graphic novel where Pinocchio is a robot (the same issue inspired Spielberg's movie *A.I. – Artificial Intelligence*) and more. Apparently, the Disney version represents the starting point of its transmedia storytelling process.

6. *Some re-writings of the story*

It is assumed that Pinocchio lives outside the pages of the *Adventures* and that his migration is partially due to the flexible universe he bears which represents the counterpart of a fixity in popular imagery that accompanies his migration. As Umberto Eco states in his essay *On Literature*, "characters migrate. We can make true statement about literary characters because what happens to them is recorded in a text, and a text is like a musical score. [Some characters] become individuals with a life apart from their original scores, and even those who have never read the archetypal score can claim to make true statements about them".[14] Pinocchio is one of those characters: being part of the collective imagination he has gained a fixity that allows him to continue his run through different media. One of the many forms of the intertextual revisitations is represented by re-writings of the story. Authors like Luigi Malerba, Giorgio Manganelli, Luigi Compagnone and Robert Coover, among others, have tried, each with a different purpose and from a different perspective, to shed light on the many aspects of the source novel through their distinctive and distinguished works. Luigi Malerba and Robert Coover offer two different examples of character migration as long as they foresee a life of Pinocchio beyond the ending written by the author. Malerba's *Pinocchio con gli stivali* (*Pinocchio in Boots*) is based on the migration of Pinocchio from the last chapter of the book into three different fairy tales: *Little Red Riding Hood*, *Cinderella* and *Puss in Boots*. Pinocchio decides that he wants to avoid the tragic ending where he becomes a boy and he enters the three fairy tales with the awareness of being a world-known puppet who deserves a place in a tale. Malerba offers an example of intertextuality mixing the personal adventure of the puppet with other well-known plots and characters that, as well as Pinocchio, have reached an archetypical fixity in popular culture. Similarly, Pinocchio is

14. Umberto Eco, "On Some Functions of Literature", in *On Literature*, ed. by Martin McLaughlin (Orlando, Florida: Harcourt, 2004), pp. 8-9.

depicted in *Shrek* as part of a team of fairy tale characters participating in Shrek's misadventures. He is sold by an old man, most likely Geppetto, and he is one of the helpers of Shrek. In *Shrek 2* he rescues Shrek, Donkey and the white horse from prison thanks to a lie that makes his nose grow. In *Shrek 3*, when Prince Charming tries to discover where Shrek is, his attempt of not lying (due to the awareness that his nose would grow) makes his speech very articulate and verbose. Here he is represented as a wooden puppet with a long nose (very similar to a tree branch) wearing a dress inspired by the Disney version.

In 1991 Robert Coover publishes *Pinocchio in Venice*, a continuation of the source novel where Pinocchio has become an *emeritus* American professor, the esteemed scholar Pinenut, who goes to Venice in order to write the last part of his most important book. As soon as he arrives in Venice, he is immediately involved in a series of misadventures where the old professor is constantly struggling between the good and the bad, meeting a lot of his old friends in a foggy Venice during a sinister Carnival. Coover re-contextualizes the source novel and puts it at the center of a rich intertextual, parodistic structure. The characters that Pinenut meet are almost all derived from Collodi, but their role and their appearance is not compliant to the source novel, thus deforming the overall story. Professor Pinenut makes a journey that connects him to his origin, thus progressively becoming a wooden puppet. The aging professor's flesh progressively decays thus revealing his wooden essence. With Coover's re-writing, the story of Pinocchio comes full circle.

Kristin Stasiowski

A *Divine Comedy* for All Time: Dante's Enduring Relevance for the Contemporary Reader

When Giovanni Boccaccio began the first series of public lectures on the *Divine Comedy* in the fall of 1373, Dante effectively became a pop icon. Known as the "Expositions on the *Divine Comedy*" Boccaccio's eloquent, impassioned and contemporary insights into the myth and meaning of Dante's epic poem translated for the first time the often opaque and ineffable aspects of the *Comedy* to a public eager to be entertained, if not enlightened. For over 700 years, the fascination with Dante's work has endured as has its status as a work for all seasons. In this sense, both contemporary and popular, the *Divine Comedy* can lay claim to a certain "timelessness" in its relevance as a "classic" and poignancy in its ability to speak to the immediacy of the world today. Therefore, to speak of the *Divine Comedy* as popular culture or to study the impact of the *Comedy* on popular culture is not wholly original in scope.

After seven centuries of commentary, criticism, cataloging and study, there are innumerable references to the many ways in which the *Divine Comedy* has produced dividends in the many "popular" cultures of history. Amilcare Iannucci's volume *Dante in Cinema and Television*[1] provides an extraordinary account of the *Comedy*'s impact on and dissemination through the world of cinema and television. Bowdoin College maintains a website dedicated to pop culture references to Dante that include everything from "Dante's Inferno balls" – a cinnamon spice candy – to Legos fashioned after the levels of Hell. *The Poet's Dante* speaks to the influence of Dante's masterwork on every great poet and writer from Petrarch to Byron and T.S.

1. *Dante, Cinema and Television*, ed. by Amilcare Iannucci (Toronto: University of Toronto Press, 2004).

Eliot; Dan Brown too has rebaptised Dante with his bestselling thriller: *Inferno*. Whether Hannibal Lector lectures in Florence on Pier della Vigna in the movie *Hannibal*[2] or Matthew Pearl reinvents Dante's sins in the context of *The Dante Club*, or *Criminal Minds*[3] features serial killers with Dantesque motives, one is certain to see Dante everywhere – especially in a 21st century global culture as fractious, contentious and commercialized as Dante's medieval Florence. All of these references speak to the impact that Dante's poem can have and has had on generations of artists, intellects and readers of all kinds. Simply put, it stirs the imagination to wonder and inspires both creative and academic endeavor and inquiry.

Therefore, scholarship can easily account for the many "texts" that have redesigned, recreated and reproduced "divine comedies" in response to Dante, but rarely outside the classroom has Dante's text been discussed for its implicit relevance to today on its own terms. Or, put in another way: to introduce the great themes, lessons and subjects of the *Divine Comedy* as "culture" for the popular issues of today. Let me be clear, the lessons of the *Divine Comedy* are always relevant to whichever epoch embraces the text. Pride, envy and lust are as eternally tempting as is the inevitable "fall" into despair as a result of following those passions; human habit may change; human nature not at all. There is, however, something *more* to the ever-contemporary nature of Dante's *Divine Comedy* which renders it truly powerful in its popularity and that lifts it from the sea of academic obscurity that threatens always to consume it. Rendering the culture of the *Comedy* in terms familiar to today's students and resonant with today's issues is as critical now as it would have been for Boccaccio's assembled Florentine audience at La Badia Fiorentina.

1. *A context for the* Comedy*: Making Dante "pop" in the classroom*

There is an awesome shock value in telling students that you "teach" Hell. It is a little more confusing when you say that you teach the *Inferno*

2. Dino De Laurentis (Producer), Ridley Scott (Director), *Hannibal*, motion picture (United States: MGM, 2001).

3. Janine S. Barrois (Writer), Karen Gaviola (Director), "Burn", television episode, in Mark Gordon (Executive Producer), *Criminal Minds* (California: Columbia Broadcast System, 2014).

and even more dubious when you confirm that the subject is really the *Divine Comedy*. Naturally, most American students who know of the *Divine Comedy* rightly assume that Dante's great poem will be read in English translation – few universities dare to offer the course to undergraduates in the original medieval Italian. Yet, despite myriad, excellent translations available to the modern American reader, the problem of translating the *meaning* of the poem has churned inside cinderblock classrooms like a restless grindstone mill-loud, constant, whittling. For contextual answers or historical relevance, scholars have amassed libraries of notes, supporting texts and critical volumes. Even the great Italian filmmaker and comedian Roberto Benigni has made an art out of drawing parallels between Dante's poem and today's contemporary world of sinful "characters" from politicians to soccer stars.[4] Though each of these approaches to teaching Dante is revelatory and therefore instructive, teaching the poem exclusively in historical context, or teaching it using modern-day stand-ins for Farinata degli Uberti or Paolo and Francesca can fall entirely short of communicating to the average student the true "relatability" of Dante's worldview and the inherent relevance of the *Divine Comedy*'s scope and power. If there is something everlasting about the *Divine Comedy*, it must be in the acuity of Dante's moral reasoning as applied to the *universality* of human frailty. But, how in a pluralistic, morally relevant, atheistic world can the sins of medieval, Christian Europe be understood as pertinent to contemporary discourse both in and outside of the classroom for students of all backgrounds?

2. *Beyond* Terza Rima*: Translating the* Comedy*'s culture for the contemporary reader*

Two examples drawn from the *Inferno* illustrate the way that the *Divine Comedy* can be instrumental in evoking relevant, pertinent conversations in regard to various aspects of 21st century economic, intellectual and creative affairs. The first example in regard to the economic climate of today can be found in *Inferno XIX* in which Dante writes of the Simonists. Secondly, in regard to the limits and boundaries of intellectual life, *Inferno XXVI* offers both a thematic and stylistic contrast in the form of Ulysses and the False

4. See Roberto Benigni, *Tutto Dante*, live performance in Piazza Santa Croce, Florence.

Counselors. Both *canti*, though different in scope and theme, represent a small sample of the many *canti* of the *Divine Comedy* that offer resonant ideas, questions and frameworks for a modern audience. Each of these two *canti* bridge the inherent gap between the medieval context in which they were written and the modern world in which they are now read. The difficulty of rendering these *canti* accessible to the modern reader abounds, but their inherent power is still derived from their enduring relevance.

One of the most challenging chapters of the *Inferno*, from this standpoint, is *Canto XIX* – the Simonists. "O Simon Magus" begins the *canto*, "and you his wretched followers, who, rapacious, prostitute for gold and silver the things of Go".[5] The first question any student would have is about Simon Magus himself. Who is he? What did he do? What offence has he levied against God? The reference, of course, is to a magician who was so impressed by the apostles – Peter and John – that he wishes to become like them. Simon witnessed Peter and John perform miracles through the Holy Spirit and he interpreted their fantastical acts not to be the stuff of faith, but rather of learned skill or trickery. He approached the apostles and asked to be given the secret to their magic. Naturally, the apostles refused to speak of the matter in those terms – insisting that the Holy Spirit alone was the cause of their blessed gifts. So, believing that Peter and John must simply be offered a more lucrative deal in exchange for their trade secret, Simon offered to *pay* them. This offer – the suggestion by Simon that Peter and John *sell* their knowledge or power for a price – is the offence for which Simon Magus is dutifully punished in Hell – his name now eponymous with the sin of simony. At this point in the *canto*, the students are amused if not intrigued – they like stories after all. But, they are certainly not enlightened. "Why does it matter that he wanted to buy a set of skills from the men?" they often object. "It doesn't make any sense; shouldn't a magician have the right to invest financially in his trade?" the business majors point out. The usual response to Dante's condemnation of the Simonists – Pope's who bought and sold "treasures" (offices) of the Church – is first confusion and then apathy: "Whatever. It's a medieval poem and Dante was pissed at everyone", they shrug. The issue of the Simonists seems just too arcane; too contextual to Dante's historical period; too "unrelatable" to offer anything culturally significant for students today.

5. Dante Aligheri, *The Divine Comedy*, Translation by John D. Sinclair (Oxford: Oxford University Press, 1961), lines 1-5.

The instructional choice is clear: either teach the historical/literary context and aim for comprehension as a purely academic exercise, or focus on the violence of the punishment in the vein of *Assassin's Creed* and let the "popular" kill the "culture". There is instead a middle way.

Michael J. Sandel's book *What Money Can't Buy: Moral Markets and the Economy* offers a critical perspective on the challenges inherent in market based economic exchanges absent of any moral or ethical guidance. He posits that most 21st century consumers care not for any moral or ethical connection to economic exchanges and that money – in and of itself – has become an absolute value. He writes:

> [...] A growing number of countries around the world embraced market mechanisms in the operations of their economies, something else was happening. Market values were coming to play a greater role in social life. Economics was becoming an imperial domain. Today, the logic of buying and selling no longer applies to material goods alone but increasingly governs the whole of life.[6]

In this new age, which he terms "the era of market triumphalism" he argues that in our need to foster a robust free market economy we have abandoned every moral law that would govern the choices that we make about what we purchase and how we purchase it. He provides a compelling list of "things" upon which a price has been placed; things that can be purchased for a value established by the market alone: "the right to emit a metric ton of carbon into the atmosphere"; "the right to shoot an endangered rhino"; "a prison cell upgrade" and so on. He cites numerous examples of market-driven exchanges of products, services and experiences where *everything* is for sale. "To contend with this condition", Sandel writes, "we need to do more than inveigh against greed; we need to rethink the role that markets should play in our society. We need a public debate about what it means to keep markets in their place. To have this debate, we need to think through the moral limits of markets. We need to ask whether there are some things *money should not buy*" (italics mine).[7]

The moral value of markets is a question that would have resonated very clearly for a medieval, Florentine, mercantile community steeped in the ethical code of a Christian worldview and its belief about the role and

6. Michael J. Sandel, *What Money Can't Buy: The Moral Limits of Markets* (New York: Farrar, Straus and Giroux, 2012), p. IV.

7. *Ibid.*, p. V.

function of commercial enterprise. What in Sandel's philosophy seems to be a great return to values was, in fact, the abiding standard of desired moral conduct in Dante's time: money should not be the ends and the means of moral life and not *everything* should be for sale.

Dante's Simonists are sinners subject to a moral authority that allowed for no ambiguity as it regarded market-based exchanges of "things" that were really not to be considered "things" at all. Those who would defile the core spiritual values of the Church by selling indulgences were acting against the accepted code of ethics that separated spiritual and economic transactions. It was inherently wrong (sinful) to take something divine and to reduce it to a commodity that could be bought and sold: "to prostitute for gold and silver the things of God". Peter and John were offended so by Simon Magus precisely because of this: their "magic" was not of this Earth and therefore not subject to the laws (or markets) of men. The suggestion that the Holy Spirit could be "bought" as though it were a commodity was the ultimate intrusion of a commercial mindset on a spiritual plane. We are tempted, as modern readers, still to ask ourselves, "what's the big deal?". Yet, Sandel argues that we do in fact have an inherent moral compass of what is right and wrong to sell; that we, like Peter and John, would also take offense at certain financial transactions. He argues that just because I *can* sell you my kidney doesn't mean that I *should.* Or, to put it another way, if everything is for sale and two partners agree, would it be *wrong* to sell you my child? Dante would not prevaricate. His medieval mindset is decidedly modern in this case: it is *wrong* to sell certain things. And it is *wrong* to purchase them. We should be outraged.

This is both the modern *and* the popular aspect of the *Divine Comedy* that is often overlooked and underappreciated. When students come to understand the significance of Simon's sin in the context of contemporary economics they also come to appreciate Dante's anger and condemnation of his peers and the institutions they represented in medieval Italy. They feel a deep stirring of emotion inside of them when confronted by the pathos of unchecked greed. Suddenly, the punishment of sinners in this circle – that they should be buried upside down – seems appropriate, not simply violent or retributive: in a world where money and greed reign supreme, everything is upside down. Students are finally moved to speak; they want to say something. And Dante gives them the words when he furnishes his pilgrim with a vitriolic reply to the Simonists he sees buried upside down in ditches with the soles of their feet on fire: "[…] thou art rightly punished [...] for your avarice afflicts the world, trampling on the good and exalting the wicked".[8] Dante sounds "badass" as he calls out the evil money grubbers before him and the students then realize that Dante has given them a voice. And the *Comedy* is their story too; that it can address with passion and acuity the pressing issues of today.

The *Canto of Ulysses* provides a similar challenge to the modern reader – and likewise a similar intellectual catharsis. Dante provides a portrait of Ulysses that differs dramatically from the one with which modern students are familiar – the Homeric hero about whom they have read in the *Odyssey*. Dante's rendering of Ulysses in the context of the *Comedy* represents an invented or extended version of Ulysses that he saw as crucial to his poetic and spiritual project; it was no mere recounting of the Greek hero's life and adventures. The central issue presented by Dante's idea of Ulysses' sin is one of excess of knowledge; knowledge beyond borders. When Dante reaches the circle of the False Counsellors in *Canto XXVI*, he must follow Virgil down into the Eighth *bolgia*. He writes: "I grieved then and grieve now anew when I turn my mind to what I saw, and more than I am wont I curb my powers lest they run where virtue does not guide them".[9]

Dante opens this *canto* by setting up a great dichotomy between archetypal figures such as Icarus or Prometheus – each who sought knowledge and power beyond their reach – and himself. As he is about to interview Ulysses and discover why he has been placed in this circle of Hell, Dante stops short and "curbs [his] powers" – tempering his writerly genius – in an attempt to avoid the disastrous fate met by both the figures of Icarus and Prometheus. Dante warns the reader that he too is tempting fate by recounting in a poem the never-before-seen world of Hell. Could he perhaps be another Icarus or Prometheus? What might he share with us that we as readers should not know? And yet here again, in a world of stem cell research and exploration of Mars, how does one find a correlation between the sins of Dante's medieval mindset and the much-praised of scientific exploration. Is not the search for new knowledge and the urge to peel back the curtain (as in the *Wizard of Oz*),[10] not the goal of 21st century living? Certainly, students can understand that Dante's worldview is formed by

8. Dante Aligheri, *The Divine Comedy*, lines 100-109.

9. *Ibid.*, lines 19-22.

10. Mervin LeRoy (Producer), Victor Fleming (Director), *The Wizard of Oz*, motion picture (United States: Loew's Inc., 1939).

Christian spirituality and the "tree of knowledge"; Adam and Eve punished for eating of the forbidden fruit. But what of Ulysses? Is he but a Greek version of that same story somehow? And even if he were to be, what remains for the student of Dante to understand about the limits he places on what we are to know? Is this *canto* nothing more than a message in a bottle from a time long since made irrelevant?

As Dante the pilgrim interacts with Ulysses he learns that after departing from Circe, Ulysses convinces his crew to continue their journey onward. Encouraging them through his bold discourse and fervent entreaties, he asks of them that they pursue the world beyond the Strait of Gibraltar which then would have represented the end of the known world – "it remains to us [...] not to deny experience, in the sun's track, of the unpeopled world".[11] In a modern context, this makes Ulysses the epitome of forward thinking; a James T. Kirk of the ancient world. How and why, then, does Dante place him in such a low circle of Hell with other False Counselors? Why was his rousing speech to his fellow sailors seen by Dante to be such an affront to the proper, moral use of reasoning and rhetoric? A student once commented, "If Dante were alive today, he'd have condemned half of America over the Freedom of Information Act". Why is having access to knowledge so wrong?

It seems obvious to students that Dante was working from a different playbook when he condemns Ulysses; they accept very easily that today's world is no longer like his and that great powers like the Church or the Holy Roman Emperor no longer have exclusive access to everything that is knowable. They take for granted that the "yesterday" of the *Divine Comedy* is nothing like their today – and *that* is where the power of this *canto* truly lies. While scholars are keen to discuss the issues of rhetoric, the real issues of *what should be known* and *who should have access to information* are perhaps the most pressing issues in *Canto XXVI and* of the post-WikiLeaks world of today. Here again, students of Dante are confronted with the difficulty of questions with no easy answers. Dante's text raises the issues posed by knowledge beyond limits not by asking *if* or *for whom* certain types of things should or should not be known. Rather, the punishment stands for the question. Students must come to question the idea of what truly represents the "sin" by recoiling at the idea of the punishment for something that – to them – seems like it should not be punished. It is as

11. Dante Aligheri, *The Divine Comedy*, lines 115-117.

though this *canto* implies a question rather than states one, as if *on purpose.* It is as if to pose a question is the very sin Dante wishes to have us avoid as it would lead to answers, and then to knowledge. And there is something volatile and unstable about knowledge; something uncontrollable. To a student today, therefore, the initial confusion of this *canto* is actually an aide to understanding. The questions they ask about this *canto*: "Why is this sinner being punished?"; "Why is knowledge so bad?" make the student reflect on their own biases about sharing or concealing information. The responsibility of information sharing is also something about which they are keenly aware – and about which this canto offers a stern warning. Just as Ulysses' men were drowned, so too can a society submit to the effects of information without borders as Assange well knows.

These two examples from the *Divine Comedy* are the cornerstone of a way to understand Dante that transcends the standard approach to both scholarship and teaching. The temptation with the *Divine Comedy* – and with many literary works deemed to be "classics" – is that they either remain rooted in the local, specific, culturally remote contexts of their time or they are used as examples of the universality of human emotion, thought, and belief. These "classical" texts are therefore texts both *of* a time and *for all* time. Dante's *Divine Comedy* clearly fits this categorization; its medieval core at once as strange and distant from us as pride, lust and greed are familiar. It is both very much drawn from the unique particularities of medieval Florence *and* representative of universal and communal human preoccupations and values. It belongs as much to its own time as it does to ours. From this standpoint, Dante's *Comedy* is every bit a "pop culture" *tour de force* for the 21st century; it has the capacity to lift itself from the past and make itself relevant to the culture of today; it is still read for entertainment and mined for enduring lessons about our humanity.

That said, the definition of the *Divine Comedy* as "pop culture" still must be qualified. Is it enough to suggest that performing a Shakespearean play in a 21st century Central Park makes Shakespeare a pop culture icon for today? Is it accurate to think that because you can purchase a Disney comic book where Mickey Mouse is Dante that Dante has attained a new status of importance as a literary figure? Can we really just extrapolate Dante from his time and the *Divine Comedy* from its context and say something profound about the nature of popular culture icons and great texts?

Quite fittingly, the standard approaches to dealing with the *Divine Comedy* from this standpoint usually fall into three categories: the historical-literary context of the medieval world of Dante; Dante as a pop culture icon for any century and the new ways in which the *Divine Comedy* appears in new media; and the teaching model that praises (and uses) Dante to comprehend universal themes and ideas seen as quintessentially human and therefore endless and enduring. All three models, while dutifully exploring and in some cases even extending our understanding of the meaning and relevance of the *Divine Comedy* fall short of embracing the broader and more subtle brilliance of Dante's masterwork as a text of a time *and* for all time at the *same* time.

Once again, take the example of the Simonists. The historical, literary and theological context for that *canto* can reveal for a student of Dante the crucial background needed for understanding Dante's fury at the Popes that so easily corrupted their church and their faith; the hypocrisy of being the guardians of all that is eternal, blessed and sacred while secretly dealing in the most earthly and sinister markets of medieval commercial gain. The appreciation of the theological and moral error goes a long way to supporting a reading of Dante that is at once fundamental to his own medieval Christianity and to his deeply rooted political convictions. Yet oftentimes, the necessary contextual work leaves Dante in the past and disallows for a reading of his critical and immediate relevance today.

We turn rather, using the same example, to what *could* be relevant today: greed. Teachings on the Simonists make Dante's treatment of them "relevant" through the suggestion that greed was no different in the Middle Ages than it would be today on Wall Street. Where Dante might have found fault with Popes – authority figures of a massive faith "industry" – we find parallels with the scions of finance and subprime mortgage debt. Greed is bad. It was bad yesterday; it is bad today. Dante just pointed our noses in it and made us reckon with it through a "close a reading". Yet, is that the real power of Dante's poem? That he catalogues examples of human wretchedness and gives us a literary model to cite when looking upon our contemporary world of upside-down morals? Does that explain the resurgence of interest in *Comedy*?

What of pop culture, then? Matthew Pearl, author of *The Dante Club*, wrote his novel set in 19th century Boston during the years in which Longfellow translated the *Comedy* for the first time into English. Naturally, a series of striking murders resembling punishments found in Dante's *Inferno* form the backbone of the narrative arc in the novel. Dante's punishments in Hell are, after all, stunningly violent. Pearl includes the punishment of the Simonists – being upside down with their feet on fire – as one of the early homicides; the shock value of the gore is enough to pull in the reader and weave a tale of deception and murder. And the reader is naturally impressed with Dante's almost "cinematic" flair for the horrid and ghastly. Dante, after all, in his infinite imagination, draws the modern reader in with what appears to be familiar to any fan of television, film or video games: "R" rated images. You need neither context, nor universal themes to make Dante popular in this manner; Dante's brand of violence is enough on its own as a subject of great interest and entertainment. The punishment of the Simonists is mild, if violent; modern "audiences" would no doubt recoil – and yet relish – the scenes of cannibalism that appear in later sections of the *Comedy.* Dante then – is he popular now because the typology of his violence can be extrapolated from the text and reused in new stories?

Each of these readings or uses of the *Divine Comedy* – historical, universal, and pop culture/new media – are illustrative; each of them communicate different aspects of the text to new audiences and underscore Dante's importance and centrality as a cultural figure. Yet, insofar as these readings delve deep into the meaning of the *Divine Comedy*, they do so only from within the shallow confines of their respective methodologies. For Dante to be seen as both popular and cultural; both of and for all time, a reading that transcends all three of these silos of understanding must take place.

The real power of *Canto XIX* and the Simonists is *not* in the lessons of medieval politics and economics as gleaned from context, nor is it in the universal condemnation of greed – nor in the extrapolated scenes of violence that appeal to readers looking for a thrill. The real power of the *Comedy* is found once we can unlock its quintessential and always relevance *method* of interpretation; the realization that the medieval lessons of a world gone mad *are* the very lessons that still matter.

Most of all, the very fact that the *Divine Comedy* still matters is a matter unto itself. Giovanni Boccaccio could only hope that his attempts to bring Dante to the people of Florence would have resulted in some modest comprehension and appreciation of the enduring brilliance of the author and inherent value of his masterwork. He could not have known that his lectures and commentary on Dante would launch a posthumous career that brings us time and time again to appreciate that there is more that unites us than what divides us. His language has become *our* language – no matter what language we speak.

BERNARDO VALLI

Italy and the Search for Modernity: At the Origins of *Made in Italy*

1. *Devastation, reconstruction and recovery*

> The Italian twentieth century, at least its first part, was a century of iron and fire, an era without equal in other European countries. We fought in the front lines in two world wars: in the Alps, Africa, Russia, the Balkans, the Mediterranean and the Atlantic. We ended the second in the country's disaster and dissolution of the State, a tragedy ending the cycle started with the unification. We created a class struggle, with the traits of a real civil war.[1]

This is how Aldo Schiavone describes Italy in the early part of the 20th century, a country that reached 1945 defeated and destroyed. What was evident after 1945, in addition to pervasive moral and political disaster, was the enormity of the damage that had affected our manufacturing facilities. The numbers spoke clearly; they reached 3.200 billion lire, which reliable estimates attributed to war damage.[2] Roads, bridges, aqueducts and other public works were razed, along with a large number of houses. Among the most ravaged productive sectors was the Merchant Navy, which was almost totally destroyed. This loss was particularly relevant since, prior to World War II, the Italian Merchant Marine had occupied sixth place in the world, with 772 vessels and 3,4 million gross tons.

The same thing happened to the aviation sector; it was particularly affected, in addition to losses due to the war, by production limitations imposed by the Armistice terms. The railways were devastated; two-thirds

1. Ernesto Galli della Loggia, Aldo Schiavone, *Pensare l'Italia* (Turin: Einaudi, 2011), p. 18.

2. Pasquale Saraceno, *Ricostruzione e pianificazione, 1943-1948* (Milan: Giuffré-Svimez, 1974), p. 218.

of the nation's rolling stock was out of operation along with 47% of the buildings and a quarter of the tracks, while the railway network concession was reduced to about 4,700 kilometers, compared with 8,603 before the war. In the mechanical sector, damages, although enormous, were quite contained, being greater in the South and lower in the North, where most companies were based. Even that figure needs interpretation; we must consider the fact that there had been a significant expansion of activities in this area during the war. At the war's end, the production of weapons could no longer be continued due to limitations imposed by the peace treaty. The situation was particularly difficult as, having lost off-shore resources, we faced a surplus of manpower that could not be used elsewhere. The country's severe lack of raw materials and energy effectively blocked any activity.

The automotive sector, represented mainly by Fiat, the most important player on the market, was in great difficulty. There was a long-standing shortage of raw or semi-finished materials and it was necessary to rebuild the devastated factories. Even if these issues were eventually resolved with the help of the Americans, for the Turin automaker, the problem related to the reorganization of production remained; namely, the reorganization of processes within company regulations.

IRI's situation was very difficult; this was the state company involved in the steel and mechanical industry and in shipyards, which had suffered because of their involvement in the war, bombing damage, which had destroyed much of the shipyards, mechanical, electric and telephone facilities. The Institute was also at the center of a fiery debate among those opposed to government intervention in the economy and those who sought more realistically to resolve problems within the existing dimension. Eventually a plan was launched for Finsider's reconstruction, better known as the "Sinigaglia Plan", pursued with great vigor by Oscar Sinigaglia, its historic and illustrious president. This plan called for significant increases in production at lower costs to bring the Italian mechanical industry to the level of more developed countries of the West. This plan was blocked, at least initially, by most of the private industry, in particular by Assolombarda and its chairman John Falk, who had interest in defending the present situation, based on production that was not supposed to exceed 2,5 million tons of steel. In this position, paradoxically, even the CGIL and some workers' unions came together, fearing trouble from an employment point of view. By the Fifties, this was all over; internal conflicts and American resistance had calmed, and in the wake of the funding arriving from overseas, the

Italian steel sector developed significantly, simultaneously the rise of the mechanical industry, led by the automotive sector.

After the war, conflict flared up over another area vital for the revival of the Country, which was energy. In particular, Ente Petrolifero di Stato (the government oil agency) was born in 1926, but it never took off permanently. After 1945, it suffered a great deal of major damage and especially the loss of plants built in the overseas territories. One of the main actors of this contention was Enrico Mattei, who would soon become one of the most illustrious stars of the country's revival. This resident of Marche, already a partisan fighter, would become the champion of all-out defense of Italy's energy independence and then of the survival of the national petroleum agency. Lined along the front against him were the international oil cartel, electrical groups that wanted to use natural gas to fuel power stations, and some liberal economists. Mattei, after getting excellent results in the discovery of deposits, reached its goal of strengthening the public presence in the fuel sector, establishing ENI in 1953.

The situation in the electricity sector was quite different; the force of the monopoly groups was crucial to block every attempt at reform. Also in the agricultural sector, the war had brought sweeping devastation, involving especially rural houses, orchards, crops and facilities used to produce income. These included cheese factories, wine cellars, oil mills, irrigation systems and substations with damage estimated at around 400 billion. Immediately after the war, the Italian government decided to intervene in the agriculture sector to remedy the enormous war damages, but also to respond to the massive unemployment problem.

Another critical aspect of these years was inflation, which had reached high enough levels to cause the allies to issue currency. This Am-lira (Allied Military Currency) flooded the market, causing a serious imbalance. The establishment of the *cento lire* (one hundred lira) against the dollar worsened the situation, increasing the price of imported products and those useful for the population's survival. At the same time, the inflation advantage was eliminated, leaving little opportunity to export abroad since the country had difficulty producing.

In such a situation, the Government action did not go beyond momentary emergency interventions; in addition to enabling a normal flow of supplies for basic needs, it enacted blockage of layoffs, wages and prices. It also promoted measures to stamp out the black market, managing to locate refugees and give proper accommodation to veterans from the war.

The United States gave Italy the chance in late 1944 to import raw materials and machinery for an estimated amount of approximately 130 million dollars. This was a breath of fresh air, in particular to address the most relevant emergencies in the central-southern regions. Despite everything, the postwar years were marked by serious problems concerning the lack of raw materials. Particularly in 1946, the insufficient amount of coal and electricity heavily influenced the country's productive activity. This was a situation that united nearly all production sectors with only half availability of useful raw materials for production, with the exception of the wool and cotton sectors, where supplies were fairly regular. In the textile industry, the productive apparatus had not suffered significant losses, and thanks to tax and foreign exchange and low labor costs, it took off with vigor, taking advantage of the favorable conditions of the international market in which there was good demand.

In 1947, many difficulties associated with procurement of raw materials were overcome, while the country's production capacity was back to satisfactory levels, if not similar to those of the pre-war period.

2. *Italy during the second postwar: Catholics, Communists and Americans*

Meanwhile, with the formation of the fourth De Gasperi government, conditions were created for a political and economic turnaround that saw Luigi Einaudi as the major protagonist. In the very problematic phase immediately after the war, faced with the need to rebuild the productive and industrial infrastructure, at the brink of deficit in a situation of rampaging inflation, various economists addressed the problem of what to do. The fundamental issue was how to deal with the reconstruction; it was possible to implement planning by intervening through Keynesian theories or favoring liberal theories and freeing the market. Liberals, highlighting the superiority of the free market, were for the abolition of all government controls, while the other side wanted to adopt an investment planning policy for private initiatives to interact with those of the State.

Behind these positions, it was not hard to glimpse a subdivision that was due largely to the two dominant economic cultures at that time, Catholic Italy and Marxism. However, between '45 and '47, through a path that was not always consistent and linear, a liberal choice increasingly consolidated to guide reconstruction. This was identified in the policy proposed by De

Gasperi to exclude the Left from the Government, aiming to close one stage and open another. He wanted to leave behind the time when a defeated and poor Italy attempted to reposition itself in the international arena by seeking acceptance from important entities. In particular, the Italian statesman, with his repeated trips to the United States, worked to rebuild a relationship of uneasy subjection to the great American nation that, having won the war, had every reason to consider the Italians as losers. In reality, the choice of excluding the Left from the Government, which took place on May 31, 1947, was the final act of a long problematic phase between the Government of the United States and the Vatican, which saw in the Italian Communist Party as a severe threat because of its close relations with Stalin's Soviet Union.

This aspect of the presence of the strongest European Communist Party in Italy is crucial to understanding the evolution of relationships between the United States and Italy. As can be seen from the large amount of documents that Nico Perrone presents in his book *De Gasperi e l'America* (*De Gasperi and America*, 1995), little benefit came from the cry of pain that Alberto Tarchiani, the Italian Ambassador to the USA, expressed with one of his writings on July 6, 1945 to President Truman. In it, as reported by Perrone in the text cited above, stated: "My country relies on the human solidarity of America and the clear sense of Justice from its President (and after a memorandum of six folders divided into eight points, the spirit of which can be summed up as follows). Italy is a poor country, lacking essential commodities".[3]

This attitude of the main Italian diplomat in the United States is a striking exemplification of the situation in which Italian diplomacy would operate. Perhaps our pleas would not have found such an ample response from across the Atlantic, if other much more important issues had not come into play. "Our requests for aid will break through, not for similar reasons, but only when the political expediency of creating a strong anti-Communist front in Italy will guide the United States to a different interest in our country".[4] However we judge this attitude of the United States toward Italy, it led to some decisive steps in the direction of Italian reintegration into the international forum.

3. Nico Perrone, *De Gasperi e l'America: un dominio pieno e incontrollato* (Palermo: Sellerio, 1995), p. 16.

4. *Ibid*., p. 17.

After De Gasperi's famous trip to America in 1947 and subsequent ouster of the left from the Government, on June 5, the US Secretary of State George C. Marshall announced the American support plan for the European Renaissance. The following year, Italy entered OEEC in NATO in 1949; in 1951 in CECA and in 1952 in CED. George C. Marshall announced the European Recovery Program (ERP); e.g. the aid program to Europe, on the occasion of receiving an honorary doctorate in law from the University of Harvard. This would have very important consequences for Europe and Italy in particular.

According to this program, the United States would appropriate 13,5 billion dollars over four years to 16 European Nations, with the stated goal of promoting reconstruction of those countries and raising a barrier to the Communist advance on the old continent. In July of that year, a Conference was held in Paris to organize the Marshall Plan. Invitations went, in addition to the sixteen countries, to the Soviet Union, Czechoslovakia, Hungary and Poland; for obvious reasons, they declined. Today, studies about this period of history agree, albeit in a varied manner, with the judgment that the Marshall Plan was instrumental in Italy's economic recovery and the subsequent "boom", but gaining membership to it was not an easy step.

Between 1948 and 1951, our country gained eleven percent of the amounts paid by the plan, or 1.470 million dollars, and 230 billion lire of loans through IMI, which went mainly to the iron and steel, oil, chemical, mechanical, and electrical sectors. One element that differed greatly from other aid for the Plan before funding arrived from across the Atlantic was that while the original funds immediately after the war were intended mainly to provide food and raw materials, a major part of Marshall Plan funds were destined for modernization of industrial plants.

The funds were decisive for the renovation and reconstruction of our country's manufacturing facilities, but also had considerable impact on the balance of external accounts. Industries such as the automotive sector and its associated steel and the electric, chemical and textile industries received a majority of the IMI-ERP loans. These, although well supported nationally and internationally, unequivocally made a great contribution to the national economy from the perspective of exports. This in turn allowed the purchase of raw materials on the international market, including cotton and food products.

The boost to exports was very important for the development of *made in Italy* products in international markets. Meanwhile, from a political point of view, the Marshall Plan as a whole gave a stronger internal and international legitimacy to the country's government, which was based on the center. Beyond the opposing factions active in Italian politics of the time, divided between supporters and those in opposition to the Marshall Plan, and the general caution with which historians have evaluated its impact on Italy, industrial production growth in the period from 1948 to 1951 is also considered. This data clearly cannot be taken as absolute or extrapolated from everything else. It is not possible to identify

> a clear demonstration of the Marshall plan playing a major and decisive role in the economic dimensions of the period in which it was implemented. There is no doubt, however, that it created multiple long-term effects, exceeding the few hundred million dollars made available by the Foreign Assistance Act of 1948. In terms of economic structures, it resulted in implementing and changing the way of thinking that it introduced.[5]

Clearly, with the Marshall Plan, the United States managed to strongly affect most of the economies of the countries concerned, in turn forcing acceptance of unsolicited goods and products that Europe neither possessed nor needed. The case of cotton for Italy is an example, but the same thing happened with tobacco, condensed milk, fresh and dried fruits, all products that the United States was interested in exporting.

In deciding to promote the Marshall Plan:

> The crucial advantage sought by the United States was acceleration of the reconstruction, weakening of the political left and the transformation of European economies debilitated in the international capitalist system. The United States specifically intended for this transformation to result in an increase in production, use of raw materials from the United States, use of capital instruments, the introduction of higher living standards, containment of inflation, wider employment, and increased exports. This in turn allowed an improvement in the balance of payments and a more competitive economy. American interests in the years of the Marshall plan coincided, in the upper echelons of politics, with the way the Italian Government defined its interests. The process itself, to offer help and to ask Europeans to make their requests, tended to bring Socialists, Centrists and conservatives to join the Coalition because they shared a common economic vision. At the same time,

5. Paolo Savona, "La stabilizzazione monetaria in Italia ed il Piano Marshall", in *Il Piano Marshall e l'Europa*, ed. by Elena Agata Rossi (Rome: Istituto Poligrafico dello Stato, 1983), p. 188.

this process excluded the Communists who were considered a very serious political threat in the light of the developing cold war.[6]

In line with this perspective, one can also say that as a whole the Marshall Plan, beyond its material existence, which was not insignificant, became an extraordinary propaganda tool. Americans in fact were quite concerned with publicizing the whole operation, with every hundredth ship in a different Italian port, organizing appropriate celebrations and special "friendship trains" that stopped along the way at various stations to distribute the goods. The American Ambassador in Rome, James Dunn, never missed an opportunity to make a political speech, highlighting the relevance of the plan with all those gifts made by the United States to the "free world" and in the specific case to Italy and the Christian Democrats who, in our country, represented the "American party".[7]

The ERP was, very briefly, a plan for free transfer of goods from the United States. This was updated annually based on a list of requests that European countries made through a four-year development plan. The sale of these assets on individual national markets gave rise to a national currency fund for use agreed between the US Government and each country. Between the summer of 1947 and the summer of 1948, Italy had to provide a multiannual plan, which focused on investment mainly in metallurgical and energy (petroleum and electricity) communications, and transport (60%), allocating just 29% to agriculture.

3. *Fiat and Olivetti: The beginning of* made in Italy

In this perspective, metallurgy played a very important role; it was the Government's intention to create three integrated plants to produce steel cheaply for mechanics. To accomplish this, the famous Sinigaglia Plan[8] was implemented. This reopened the never entirely dormant conflict between public and private steel industry and disputes with other European manufacturers. These, considering Italy a target market, did not look kindly

6. Nicola White, *Ricostruire la moda italiana. Il ruolo chiave degli Stati Uniti d'America nello sviluppo del sistema industriale del Made in Italy* (Monza: Deleyva Editore, 2013), pp. 52-53.

7. *Ibid.*, p. 54.

8. Oscar Sinigaglia, Finsider President since 1945, was an important Italian manager with a long and reach record of experiences both in the private and public sectors. He is one of the leading figures among the promoters of Italian development during the postwar period.

on the development of a steel industry in our country. This defense of the Italian steel industry was not an end in itself, but was designed according to the mechanical industry's development.

All these focused efforts soon led to mechanics becoming the leading sector of Italian industry.

> Restructuring and reorganization of the mechanical sector proceeded, of course, on much more decentralized and fragmented lines than the metal sector, and took a long time, partly because it needed those broader domestic and international markets that were opened only later. But no production line remained intact: from the car to the tractor, from the Vespa to the Lambretta, from sewing machines to machinery for paper mills, calculators to electrical equipment, refrigerators to washing machines, typewriters to packaging machines, attempts were made to produce everything, with more or less luck but with great promptness.[9]

Moreover, the Sinigaglia Plan, putting the mechanical industry at the center of the Italian system, in which the steel industry was upstream, was confident that the success of these two sectors would lead to absorption of rampant unemployment and a realignment of the balance of payments. In such a context, major automotive development reached very positive results between 1953 and 1960.

Fiat was the industry leader that in ten years quadrupled manufacturing, covering 90% of civil production. This contradicted the widespread opinion that it was not possible for Italy to create a competitive car industry since the great American industry in the sector would try to prevent it.

Fiat developed its own complete automobile cycle, but also produced commercial vehicles, agricultural machinery, and aeronautical and railway products. At the head of this company was Valletta, surrounded by prestigious directors like Dante Giacosa and Gaudenzio Bono. The group included Cinzano in the food sector, Manchino in cement, SAI in the insurance sector, Rinascente Upim, and SMA in mass retailing. The great success of the Turin company depended on many factors, but especially the work of Valletta, who, from the beginning of his activity, had started a massive investment policy. In 1953, he had earmarked 300 billion for the assembly line of the *Seicento* (600), which was to become the means of transport that, after the Vespa and Lambretta, would give mobility to the Italians. In 1957, the Turinese giant was already churning out more than 300.000 cars a year

9. Vera Zamagni, *Dalla periferia al centro. La seconda rinascita economica dell'Italia (1861-1990)* (Bologna: Il Mulino, 1990), pp. 420-421.

and put into production the *Cinquecento* (500), the legendary small car with an affordable price. With the huge growth of the factory, downstream activities also grew. The outskirts of Turin became the home to a myriad of small companies producing semi-finished products and accessories for the parent company. Because of the immigration phenomenon, the city of Piedmont saw an exponential increase in its inhabitants at the beginning of the Sixties, 42% compared to 1951.

In the remaining mechanical sectors, sewing machines for use at home had particular relevance along with accounting machines. Among the first are Italian companies Necchi and Borletti and American Singer, while regarding the latter, it is necessary to mention Olivetti with Adriano Olivetti as president, manager and innovator, but also a refined man of profound culture attentive to Italy's social and political problems.

Adriano, after taking over the company after the war, launched a major plan for investments and projects. This partially overlapped with the climate generated by the process of rebuilding the country and partly put in the foreground the ideal complex of "community". He had worked on this in the years before and between 1946 and 1947, he devoted to it a magazine, a publishing house and a political and cultural movement. In the same period, while the original company of Ivrea was expanded, the facilities in Turin and the one in Glasgow were also opened; the one in Massa was rebuilt and British Olivetti was established in London. Meanwhile, in line with the resumption of office work in Italy and Europe, the *Divisumma 14* was launched.

This was a calculator capable of performing four operations and accompanied the typewriter from the Lexicon workshop. Both these machines were designed by Nizzoli,[10] one of the founding fathers of Italian design, a discipline that would contribute to the success of *made in Italy* in the world. Also designed by Nizzoli was the *Lettera 22* portable typewriter, released in 1950. In 1954, it received the "Compasso d'Oro", a prize established that year to indicate the best works of Italian design. It was built at the new Agliè plant at Ivrea and soon became a symbol of the rebirth of Italy, a cult object, along with the Vespa, Lambretta, *Cinquecento* and Riva

10. Marcello Nizzoli, Italian architect and designer that started his collaboration with Olivetti in 1938, was also a set designer and a poster designer. For Olivetti, he designed: calculator *Summa* in 1940; typewriter *Lexicon 80* in 1948, the popular portable typewriter *Lettera 22* in 1950 as well as the calculator *Divisumma 24* in 1956.

motorboats, with Acquamarina leading the new *made in Italy* movement. Olivetti production in 1955 was strongly directed toward the calculator machine, manufacturing of which exceeded the number of typewriters produced. The *Divisumma 24*, designed from a mechanical point of view by Giovanni Cappellaro and from the aesthetic by Marcello Nizzoli, in 1956 marked the transition from mechanical to electromechanical technology.

Meanwhile, Olivetti, after putting together a powerful design workshop composed of 400 people, dedicated to the development of electronic products, in 1959 made the first electronic computer, the *Elea 9003* designed by Ettore Sottsass,[11] and subsequently the *Programma 101*, which was presented at the fair in New York in 1965. The latter machine, designed by noted designer Mario Bellini,[12] among others, was a remarkably advanced computer. Its competitors, led by the Americans, called it the first personal computer in history. Unfortunately, the large expansion in Italy and abroad, the huge effort to conquer the American market, including the costly acquisition of Underwood, and the inability to enter the new electronic computer market, led to an unsustainable financial situation for Olivetti, which was aggravated by the death of Adriano Olivetti in 1960.

Today the Olivetti remains an extraordinary example, and one of the cornerstones of a phenomenon that would become central to our country. At its base, there is a style and a number of values that we now call *made in Italy*. The work of Adriano Olivetti developed scenarios that were unknown at that time, involving in its design writers, sociologists, economists, architects, poets, artists, graphic artists and designers. In particular, Olivetti developed a special focus on communication because he was convinced that the company, in addition to pursuing excellence, should be able to transmit its values including aesthetic ones that were very important for building an image. In fact, Olivetti was able to do this through the design of its products, the architecture of its factories, the graphics of the posters, the

11. Ettore Sottsass starts his collaboration with Olivetti in 1958 in the computer design department. He will work for Olivetti for 30 years. His remarkable contribution was able to impose a new style for the many types of office products realized by Olivetti group. Among the designed objects we can identify both calculators (*Elea 9003*, *Summa-19*, *Logos 27*) and typewriters (*Praxis 48* and *Valentine*). Finally, he also was awarded the "Compasso d'Oro" thanks to the computer mainframe *Elea 9003*.

12. Mario Bellini, prominent designer within the International environment has been chief design consultant for the Olivetti group. Among his projects: *Programma 101*, calculator *Divisumma 18/28* (1973) and typewriters *Praxis 35* and *Praxis 45* (1981).

stores' furnishings and how its advertising was done. The aesthetics of the products and all other components gravitating in the Olivetti universe was not limited to being a simple formal matter, but were substantive choices, as were technological, economic and managerial ones.

At a time in Italy when design had still not entered the University fully, Sottsass, Nizzoli and Bellini worked with Olivetti, producing extraordinary machines, not in a subordinate position but in perfect symbiosis with the engineers and technicians, in order to give each form a complete sense and justified from a functionally ergonomic and communicative perspective. From this, the Olivetti style was born and with it, a way of operating that permeated every phase of corporate life. This gave the product and its design an extraordinary weight that would become an absolute model and a reference point for the best *made in Italy*.

In such a context, although in a less inspired manner, within the revival of the so-called Italian mechanics, a prominent place was definitely held by household appliances, namely washing machines, refrigerators, stoves, home accessories and later also television sets. This sector, not very high-tech and characterized by low capitalization, was penetrated by many semi-artisanal businesses. Some among these reached significant levels, not only on the domestic market, such as Zanussi, Rex-Naonis, Ignis, Candy, Zoppas, and Indesit, but also found themselves faced with foreign competitors, which, having long since consolidated their image, could count on the most qualified brand.

In such a situation, larger Italian companies along with smaller ones, placed in famous districts, developed so-called outsourcing; e.g., production of components and intermediate processing, with assembly done by the most prestigious companies. Among the factors contributing to the success of this sector was the fortune of liquid gas related to replacement of economical stoves, spread mainly in small and medium-sized urban centers or in the countryside, and electric or gas stoves operated with LPG. Liquid gas distributors were often Liquigas in Milan, but also Agipgas and Pibigas, to encourage the purchase of stoves built especially for use with this type of gas. In the years between 1949 and 1954, the market was flooded with a disproportionate number of these devices (4 millions), which were produced by small semi-artisanal companies or semi-industrial production. After an initial phase in which the imitation of foreign products prevailed, they switched to designing and producing original equipment, technologically mature and with good design, which allowed the use of a common brand. The development of this sector is considered the historical forerunner of domestic appliances, as technological and distributive convergences were created between the two areas.[13] Around 1953, some companies essentially producing gas saw the opportunity to engage in the production of another kitchen appliance, the refrigerator, which shortly thereafter became a symbol of new balances that would be established in homes and in the lives of Italians.

4. *The birth of the Italian fashion system*

Another story is that of fashion, at least for the historical relevance that would make *made in Italy* great. The time that everyone mentions to evoke those events is February 12, 1951 when Giovan Battista Giorgini, "Bista," organized a fashion show in his Florentine villa. It would become an epochal event that effectively sanctioned the birth of Italian fashion and more. Giorgini was born in Forte dei Marmi, but already by the early Twenties he had moved to Florence where he started his career as exporter of Italian crafts to the United States. After the break due to the crisis of 1929, he opened a US craft shop in Florence on behalf of one of his American clients. At the end of the war, he began to work closely with Allied Command and so in 1944 assumed the task of organizing the Allied Forces Gift Shop, a gift shop for Allied troops. This activity was very successful, as was the exhibition *Italy at work* at the Museum of Modern Art in Chicago; these activities solidified his relationship with major American and Canadian importers and distributors. Reports that Giorgini had developed over twenty-five years of work as a purchasing agent and attentive explorer, on behalf of the largest and most prestigious department stores in New York, San Francisco, Dallas, Chicago, refined Italian handicrafts. Ambassador of taste and *bello italiano* (Italian beauty) for the overseas market, he learned about consumer trends, styles and needs. When Giorgini put his mind to exporting Italian fashion to the United States, he realized that Americans enjoyed less sophisticated clothes than those of Parisian fashion, because they were more practical and suitable to their dynamic and constantly evolving lifestyle. Giorgini was sure that products of unorganized Italian

13. Carlo Castellano, *L'industria degli elettrodomestici in Italia* (Turin: Giappichelli, 1965), p. 61.

fashion, still unaware of its strength, could meet the tastes, customs and way of life of Americans.

For this reason, he opened the Serragli runway with products that only by appearance, could be judged as minor, such as swimwear, hosiery, and fashion boutiques. In the neo-classical salon of villa Torrigiani in Florence, where the architectural scenario was significant, on February 12, 1951, on an artisanal runway, with no stage, simply filing between chairs and armchairs, Giorgini coolly played his cards, facing the American buyers who had to be convinced right away that a market full of prospects was going to open. On February 12, before the day dresses, the boutique models paraded a new genre dedicated to leisure and sport. These products were far from those of Paris, at prices that were very interesting. Giorgini, in making this choice, showed an extraordinary talent as a strategist that transcended the narrow world of fashion. He had decided to present, to a chosen audience of qualified buyers, what would become the values on which all the fashion *made in Italy* would subsequently be built.

In the invitation to the big final dance on the evening of February 14 was written: "The purpose of the evening is to promote our fashion. Ladies are strongly urged to wear clothes of pure Italian inspiration".[14] Even with a bit of irreverence, Giorgini did what Mussolini had failed to do, imposing Italian fashion in a world dominated by French style, which Italy viewed with a sense of worship and awe. Especially Italian fashion houses, which Giorgini contacted before organizing the event in Florence, were paralyzed with fear of missing the French atelier circuit, where they usually went to take ideas, models and clothes, and even to buy exclusive items they would reproduce later in multiple copies with some variations of fabric and cut. They in particular knew that Italian customers had French fashion in mind, considering it the best in elegance and refinement. In such a context, after receiving a series of refusals by the most renowned tailors, Giorgini stayed calm and turned to those who could be considered emerging or recently successful. Fashion houses that joined the initiative were Carosa, Sorelle Fontana, Fabiani, Simonetta, Shuberth Noberasco, Maduka, Veneziani and Vanna, representing high fashion, while boutique clothes included Mirsa, Pucci, Bertoli and Tessitrice dell'Isola. Since the tailors and the models were few, Giorgini decided to group them by style and use, to best display

14. Sofia Gnoli, *Moda. Dalla nascita della haute couture a oggi* (Rome: Carocci, 2012), p. 169.

most of their features. The first on the runway were boutique clothes, a type of product presented in Paris and which turned out to be the trump card of the event of February 12, 1951.

These clothes were cheerful, young, colorful and of high quality, but their cost was about 50% less than French products. The success of this type of clothing showed the existence of Italian style that made the event successful and would become strategic for the launch of the Italian market. Giorgini had realized that to make the Italy a country acceptable to North American buyers, in particular, it was necessary to combine the image of Italian beauty with the image of fashion. "Fashion, or rather high fashion, would constitute a 'trait d'union' between the commercial world and much more artistic craftsmanship. It was linked to the world of dreams, wealth and the cinema, with its divas representing its essence. The media then fed the myth. There was no newspaper that did not cover the great tailors, their creations, and the vagaries and whims of the characters in view of wearing their style-making fashions. Only the allure of beautiful fashion would have the ability to make itself heard, attracting journalists and buyers from all over the world".[15] In the room were a few but very important American buyers; those of B. Altmann & Co, Bergdorf Goodman, Leto Cohn Lo Balbo of New York, Magnin of San Francisco and Henry Morgan of Montreal. Five journalists were also called to attend the event: Elisa Massai, correspondent of *Women's Wear Daily*; Elsa Robiola, Director of *Bellezza* and representative of the weekly magazine *Tempo*; Gemma Vitti of *Corriere Lombardo*; Vera Rossi of *Novità*; Misia Armani of the newspaper *I tessili Nuovi* and *Omnibus*, and Sandra Bartolomei Corsi from *Secolo XIX*.

Subsequent history is well known; the great success of the first fashion show led Giorgini to organize a second in July of that year in the salons of the Grand Hotel in Borgo Ognissanti. This choice was required by the large number of spectators who had asked to participate in the event. The journalists included Bettina Ballard, fashion editor of the American edition of *Vogue* and her historic antagonist, Carmel Snow, the all-powerful editor in chief of *Harper's Bazaar*. As a result of these successes, after an excellent third event organized again at the Grand Hotel from January 18 to 22 1952, the fourth was held July 22 of that year in the prestigious Sala Bianca at Palazzo Pitti, where, along with to nine houses of *haute couture*, sixteen fashion and leisure boutique firms turned out, presenting

15. *Ibid.*

a kind of product that the French tailors were not able to offer. It was the phenomenon of fashion boutique, together with the growing importance of accessories, that brought to the explosion of the "Italian style". But the phenomenon had become too impressive and able to carry with it the whole *made in Italy* sector. Meanwhile, with the season of the great designers and the rise of prêt-à-porter, Milan managed to establish itself permanently as a fashion capital, finally overcoming Rome and Florence, triggering a massive financial horizon, which would become triumphant for Italy's image in the world.

Contributors

PAOLO BIONDI holds a Ph.D. in Intercultural relation and processes. Since 2013 he collaborates to the teaching and research activities of the chair of Political Philosophy at the University of Molise (Italy). His research interests include: anarchism and its contemporary reprise, philosophy of the social sciences, feminism and gender studies, queer theories, intercultural communication and dialogue theories, with particular attention to their application to group communication. Moreover, his activity is intended to connect his personal interest and appreciation for the so called popular culture (above all, for comics) with philosophical and scientific research and analysis. Among his published works: *Il criterio del genere: rappresentazioni della maschilità nell'horror italiano*, in *Schegge di genere. Dagli stereotipi alla cittadinanza*, ed. by F. Corsini and F. Monceri (Pisa: ETS, 2013, pp. 61-82); *'Serialità' e 'fumetto': problemi di definizione*, in *Mediascapes journal*, 6 (2016), pp. 140-154; *The Epistemological Foundations of David's Bohm Dialogue*, in *Teoria*, 1 (2016), pp. 75-93); the Italian translation of David Bohm's classic *On Dialogue* (*Sul dialogo*, Pisa: ETS, 2014) and the book *Maschere. V per Vendetta* (Pisa: ETS, 2016).

MARCO BRACCI got his B.A. degree in Political Sciences, his M.A. in Communication and Media and his Ph.D. in Sociology of Communication at the University of Florence. From 2002 to 2012 he taught sociological courses and was research collaborator at the Department of Sociology and Political Sciences, University of Florence. He is adjunct professor at Kent State University, Florence Center, at Gonzaga in Florence, at University of Minnesota-Florence, and at Richmond University-Florence. He is a member of the international research group "Personal Development" (UCAM-Spain), of the Italian Sociological Association, of the American Sociological Association, and of the Steering and Monitoring Committee of IRPET. His research interests focus on social and cultural changes in late modernity, media, popular music, sports, deviance and identities. His publications include monographs, essays and chapters in books. Some of his books are: *Da Modugno a X Factor. Musica e società italiana dal dopoguerra a oggi* (Rome:

Carocci, 2010); *Radici di Ferro e Futuro d'Acciaio* (Naples: Liguori, 2012); and *The Dark Side of the Moon. Viaggio nell'identità dei Pink Floyd* (Milan: Aerostella, 2013). Some of his latest chapters are: *The "journey" of personal identity in The Dark Side of the Moon*, in *Human development*, ed. by Beatriz Pena Acuna (Japur: Yking Books 2013) and *On line music listening and consumption, and the re-definition of personal identities in our radical modernity*, in *Popular culture: A Reader*, ed. by Beatriz Pena Acuna and Otto Von Feigenblatt (Newcastle upon Tyne: Cambridge Scholars Publishing, 2013).

Milly Buonanno is former Professor of Television Studies in the Department of Communication and Social Research at "Sapienza", University of Rome. She is the founder and head of the Observatory of Italian TV Drama (1988-present), the co-director of the research group GEMMA GEnder and Media MAtters (2010-present), and has been the coordinator of the Eurofiction Project (1996-2004) on the European television industry. She sits in the editorial board of several international journals and is the associate editor of the *Journal of Italian Cinema and Media Studies.* She has extensively researched and written on television theory, television drama, gender and media, journalism, and has authored and edited more than 50 books, in addition to being the author of several articles in scholarly journals and chapters in edited collection; her works have been published in English, Spanish, Portuguese, and French. Her main publications over the last decade include: *The age of television* (Bristol: Intellect, 2008), acknowledged as "one of the fundamental texts in television studies"; *Italian TV Drama and Beyond* (Bristol: Intellect, 2012); *The Sage Handbook of Television Studies* (Sage, 2014, co-edited with Manuel Alvarado, Herman Gray, Toby Miller); the edited collection *Television antiheroines. Women behaving badly in crime and prison drama* (Bristol: Intellect, 2017). She is currently working on the disruption of seriality as-it-was-formerly-known in the age of Netflix.

Fabio Corsini, Ph.D. in Sociology and Social Research, is the coordinator of the Communication Program – College of Communication and Information, at Kent State University, Florence Center where he serves as adjunct professor since 2010 teaching Intercultural Communication and Fashion in the Media. He has been Research Fellow at the University of Urbino for the past three years (2014-2017) and since 2015 he is also adjunct professor of Fashion Branding at Sapienza, University of Rome. As a researcher he is interested in the role played by the media in the development of a new intercultural globalized context. He also investigates brands and brand communication strategies. He is member of Italian research projects about the representation of gender in audiovisual products and about young adult media consumption practices. He has published various articles focused on mediated representations – mainly television narratives – in relation to gender and sexual orientation. In 2014 he co-edited with F. Monceri *Schegge di genere. Dagli stereotipi alla cittadinanza* (Pisa: ETS, 2013). Together with P. Biondi and F. Monceri he co-authored *UniversiCorti I. Tre Sguardi sulla Diversità* (2014); and *UniversiCorti II. Immagini da altrove* (2015), two volumes on short movies and the representation of diversity. Currently he is working as co-editor on a book about *made in Italy* by the title *Quel che resta del made in Italy* (forthcoming).

FLAVIA MONCERI is professor of Political Philosophy at the University of Molise, where she teaches also Gender Studies and Multiculturalism and Intercultural Communication. She got her M.A. in Political Sciences at University of Pisa, Ph.D. in Philosophy of the social sciences at Scuola Superiore Sant'Anna, Pisa, and Diploma di pianoforte at the Istituto Musicale Pareggiato "Luigi Boccherini", Lucca, in 1986. She is series editor of "Difforme" and "Sakura. Filosofie e società nei prodotti culturali" (Edizioni ETS, Pisa). Her main research interests are: political philosophy, social philosophy, philosophy of the social sciences; theory and practice of intercultural communication, intercultural studies, dialogue; queer and transgender theories and studies; disability studies; film philosophy; complexity and systems theories; radical constructivism; globalization and multiculturalism; anarchism and postanarchism; East Asian religions and philosophies (esp. Japan). She has presented papers to several national and international conferences and workshops in Italy and abroad (including Japan and the USA) and is the author of a number of books and articles in Italian and in English, among them: *Etica e disabilità* (Brescia: Morcelliana, 2017); *Connessioni Fatali.* La storia dei tre Adolf *di Tezuka Osamu* (Pisa: Edizioni ETS, 2016); *Oltre l'identità sessuale. Teorie queer e corpi transgender* (Pisa: Edizioni ETS, 2010); *Ordini costruiti. Multiculturalismo, complessità, istituzioni* (Soveria Mannelli: Rubbettino, 2008); *Interculturalità e comunicazione. Una prospettiva filosofica* (Roma: Edizioni Lavoro, 2006); *Dialogue and Power: Preliminary Steps to Overcoming an Opposition*, in *Teoria*, 36/1 (2016), pp. 45-62; *The Nature of the "Ruling Body": Embodiment, Ableism and Normalcy*, in *Teoria*, 34/1 (2014), pp. 183-200; *Citizenship on trial: 'Disability' and the borders of gender*, in *AG-About Gender*, 1/2 (2012), pp. 51-72; *Sguardi prospettici. La filosofia del film fra etnocentrismo e interculturalità*, in *Imago*, I/2 (2010), pp. 73-85.

ANNA LUCIA NATALE is Associate Professor at the Department of Communication and Social Research (CORIS), "Sapienza", University of Rome. She teaches History of Radio and Television and Contents and Markets of Radio. Her main fields of interest concern: the social history of Italian radio; narrative forms and social representations in the television drama. These themes are based both on recognizing the centrality of the media as a technological means, which can influence the social transformation process, and as symbolic forms, that is place of expression, storage and processing of culture. Among her most significant publications: *Gli anni della radio (1924-1954)* (Naples: Liguori, 1990); *Immagini di realtà. L'informazione d'attualità nella televisione pubblica e privata (1988-1994)* (with Guido Gili, Milan: Angeli, 1995); *Reinventare la tradizione. Novità e ripetizione nella fiction tv in Italia* (Mediascape 2004); *Il senso del luogo. I protagonisti della fiction fra qui e altrove*, in *Tempo di fiction*, ed. by Milly Buonanno (Naples: Liguori, 2013); *Non più e non ancora. Il protagonismo femminile nella fiction italiana*, in *Il prisma dei generi*, ed. by M. Buonanno (Milan: Angeli, 2014); *Sulle onde sonore. Strategie e usi sociali della musica alla radio (1924-1940)*, in *La musica alla radio: 1924-1954*, ed. by A. I. De Benedictis and F. Monteleone (Rome: Bulzoni, 2015).

NICOLETTA PELUFFO serves as coordinator for the College of the Arts & Sciences and Italian Language at Kent State University, Florence Center, where she also teaches Italian language and culture. She has been working for Kent State University Florence Center for 15 years, contributing in the development of the Italian language program, Internships Program for EHHS (she has served as EHHS local coordinator until 2016), and the Exchange Program with Italian schools. She earned her B.A. and M.A. in Modern Languages and Literature at IULM (University of Language and Communication) in Milan and her diploma as Interpreter and Translator at Scuola Interpreti in Florence. In 2004 she earned her certificate for Teaching Italian as a Second Language (Ditals) from the University of Siena. In 2010 she earned her Second Level Master degree in Teaching Italian as a Second/Foreign Language from the University Ca' Foscari in Venice. Actually, she is Ph.D. candidate at IULM: her final dissertation focuses on transmedia narrative and parody in the novel *The Adventures of Pinocchio*. Her publications and lectures focus on transmediality, narratology and language teaching.

KRISTIN STASIOWSKI, Ph.D., is the Assistant Dean of International Programs and Education Abroad for the College of Arts and Sciences and Assistant Professor of Italian Language and Literature in the Department of Modern and Classical Languages at Kent State University. She received her Ph.D. from Yale University in Italian Language and Literature and has taught Italian language, literature, cinema, history and culture in both the United States and Florence, Italy prior to arriving at Kent State where her current responsibilities are focused on promoting study abroad opportunities to undergraduates. Her research interests include Dante; Boccaccio; Renaissance astrology in Luigi Pulci's *Morgante*; and the poetic works of Clemente Rebora.

EDOARDO TABASSO, Ph.D. in Sociology of Communication at the University of Florence, is professor at the Master in Institutional Advertising, Multimedia Communication and Event Creation, University of Florence, and at the Italian

Diplomatic Academy (Ministry of Foreign Affairs Italian Government). He is research collaborator at the University of Florence and founding member of the Italian-French university study center *Réseau pour l'étude des thèories du complot* and scientific director of *ThinkThankYou*, research center aimed at promoting and creating original cultural economy proposals. He has multiple research interests: sociological and ethnographic research, media, new organizational paradigms and cultural and creative industries (in particular cinema, TV, pop music and digital media). Member of the scientific committee of the journal *Mirabilis* (Nivi Group). Journalist and TV commentator of foreign policy analyst for Italian and international newsmedia. Author of many books and articles in Italian, English and Spanish. Among his works: *The Cinematographic Italian Miracle. Producers Among Colossal Ambitions, Authorial Disasters and Flights from the Genres*, in *Popular culture: A Reader*, ed. by Beatriz Pena Acuna and Otto Von Feigenblatt (Newcastle upon Tyne: Cambridge Scholars Publishing, 2013); *Breve storia sociale della comunicazione* (with Zeffiro Ciuffoletti, Rome: Carocci, 2007); *Raccontarsi. La passione narrativa nel cinema e nella Tv* (Florence: Le lettere, 2008); *Da Modugno a X Factor Musica e società italiana dal dopoguerra a oggi* (with Marco Bracci, Rome: Carocci, 2010).

Bernardo Valli is professor of Media and Brand Studies at the Universiy of Urbino "Carlo Bo". He teaches Sociology of Mass Media and Brand Languages for the M.A. in Information, Media and Advertising and Sociology of Brand for the B.A. in Communication and Promotion for Organizations. He is Provost for External Relations at the same university where he also founded and directs the Research Labarotory "Image Lab" on audiovisual languages. During the last years he has been investigating the topics of fashion, branding and the development of *made in Italy*. He has been Dean of the School of Sociology at the University of Urbino from 2005 till 2013 and Director of the School for Fashion Designers at the same University from 1996 till 2005. He is the director of the editorial series "Materiali per la Comunicazione" for the publishing house Liguori. Among his most important publications: *La comunicazione dell'Immateriale* (Naples: Liguori, 2003); *Il luogo dell'abitare. Una ricerca sociologica sul design della terza età* (Naples: Liguori, 2012) e *L'immagine del made in Italy* (Soveria Mannelli: Rubbettino Editore, 2012).

Finito di stampare
nel mese di giugno 2018
da Arti Grafiche CDC s.r.l.
Città di Castello (PG)